T0339426

Public Sector Transformation through E-Government

RIOT! Routledge Studies in Innovation, Organization and Technology

Public Sector Transformation through E-Government

Experiences from Europe and North America

Edited by Vishanth Weerakkody and Christopher G. Reddick

Routledge
Taylor & Francis Group
New York London

First published 2013
by Routledge
711 Third Avenue, New York, NY 10017

Simultaneously published in the UK
by Routledge
2 Park Square, Milton Park, Abingdon, Oxon OX14 4RN

First issued in paperback 2017

*Routledge is an imprint of the Taylor & Francis Group,
an informa business*

Library of Congress Cataloging-in-Publication Data
Public sector transformation through e-government : experiences from
    Europe and North America / edited by Vishanth Weerakkody and
    Christopher G. Reddick.
        p. cm. — (Routledge studies in innovation, organization and
technology ; 26)
    Includes bibliographical references and index.
    1. Public administration—Technological innovations.   2. Internet
in public administration.   3. Public administration—Technological
innovations—Europe.   4. Internet in public administration—Europe.
5. Public administration—Technological innovations—North America.
6. Internet in public administration—North America.   I. Weerakkody,
Vishanth.   II. Reddick, Christopher G.
    JF1525.A8P833 2012
    352.3'802854678—dc23
    2012010061

Typeset in Sabon
by IBT Global.

ISBN 13: 978-1-138-11559-0 (pbk)
ISBN 13: 978-0-415-52737-8 (hbk)

Contents

Figures

Tables

1 Public Sector Transformation through E-Government

Vishanth Weerakkody and
Christopher G. Reddick

TRANSFORMATION AND E-GOVERNMENT

Over the last decade, governments in Europe and North America in particular have intensified their efforts to improve efficiency of public services through electronic government (e-government) influenced transformation of public institutions. It is in every government's interest to make their public services more efficient and available in order to gain citizens' trust, which has often eluded many governments and political leaders in modern society. Such efforts are now seen by governments as a necessity rather than an option, whereas citizens consider it as their right to have access to government services at anytime from anywhere. In this backdrop, *Public Sector Transformation through E-Government* explores the influence that e-government has on transforming public sector institutions and the resulting organizational complexities that need to be tackled as well as its impact on citizens and democratic society. This book does this in the context of experiences in governments in Europe and North America.

E-government can be broadly viewed as the adoption of information and communications technologies (ICTs) in government institutions to improve public services. For many countries, e-government implementation efforts began in the late 1990s. Since then, the e-government influenced implementation of ICT in public administration has enabled governments to offer better, faster, and a more transparent way of delivering services to citizens and other stakeholders. Equally, it has also created a platform for better collaboration and information sharing between various government institutions. In the last few years in particular e-government implementation efforts in most countries have evolved from basic information provisioning online to more integrated service offerings. The implementation of such integrated online services has enabled public institutions to offer more joined-up and citizen-centric service facilitated primarily through cross-agency process and information systems transformation. However, public sector service transformation is a complex undertaking involving distributed decision-making that requires a good understanding of the political context, business processes and technology as well as design and engineering methods capable of transcending the traditional boundaries that exist between departmental silos in public institutions. Conversely, from a demand perspective extensive efforts are required to increase citizens' awareness about the transformation of the delivery of government services and their online availability.

Transformation through e-government involves fundamentally changing the relationship between how governments interact with citizens as well as other stakeholders such as businesses and non-governmental organizations. In the context of highly strained economic resources and related social consequences, governments have been devoting significant effort on reorganising public institutions through examining strategies for eliminating non-essential back office operations and management activities and providing platforms for different stakeholders to collaborate, participate, share resources to undertake work traditionally seen as the sole preserve of the public sector. In this respect, many governments have embraced new technologies such as Web 2.0 based social media applications to engage citizens in policy modelling through e-participation and worked towards enhancing transparency of their governance processes.

Yet, sceptics have argued whether these new ICT tools save the public sector money and make it more productive, as well as provide more trustful, engaging and useful services for citizens. Further, the continued debate about adoption looms large particularly in Europe as the take up of e-government services have been disappointing due to issues such as digital divide and social exclusion. In fact, the European Commission has repeatedly called for research into social inclusion in the realm of public service transformation and digital era government. In order to prevent digital divide and social exclusion in terms of using e-government services, it is necessary that citizens from all facets of society are equipped with basic ICT skills as well as access to high-speed Internet connections. Yet, despite the availability of innovative technologies, governments are faced with many technical, organizational, and socio-economic challenges that need to be addressed when developing, adopting, and diffusing e-government systems and services. Furthermore, from an organizational perspective e-government has introduced an environment where most public institutions such as healthcare, social services, education, employment and law enforcement have struggled with the need to balance issues such as transparency and opaqueness, or social inclusion and professionalism.

Consequently, there has been increasing pressure on the academic and practitioner communities for research that focuses on bridging the gap between e-government theory and practice as well as availability versus demand for services. In such as backdrop, various researchers and practitioners have attempted to offer insights into the implementation (Irani et al., 2007; 2008; Weerakkody & Dhillon, 2008; Weerakkody et al., 2007a; Janssen et al., 2007; Weerakkody & Choudrie, 2005; Kamal et al., 2009; Beynon-Davies & Martin, 2004), acceptance (Carter & Belanger, 2005), and diffusion (Alshafi & Weerakkody, 2008; Warkentin et al., 2002) of e-government services. The last few years have seen e-government being regarded with the same level of importance that electronic business (e-business) was treated with in the mid-1990s.

When examining e-government literature, it can be concluded that principally *three* key themes have emerged in published research on e-government. These include (a) research that examine the implementation of e-government from a policy-oriented perspective that includes strategic, organizational, technical, and wider socio-political dimensions (Irani et al., 2007; 2008; Weerakkody & Dhillon, 2008; Beynon-Davies & Martin, 2004; Ramaswamy &Selian, 2007; Janssen et al., 2005; 2007); (b) studies that take a citizen-centric perspective on e-government through adoption and diffusion or in other words e-participation research (Niehaves et al., 2009; Niehaves & Becker, 2008; Al-Shafi & Weerakkody, 2008; Carter & Belanger, 2005; Warkentin et al., 2002; Welch et al., 2005; Huang, 2007); and (c) research that explore the complexities of transforming governance practices in an e-government context (O'Donnel et al., 2003; Ramaswamy & Selian, 2007; Irani et al., 2007; Weerakkody at al., 2007b). Therefore, the themes of policy modelling, participation and governance emerge as key areas for research in the area of e-government influenced public sector transformation as this book explores.

From a conceptual angle, a review of the extant literature also suggests that despite committed efforts, many countries have struggled to successfully achieve transformational change in public institutions due to various organizational, social, political and technology related challenges (Irani et al., 2007; 2008; Beynon-Davies & Martin, 2004). Studies have confirmed that implementing transformational change in the public sector through e-government involves a radical paradigm shift in comparison to any previous efforts of organizational change seen in the public sector. Moreover, to realize transformational change, public institutions will need radical changes in core processes across organizational boundaries, in a manner that has not been seen before in the public sector (Andersen & Henriksen, 2006; Kim et al., 2007; Weerakkody, & Dhillon, 2008).

Consequently, success will require the ability to rethink processes in a cross-functional way as championed by management approaches such as business process reengineering (BPR). In this respect, public sector agencies have indeed tried to replicate concepts such as BPR, Lean Management, Total Quality Management, and Public Value Management with a view of improving key public services such as healthcare, social service, education, transportation and local government. Yet, although large sums of money have been invested in transforming such key public services in recent years, research has shown that these initiatives have not met the expectations of stakeholders and delivered policy outcomes which have resulted in services that facilitate social inclusion and democratic processes. Rather, the application of these management concepts to transform public institutions has resulted in the tax payers' money not being sensibly utilized and in some cases created social exclusions. A broader example would be that of e-business ideas being borrowed from the private sector and applied in the context of e-government resulting in major digital divides and exclusions among citizens and inequality of service provision. While the implementation of such approaches and management concepts have proven difficult in the private sector, research suggests that government entities face even greater challenges (Fagan, 2006; Tan & Pan, 2003). Indeed, while much of the early e-government research efforts have focused on identifying and analysing these challenges that impact implementation, more recent research has emerged that identifies determinants of adoption and diffusion from a citizen-centric perspective. Nonetheless, very few studies have attempted to systematically synthesise theory with practice to generate knowledge about the gaps that exist between *implementation* and *diffusion* (service provider or government's perspective on policy formulation and governance) and *adoption* (service recipient or citizens' perspective on participation). This book attempts to provide both theory and practice of transformational change from e-government. This book offers readers the theoretical context of the potential of e-government to transform public services, and practical examples are provided from leading public sector institutions that have attempted to use e-government to bring about transformational change.

2   PLAN OF THE BOOK

The *four* main objectives of this book are to:

1. Understand the importance of e-government as a force for change in public sector organizations and how it has changed, or has not changed, service delivery in European and North American governments.
2. Understand both the benefits of e-government and transformational change for government and citizens and some of the challenges and complexities in its implementation in Europe and North America.
3. Explore the major schools of thoughts on e-government and related transformational change, and provide examples of public sector institutions through case studies that have used e-government to change their organization.
4. Understand the relationship between citizens and government and how they are affected by transformational change through e-government policies and programs.

There are three sections to the book that examine these objectives: (I) Transformation E-Government, (II) Benefits and Barriers to Transformation, and (III) T-Government and Public Service Delivery. Section I has chapters that deal with the important theories and concepts in transformational e-government research such as open government, service delivery reform, economic constraints, internal organizational change, and performance improvements. The overriding contribution to the research on transformational e-government is that change can occur as a result of e-government, but it is a slow process and often incremental process.

Section II discusses some of the benefits and barriers to transformation change from e-government. Again repeating some of the themes from Section I, the benefits are improvements in service delivery and increased participation by citizens in the process of governance. However, the barriers are the digital divide, or those groups that are left out of the development of e-government for transformation change.

Section III, the final section of the book, focuses on transformation government or T-Government and public service delivery. As we learned from previous chapters the overriding and notable contribution of T-Government is to improve service delivery for public sector organizations. This chapter as a result provides examples of improvements in service delivery through increased collaboration, improved technologies, shared services, and increased channel choice.

REFERENCES

Alshafi, S., & Weerakkody, V. (2008). The use of wireless Internet parks to facilitate adoption and diffusion of e-government services: An empirical study in Qatar, Americas Conference on Information Systems (AMCIS), Toronto, Canada, August.

Andersen, K., & Henriksen, H. (2006). E-government maturity models: Extension of the Layne and Lee model. *Government Information Quarterly, 23*(2), 236–248.

Beynon-Davis P., & Martin S. (2004). Electronic local government and the modernization agenda: Progress and prospects for public service improvement. *Local Government Studies, 30*(2), 214–229.

Carter, L., & Belanger, F. (2005). The utilization of e-government services: Citizen trust, innovation and acceptance factors. *Information Systems Journal, 15*(1), 5–25.

Fagan, M. (2006). Exploring city, county and state e-government initiatives: An East Texas perspective, *Business Process Management Journal,* 12(1), 101–112.

Huang, Z. (2007). A Comprehensive analysis of US counties' e-Government portals: Development status and functionalities. *European Journal of Information Systems, 16*(2), 149–164.

Irani, Z., Elliman, T., & Jackson, P. (2007). Electronic transformation of government in the UK: A research agenda. *European Journal of Information Systems, 16*(4), 327–335.

Irani, Z., Love, P. E. D., & Jones, S. (2008). Learning lessons from evaluating e-government: Reflective case experiences that support transformational government. *The Journal of Strategic Information Systems, 17*(2), 155–164.

Janssen, M., Joha, A., & Weerakkody, V. (2007). Shared service arrangements in the public sector: An exploratory study. *Transforming Government: People, Process and Policy, Emerald, 1*(3), 271–284.

Janssen, M., Kuk, G., & Wagenaar, R. W. (2005). A Survey of E-Government Business Models in the Netherlands, Proceedings of the 7th International Conference on Electronic Commerce (ICEC), Xi'an, China.

Kamal, M. M., Weerakkody, V., & Jones, S. (2009), The case of EAI in facilitating e-government services in a Welsh authority. *International Journal of Information Management, 29*(2), 161–165.

Kim, H., Pan, G., & Pan, S. (2007). Managing IT-enabled transformation in the public sector: Case study on e-government in South Korea. *Government Information Quarterly, 24,* 338–352.

Niehaves, B., & Becker, J. (2008). The age-divide in e-government—Data, interpretations, theory fragments. *Towards Sustainable Society on Ubiquitous Networks,* Volume 286, 279–287.

Niehaves, B., Ortbach, K., & Becker, J. (2009). The demographic challenge: aging and depopulation and their consequences for O'Donnel, O., Boyle, R., & Timonen, V. (2003). Transformational aspects of e-government in Ireland: Issues to be addressed. *Electronic Journal of e-Government, 1*(1), 23–32. Retrieved May 24, 2007, from http://www.ejeg.com

Ramaswami, M., & Selian, A. (2007). E-Government in Transition Countries: Prospects and Challenges, Proceedings of the 40th Hawaii International Conference on System Sciences, IEEE, 1–10.

Tan, C., & Pan, S. (2003). Managing e-transformation in the public sector: An e-government study of the Inland Revenue Authority of Singapore (IRAS). *European Journal of Information Systems, 12,* 269–281.

Warkentin, M., Gefen, D., Pavlou, P., & Rose, M. (2002). Encouraging citizen adoption of e-government by building trust. *Electronic Markets, 12*(3), 157–162.

Weerakkody, V., & Choudrie, J. (2005). Exploring e-government in the UK: Challenges, issues and complexities. *Journal of Information Science and Technology, 2*(2), 25–45.

Weerakkody, V., & Dhillon, G. (2008). Moving from e-government to t-government: A study of process re-engineering challenges in a UK local authority perspective. *International Journal of Electronic Government Research, 4*(4), 1–16.

Weerakkody, V., Janssen, M., & Hjort-Madsen, K. (2007a). Realizing integrated e-government services: A European perspective. *Journal of Cases in Electronic Commerce, 3*(2), 14–38.

Weerakkody, V., Jones, S., & Olsen, E. (2007b). E-government: A comparison of strategies in local authorities in the UK and Norway. *International Journal of Electronic Business, 5*(2), 141–159.

Welch, E. W., Hinnant, C. C., & Moon, M. J. (2005). Linking citizen satisfaction with e-government and trust in government. *Journal of Public Administration Research and Theory, 15*(3), 371–391.

Part I

Transformational
E-Government

2 Open Government as a Vehicle for Government Transformation

Dennis Linders, Susan Copeland Wilson, and John Carlo Bertot

CHAPTER OVERVIEW

In 2009, the Obama administration launched a comprehensive open government initiative—operationalized through agency open government plans, transparency portals, open data, and Web 2.0 technologies—that sought to realize greater transparency, accountability, and collaboration in the government's interactions with the public. This sparked a global movement around innovative new ways to partner with citizens and deliver public services. Inspired nations look to the early pioneers for guidance but no definitive model or best practices yet exist. Yet while open government approaches have evolved in different ways, all point to the goal of transforming the role of the citizen from customer to collaborator. Building on this, the authors argue that open government initiatives, when well designed and implemented, can become vehicles for realizing genuine government transformation. To support this claim, the chapter draws from the United States (U.S.) experience and other countries' national action plans to identify the open government enablers for specific government transformations. Evaluating early lessons learned, the chapter demonstrates the importance of a targeted strategic vision; clear implementation guidance and metrics; and citizen-centricity. It concludes that open government offers new forms of citizen participation and collaboration that, when combined with the right strategic approach, promise a profound transformation of the social contract.

1 ABOUT THIS CHAPTER

The Obama administration's open government initiative (OGI) gave voice to an emerging global open government movement that has redefined government transparency around wholesale data publication; embraced Web 2.0 interactivity for improved citizen participation and collaboration; and promoted government planning and management strategies for open government. These emerging efforts, however, lack best-practice models from which to draw lessons, aspiration, and guidance. It is essential, therefore, to evaluate current initiatives to identify patterns for success, lessons learned, and pitfalls to avoid (Lee & Kwak, 2011).

To frame this analysis, the chapter first covers the characteristics of open government and transformation, and discusses how open government offers the vehicle for government transformation. This is followed by an evaluation of the U.S. OGI's accomplishments and the rise of a global open government movement. It then synthesizes the national action plans produced for the international Open Government Partnership (OGP) (2011) to explore how governments intend to leverage openness to enable transformation. The chapter concludes with an assessment of the status of the OGI, the challenges encountered, and lessons learned to date.

2   OPEN GOVERNMENT AND TRANSFORMATION

When implemented, the open government and transformational government models promise greater innovation, efficiency, and accountability in public services by opening the government's functions to greater public oversight and participation. In so doing, they introduce new frameworks for collaboration that could spark a reinterpretation of the roles and responsibilities of citizens and governments.

2.1   Open Government

How open government is implemented—the legal and policy frameworks used, the strategies articulated, and the processes adopted—varies with a country's culture, needs, inclinations, and technology maturity (OASIS, 2010; Bicking & Wimmer, 2011; OECD, 2011). The normative protocols for implementing and assessing open government are still evolving: no common set of accepted practices or implementation strategies exists. Rather, each implementation has its own interpretation of the problems to solve, paths to sustainability, impacts sought, measurability, and good practices.

At a high-level, the OECD provides a characterization of open government that is consistent with the literature, that is, government initiatives which:

1. "Strengthen the public debate to create ownership for objectives and methods used" and
2. "Demonstrate results for the purpose of being accountable and building trust." (p.6, 2011)

Many of the open government strategies commonly employed support these characteristics, including making government data open for public re-use and validation; collaboratively developing solutions with citizens; and fostering a culture of presumed, proactive transparency (Lukensmeyer, Goldman, & Stern, 2011; Kundra, 2010). While flexible in language, these strategies each embody the most common aims of open government: accountability, trust, and collaboration.

A decomposition of the U.S. Open Government Directive (OGD), policies, speeches, and discussions within the U.S. open government community suggests six discrete objectives for open government (Linders & Wilson, 2011):

- Improved accountability;
- Public reuse of data;
- Citizen engagement;
- Open innovation and crowd sourcing;
- Collaborative service delivery; and
- Interagency partnering.

These objectives are pushed by four clusters of advocates—transparency and oversight watchdogs; technologists; e-democracy and citizen participation supporters; and bureaucratic reformers—that both complement and compete in their interests. But their collective voice presents no clear, overarching vision. As a result, "the idea of open government is still an abstract one–to-many" (Montalbano, 2010b).

2.2   Transformational Government

Transformational government is often viewed as e-government's next evolutionary step, requiring technology for its implementation (Jansseen & Shu, 2008). But it is similarly unscoped, leaving a number of unanswered questions (OASIS, 2010; Bertot, Jaeger, & Grimes, 2010), such as:

- Which government structures should be transformed, to what extent, and how?
- Should transformation depend on using technology?
- Does openness provide the venue for transformation?
- Who should participate?
- How should transformation be measured?

At a high level, consensus is developing regarding the characteristics of government infrastructures that are transformational (Bannister & Connolly, 2011):

- *Transparency and open access to information*: tools and data that facilitate public engagement in decision making, expand situational awareness, challenge the validity of information and practices, and encourage innovative reuse.
- *Participation and collaboration*: citizen partnerships with government entities, using government resources and information to identify specific problems, and co-design/co-produce resolutions.

Importantly, these characteristics directly mirror the key principles of open government. Whereas this is in part due to conceptual overlaps, it also suggests opportunities for complementarity. For instance, transformation requires an environment of mutually assumed trust and transparency that gives the agency and stakeholders the confidence to accept the new norm change brings (Bannister & Connolly, 2011). Open government can provide the mechanism for building this public trust (Freed, 2010; Nye, Zelikow, & King, 1997). Indeed, open government has tremendous potential to enable and give meaning to the concept of government transformation.

2.3   Open Government and the Transformation of the Social Contract

If government is to transform through ICTs, it will likely be the interaction between people and the technology that creates something new and valuable, not the technology itself (Scholl, 2005). Likewise, open government is not so much an end in itself as a means to *fundamentally evolve* the relationship between governments and their citizens toward a collaborative partnership. In particular, governments can today leverage the information revolution to offer their citizens the means to genuinely "ask what you can do for your country" (Cameron, 2010). This has come not a moment too soon, as budget-crunched governments can no longer afford to act on their own. Recognizing this, politicians have begun to reshape their governing philosophy around transferring power and decision-making to their citizens in exchange for added public responsibility.

It is likely in these newly enabled forms of citizen participation and collaboration that government's true transformational potential lies. With ICTs enabling "many more people to work together," it is possible that "we can redesign our institutions" around collaborative problem-solving and thereby deliver a "new kind of democratic legitimacy" (Noveck 2009, p. xiv). In this new arrangement, "government becomes a platform for the creation of public value and social innovation. It provides resources, sets rules, and mediates disputes, but it allows citizens, nonprofits, and the private sector to do most of the heavy lifting" (Tapscott, 2010, p. xvii). Open data, for instance, enables the public to "do things government employees might not think to do, to achieve objectives far beyond those of government organizations" (Lakhani, Austin, & Yi, 2010, p.1). Indeed, the tools of open government present an unprecedented opportunity to *transform* the social contract by transitioning from a focus on entitlements and a "citizen-as-customer" transactional relationship towards shared responsibilities via government-citizen collaborations (Linders, 2011). To examine this changing relationship in detail, it is important to explore the evolution of open government.

3   EVOLUTION OF OPEN GOVERNMENT

3.1   Historical Support

Open government is not a new concept. Dating back to Sweden's 1766 Freedom of the Press Act, it is reflected in the U.S. Declaration of

Independence and is integral to the Constitution (Article 1, Section 5). This commitment is strengthened through legislation, executive orders, and administrative policies that protect citizens' right to understand the government's business, influences, and decisions. While their motives varied, nearly every president since 1900 has contributed to these policies and reforms (Peri, 1995). Institutions such as the Government Printing Office and Federal Depository Libraries further ensure that the public has access to government information and data (Jaeger, Bertot, & Shuler, 2010). But these measures to ensure openness are often counterbalanced by efforts to restrict access to government information and operations, usually in the name of national security (Gorham-Oscilowski & Jaeger, 2008). The OGI marks a significant rebalancing of such policies in favor of openness.

3.2. The U.S. Open Government Directive

Building on his campaign's successful use of the Internet and social media, President Obama based the OGI around the principles of transparency of information; participation in decision-making; and collaboration in problem-solving (Orszag, 2009). Through agency Open Government Plans, the OGD instilled these principles into the functions of government by instructing agencies to:

- Identify key stakeholders;
- Make "high-value" datasets available;
- Design flagship initiatives; and
- Explore new ways of engaging and collaborating with the public.

The process of developing the plans generated extensive discussions and partnerships between agency open government representatives and advocates, academia, and commercial vendors via open forums, workshops, seminars, and an emerging community of practice (Bertot, Smith, & McDermott, 2012). An independent audit[1] suggested that many agencies innovatively used the OGD as a tool to further their existing open government activities, even if the Directive was often viewed as yet another compliance mandate (Wilson & Linders, 2011).

3.3 Initiatives and Accomplishments

To date, federal agencies have launched over 350 initiatives that have helped to reshape the government's interactions with the public while making vast stores of federal data available for public reuse and validation (Vein, 2011). Table 2.1. identifies some of the chief accomplishments.

Table 2.1   Selected Accomplishments of the U.S. Open Government Initiative

Data Publication	Citizen Engagement
• *Data.gov* provides access to about 380,000 government datasets in usable formats on subjects ranging from budgets to demography to astronomy. • *Recovery.gov* provides transparent access to Recovery Act spending for public oversight. • Mash-ups of many different data streams (e.g., *On the Map for Emergency Management*) enable comprehensive analysis by the public. • *E-FOIA reading rooms* post Freedom of Information Act (FOIA)-released documents on agency websites.	• Commercial entities are shaping new businesses around open government data; *Data.gov* cites over 230 citizen-developed applications (Kundra, 2011). • The *America COMPETES Act* promotes using prizes and challenges to incentivize citizen and private sector contributions such as through *Challenge.gov*. • We *the* People (https://petitions.whitehouse.gov/) encourages the public to post online petitions for White House review. • *Regulations.gov* posts proposed regulations for citizen comment. • The White House hosts virtual town hall meetings, and most of the 24 major departments have a presence on Facebook, Twitter, YouTube, or other platforms.

3.4   Towards a Global Movement

The OGI gave rise to a global open government movement. Close on Obama's heels, Prime Minister David Cameron of the United Kingdom's (U.K.) began a radical push for "the Big Society" that aims to leverage modern ICT infrastructure to shift government functions back into the hands of the people. Parallel efforts elsewhere—from Singapore's "Government-with-You" strategy to Kenya's ground-breaking open data portal—are more disjointed but share many drivers, objectives, and policy arguments. More are likely to follow, with the U.S. and Brazil launching a prominent Open Government Partnership (OGP) to guide and incentivize similar initiatives across the globe.

4   OPEN GOVERNMENT AS A VEHICLE FOR TRANSFORMATION

The varied experiences of U.S. agency implementations demonstrate that open government for its own sake may not be sufficient to unlock the information revolution's potential to reshape the government/citizen relationship. Rather, this transformation must be strategically targeted using openness as a tool rather than an end-goal in ways that align with the agency's mission (Lee & Kwak, 2011). The most successful U.S. agency transformations validate this assertion, such as:

- The Department of Health and Human Services has implemented an open infrastructure to spark an entirely new Health 2.0 industry via public-private partnerships around data-driven healthcare, electronic health records, and innovative healthcare service delivery.
- The State Department is enlisting the public in its on-line diplomatic efforts (e.g., Virtual Student Foreign Service) and rejuvenating its promotion of transparency and good governance via the OGP.
- NASA has centered its initiatives around open innovation to create public value through open source technologies and scientific projects, while benefiting from valuable contributions from the public through competitions.
- The Federal Communications Commission is expanding inclusive e-rulemaking through crowd-sourcing technologies to "open a process that was closed for too long" (VanRoekel, 2010).

These successful strategies leverage open government for strategic transformation. This pattern of success is consistent worldwide, from Singapore tapping openness to combat citizen apathy; Kenya connecting open government to the devolution of power to local governments; and to the World Bank embracing open development to reshape its role in an increasingly multi-polar and networked world.

Adopting a similarly targeted approach, the international Open Government Declaration issued by the OGP explicitly structures open government commitments around a set of goals, or "grand challenges." Analysis of member nations' action plans demonstrates that governments intend to address these challenges by operationalizing the OGP's core principles—transparency/accountability, citizen participation, and technology/innovation—through deliberate actions that enable specific government transformations (Table 2.2).

Table 2.2 Transformation Goals Targeted to Address Grand Challenges through OGP Principles

	OGP Core Principles		
OGP Grand Challenge	*Transparency/ Accountability*	*Citizen Participation*	*Technology/ Innovation*
Improved public services	Citizen choice & informed decision-making	Collaborative service delivery & open innovation	Citizen-centric, digital service delivery
Increased public integrity	Open book government	Real-time citizen feedback	eProcurement
More effective public resource management	Open data	Participatory planning & budgeting	Shared services

Table 2.3 synthesizes the toolbox of open government policy, business, technology, and community enablers that governments are employing to realize these transformation goals as identified by the action plans, which for the first time, provide a standardized way to look across national open government initiatives. In so doing, it provides a preliminary framework for how open government can drive transformation.

Table 2.3   Open Government Enablers for Transformation

Transformation	Examples	Enablers		
		Policy/Business	*Technology*	*Community*
Citizen choice & informed decision-making	▪Police.uk (U.K.) ▪Performance.gov (U.S.) ▪ "Know your service rights" (South Africa)	▪Results-based management ▪Performance indicators ▪Data publication guidelines ▪Public awareness campaigns	▪Performance dashboards portal ▪Crime mapping ▪Open agency information systems ▪National geographic information system	▪Citizen report cards
Collaborative service delivery & open innovation	▪Open Data Communities, ExpertNet (U.S.) ▪Space App Competition (U.S.) ▪Regulations.gov (U.S.)	▪Open government license ▪Competitions ▪Public-private partnerships ▪Scientific data guidelines ▪Open rulemaking framework	▪Open APIs ▪Online communities/ collaboration spaces ▪E-rulemaking ▪Ideation platforms	▪Government data reuse ▪Civil society partnership on implementation projects ▪Expert networks
Citizen-centric, digital service delivery	▪Gob.mx (Mexico) ▪Plain language project (Norway) ▪Household targeting system for social services (Philippines)	▪Business process improvement ▪Administrative simplification ▪Consolidation of service delivery channels ▪Citizen charter	▪One-stop interactive citizen service delivery portal ▪Household electronic registry, targeting system ▪Zero-touch technologies	▪Citizen surveys ▪Assisted digital service providers
Real-time citizen feedback	▪Presidential Hotline (South Africa) ▪FixMyStreet (U.K.) ▪Open311 (U.S.)	▪Citizen complaints management ▪Open forums, town halls, workshops ▪Whistleblower protection	▪Social participation systems ▪Online feedback mechanisms ▪Online reporting, hotlines ▪Crime mapping	▪Online/ mobile reporting ▪Civil society services monitoring

(continued)

Table 2.3   (continued)

Transformation	Examples	Enablers		
		Policy/Business	Technology	Community
Open book government & Open data	•Data.gov.uk (U.K.) •Recovery.gov (U.S.) •Open Gov Plans (U.S.)	•Right to information •Proactive data publication •Open data standards •Public sector transparency board •Digital records management •Agency open government plans •Declassification regimes	•Open data portal •Expenditure tracking system •Information registry •Agency data inventories •Unified data warehouse •Electronic records	•Partnerships with developers, civil society, students, etc.
Participatory planning & budgeting	•Participatory Budgeting (Brazil) •We-*the*-People (U.S.) •EITI (Indonesia)	•Participatory budgeting and development planning •Social audits •Transparent budgeting	•E-petitioning •Online dialogs and town halls •Fiscal transparency system	•Consultative National Conferences, Councils
eProcurement	•Comprasnet (Brazil) •CompraNet (Mexico)	•Consolidated bidding •Civil recruitment transparency •Anti-corruption conventions	•Electronic procurement system	•Civil society oversight
Shared services	•Data center consolidation (U.S.) •Directgov (U.K.)	•Business process improvement •Consolidated sites, data center •Whole-of-government architecture	•Consolidated digital services •Integrated financial information system •Cloud computing	•Open source solutions

The interplay among these enablers is complex, but the findings suggest that each targeted transformation necessitates a somewhat different set of actions. This argues against adopting foreign open government models wholesale; rather, governments should tailor implementations to their particular strategic goals and ensure that they suit local contexts, needs, and opportunities.

That said, the action plans also demonstrate strong consensus around a common set of basic enablers: a right to information; transparency of planning, process, and systems; and platforms for data publication, public engagement, and online service delivery. While the specific implementation will differ based on goals and circumstance, virtually all genuine open government initiatives require this baseline infrastructure and enabling policy environment.

Indeed, perhaps the most exciting characteristic of the OGP is that it offers the catalyst and means for developing countries to realize the level of transparency, citizen engagement, and good governance that have largely remained the reserve of mature democracies. In these more nascent environments, even the first steps towards open government represent not incremental improvements (as in the U.S.) but a fundamental *transformation* of their governance model.

5   LESSONS FROM A PIONEER: THE STATE OF U.S. OPEN GOVERNMENT

While the pioneering U.S. experience has rightly served as a model for those who have followed, it is important also to explore opportunities for improvement and appropriate differentiation. Accordingly, this section identifies several obstacles encountered by the OGI, with a particular focus on the challenges to sustainability.

5.1   One Year After the Directive

Early in 2011, rising budgetary pressures for a more cost-effective government pushed agencies to focus on mission-critical activities only—a condition few open government initiatives met. Looking to cut costs, Congress reduced the 2011 budget for federal e-government programs by 76 percent, shuttering or slowing federal shared services and open government efforts (Serbu, 2011). Meanwhile, the White House's rhetoric has shifted to a focus on customer service, which downplays the role of citizens as partners (Executive Order 13571), just as many of the open government champions—including the first Federal Chief Information Officer (CIO)—have left their White House posts (Howard, 2011). In this shifting policy environment, few agency plans have been updated since the last review, a number of efforts remain incomplete, and little new data is posted to *Data.gov* (Perera, 2011; Lukensmeyer et al., 2011).

The future of open government therefore remains unclear; some even predict its "slow, inevitable death" (Wadhwa, 2011). But perhaps open government has simply entered what Gartner's hype cycle identifies as the "trough of disillusionment" with the deflation of the impossible expectations that had been placed upon it (Fenn & Raskino, 2011).

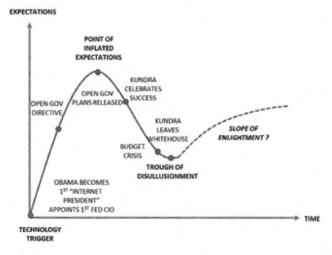

Figure 2.1   U.S. Open Government Initiative on the Gartner Hype Cycle.

The question now is whether and how the U.S. can re-energize its efforts to reach the cycle's "slope of enlightenment" (Figure 2.1).

5.2   Overcoming the Challenges

Fiscal pressures need not mean the end of open government efforts. To the contrary, openness can form *the* central strategy in today's dominant narrative of budget cuts, smaller government, and the elimination of waste—as it has in Britain under Prime Minister Cameron. He declares that transparency is at the heart of his government's agenda of improving services without spending more money by "radically redistributing power away from government and to communities and people" (Cameron, 2011b). Indeed, despite similar budget shortfalls, the U.K. government has committed to "the most ambitious open data agenda of any government in the world" (2011a), an assertion supported by the *Guardian* (Rogers, 2011).

Beyond the failure to effectively tie open government to the changing political winds in favor of small government, the literature points to other potential pitfalls that may have been inherent to the OGI implementation approach. Conditions which often derail technology products include: lack of standards and measurements; little top-level governance; unmaintained efforts; inhibited data sharing; legal barriers; and limited funding, experience, and training (OASIS, 2010). Likewise, a lack of clear direction risks disintegrating transformational efforts "into a set of unrelated and confusing directives and activities" (Fernandez & Rainey, 2006, p. 169). Some of these conditions were present in the

OGI. Specifically, research and interviews with government administrators conducted by the authors (Wilson & Linders, 2011) identified the absence of three critical success factors:

1. *Factor 1: Clear Vision and Leadership.* Taking an agency-centric perspective, the U.S. has promoted change from the bottom. But agencies often meet unfunded mandates with recalcitrance in favor of funded priorities; combined with the OGD's lack of specificity, this limited the ability to create significant change. The OGD also did not clearly articulate strategy and definitions by focusing on abstract principles, leaving agency CIOs "fuzzy" about open government and needing more "direction and clarity" (Montalbano, 2010a). Without clear guidance, agencies developed their own definitions and policies with little cross-agency cohesion.

2. *Factor 2: Specific Implementation Guidance and Success Measurements.* Lack of a robust, consensus-based implementation framework made "success" nearly impossible to define. Thus, agencies struggled to build internal business cases or demonstrate value. The OGD also indirectly encouraged pro-forma compliance (e.g., publishing "high-value data sets" for compliance rather than for their value) by requiring immediate outputs and technology implementations rather than the patient organizational reform needed for institutionalization within day-to-day operations.

3. *Factor 3: Citizen-Centricity.* A focus on building a vast catalog of raw data—much of questionable quality—rather than directly delivering a coherent set of citizen-centric services meant that a large share of the OGI efforts were not immediately usable by the broader public. Many required intermediary citizen "hactivists" and developers to create applications and visualizations to make the data useful. This reliance on the "invisible hand of data"—"release it and they will build apps" (Robinson et al, 2009)—proved inferior to more citizen-centric efforts, such as Britain's data.gov.uk which focused on collecting centrally identified high-value datasets and on filtering data down to a citizen's postal code to deliver localized mash-ups, tools, and services for informing citizen decision making (e.g., on hospitals, schooling, local street crime, commuting, etc.) (Rogers, 2011).

The White House recognizes the challenges and endeavors to return open government to prominence, particularly via the OGP and the release of the U.S. *Action Plan*, which recommits the federal government to deepening FOIA and transparency, promoting greater participation in policy making, expanding access to data, and modernizing recordkeeping (Open Government Partnership, 2011). While these commitments are neither dramatic nor new, planned implementing guidelines will provide more actionable protocols for agency implementations so that outcomes can be measured across the federal space, and lessons can be shared with international partners.

6 CONCLUSIONS

The relationship between openness and transformation is symbiotic: openness is essential for providing the tools and guiding principles that enable transformation, whereas transformation provides purpose and concrete policy challenges for impactful open government. However, both concepts continue to lack clearly defined characteristics or thresholds from which to develop measurable outputs, pin-point maturity, or assess outcomes (Wilson & Linders, 2011). Likewise, no consensus framework yet exists to enable consistent interpretation, and no critical analysis has been performed to understand the impact of transformation on those with the least clout (e.g., the poor, minorities, and the disadvantaged)—that is, will they be more deliberately engaged or further marginalized?

Not waiting for theory to catch up with practice, the Obama administration's OGI spawned a global movement that focuses government transparency around proactive, wholesale data publication and that spearheads adoption of Web 2.0 interactivity for improved citizen participation and collaboration. Many nations are actively adapting these principles to their needs, cultures, and conditions, ranging from Norway's emphasis on extractive industry transparency to the Philippines' focus on combating a culture of corruption by institutionalizing "People Power." With efforts still new, many of these transformational efforts have yet to show significant measurable value and impact. But the experiences of the pioneers offer early lessons that can provide a foundation for the transformation of the government/citizen relationship worldwide.

NOTES

1. Described fully at https://sites.google.com/site/opengovtplans/home.

REFERENCES

Bannister, F., & Connolly, R. (2011). Trust and transformational government: A proposed framework for research. *Government Information Quarterly*, *28*(2), 137–147.

Bertot, J. C., Jaeger, P. T., & Grimes, J. M. (2010). Using ICTs to create a culture of transparency: E-government and social media as openness and anti-corruption tools for societies. *Government Information Quarterly*, *27*(3), 264–271.

Bertot, J. C., Smith, T., & McDermott, P. (2012). Measurement of Open Government: Metrics and Process. Hawaii International Conference on System Sciences. *(January 4–7)* (pp. 2491–2499). Maui, HI: IEEE.

Bicking, M., & Wimmer, M. A. (2011). A scenario-based approach towards open collaboration for policy modelling. In M. Janssen, H. Scholl, M. Wimmer, & Y.-h. Tan (Eds.), *Electronic Government* (Vol. 6846, pp. 223–234). Heidelberg: Springer Berlin.

Cameron, D. (2010, February). The next age of government. *TED Talk*. Retrieved October 1, 2011, from http://www.ted.com/talks/david_cameron.html

Cameron, D. (2011a, July 7). *Letters to Cabinet Members on Transparency and Open Data*. Retrieved October 2, 2011, from Number 10: http://www. number10.gov.uk/news/letter-to-cabinet-ministers-on-transparency-and-open-data/

Cameron, D. (2011b, July 7). PM on Government Transparency. Retrieved October 1, 2011, from http://www.youtube.com/watch?v=tQTt4l2Qmd4&feature=player_embedded

Fenn, J., & Raskino, M. (2011). *Understanding Gartner's Hype Cycles*. Stamford, CT: Gartner, Inc.

Fernandez, S., & Rainey, H. (2006). Managing Successful Organizational Change in the Public Sector. *Public Adminisration Review* , 66(2), 168–176.

Freed, L. (2010, October 26). *American customer satisfaction index: E-government satisfaction index*. Retrieved November 2, 2010, from American Customer Satisfaction Index: http://www.foreseeresults.com/research-white-papers/_downloads/foresee-results-acsi-egov-index-q3-2010.pdf

Gorham-Oscilowski, U., & Jaeger, P. T. (2008). National Security Letters, the USA PATRIOT Act, and the Constitution: The tensions between national security and civil rights. *Government Information Quarterly* , 25(4), 625–644.

Howard, A. (2011, July 9). *Open Government Grows Globally Despite Whitehouse*. Retrieved October 2, 2011, from Governing People: http://governingpeople. com/alexander-howard/23218/white-house-tech-talent-comes-and-goes-open-government-continues-grow-globall

Jaeger, P. T., Bertot, J. C., & Shuler, J. A. (2010). The Federal Depository Library Program (FDLP), Academic Libraries, and Access to Government Information. *Journal of Academic Librarianship* , 36(6), 469–478.

Jansseen, M., & Shu, W. S. (2008). Transformational government: Basics and key issues. *Proceedings of the 2nd international conference on Theory and practice of electronic governance (ICEGOV '08)* (pp. 117–122). New York: ACM.

Kundra, V. (2010, March 23). Removing the Shroud of Secrecy: Making Government More Transparent and Accountable. *CIO*.

Kundra, V. (2011, May 20). *From Data to Apps: Putting Government Information to Work for You*. Retrieved September 21, 2011, from White House Blog: http://www.whitehouse.gov/blog/2011/05/20/data-apps-putting-government-information-work-you

Lakhani, K. R., Austin, R. D., & Yi, Y. (2010). *Data.gov*. Boston, MA: Harvard Business Publishing.

Lee, G., & Kwak, Y. H. (2011). *An Open Government Implementation Model: Moving to Increased Public Engagement*. Washington, DC: IBM Center for the Business of Government.

Linders, D. X. (2011). We-government: An anatomy of citizen coproduction in the information age. *Proceedings of the 12th Annual International Digital Government Research Conference: Digital Government Innovation in Challenging Times (June 12–15)* (pp. 167–176). College Park, MD: ACM.

Linders, D. X., & Wilson, S. C. (2011). What is Open Government? One Year after the Directive. *Proceedings of the 12th Annual International Digital Government Research Conference: Digital Government Innovation in Challenging Times (June 12–15, 2011) (pp. 262–271). College Park, MD: ACM.

Lukensmeyer, C. J., Goldman, J., & Stern, D. (2011). *Assessing Public Participation in an Open Government Era: A Review of Federal Agency Plans*. Center for the Business of Government. Washington, DC: IBM.

Montalbano, E. (2010a, March 23). Federal CIOs seek direction on open government. Retried on May 1, 2011, from *Information Week*: http://www.informationweek.com/news/government/info-management/224200101

Montalbano, E. (2010b, March 24). Kundra outlines open government progress. Retrieved May 1, 2011, from *Information Week*: http://www.informationweek.com/news/government/leadership/224200264

Noveck, B. S. (2009). *Wiki Government: How Technology Can Make Government Better, Democracy Stronger, and Citizens More Powerful*. Washington, DC: Brookings Institution Press.

Nye, J. S., Zelikow, P. D., & King, D. C. (1997). *Why People Don't Trust Government*. Cambridge, MA: Harvard University Press.

OASIS. (2010). *Avoiding the Pitfalls of eGovernment: 10 lessons learnt from eGovernment deployments*. eGov. Retrieved April 27, 2011 from Organization for the Advancement of Structured Information Standards: http://www.oasis-egov.org/sites/oasis-egov.org/files/eGov_Pitfalls_Guidance%20Doc_v1.pdf

OECD. (2011). *The Call for Innovative and Open Government: An Overview of Country Initiatives*. Paris: Organisation for Economic Co-Operation and Development.

Open Government Partnership. (September 20, 2011). *U.S. National Action Plan*. Retrieved April 27, 2011 from http://www.whitehouse.gov/sites/default/files/us_national_action_plan_final_2.pdf

Orszag, P. (2009). *Open Government Directive: Memorandum for the Heads of Executive Departments and Agencies*. Washington, DC: Office of Management and Budget.

Perera, D. (2011, August 24). *Participation lacking from open government plans*. Retrieved August 25, 2011, from Fierce Government: http://www.fiercegovernmentit.com/story/participation-lacking-open-government-plans/2011–08–24

Peri, A. (1995). Reform's changing role. *Public Administration Review* , 55(5), 407–417.

Robinson, D. G., Yu, H., Zeller, W. P., & Felton, E. W. (2009). Government data and the invisible hand. *Yale Journal of Law and Technology* , 11, 160–175.

Rogers, S. (2011, July 7). The government's new transparency intitiatives: What data will they release and how big a deal is it? *Guardian*.

Scholl, H. J. (2005). Hans Jochen Scholl. In M. A. Wimmer, R. Traunmüller, Å. Grönlund, & K. V. Andersen (Ed.), *Lecture Notes in Computer Science*. 3591. Copenhagen, Denmark: 4th International Conference, EGOV 2005, Proceedings.

Serbu, J. (2011, April 23). Six-month budget slashes e-gov fund by 76 percent. *Federal News Radio*.

Tapscott, D. (2010). Foreward. In D. Lathrop & L. Ruma, Eds. *Open Government: Collaboration, Transparency, and Participation in Practice*. O'Reilly Media.

VanRoekel, S. (2010, December 7). *The FCC and First Year of Open Government*. Retrieved October 2, 2011, from FCC Blog: http://www.fcc.gov/blog/fcc-and-first-year-open-government

Vein, C. (2011, April 7). *Open Government Plans' Anniversary is a Testament to Hard Work at Agencies*. Retrieved September 23, 2011, from White House Blog: http://www.whitehouse.gov/blog/2011/04/07/open-government-plans-anniversary-testament-hard-work-agencies

Wadhwa, V. (2011, June 21). The death of open government. Retrieved May 1, 2011, from *The Washington Post*: http://www.washingtonpost.com/national/on-innovations/the-coming-death-of-open-government/2011/06/21/AGP-K3afH_story.html

Wilson, S. C., & Linders, D. X. (2011). The Open Government Directive: A Preliminary Assessment. *Proceedings of the iConference, February 8–11* (pp. 387–394). Seattle: ACM.

3 E-Government and the Evolution of Service Canada

Transformation or Stagnation?

Jeffrey Roy

CHAPTER OVERVIEW

The purpose of this chapter is to critically examine the Government of Canada's service transformation efforts over the past decade. Although e-government denotes a wider reform lens than service architecture and delivery strategies, for many countries, certainly Canada among them, service became the starting point and hallmark of online efforts at the turn of the century as Internet usage exploded. The example of Service Canada was widely regarded as an international leader, propelling Canada to or near the apex of many surveys such as those completed by Accenture Consulting and the United Nations. In recent years, however, Canada's relative performance has stagnated (reflected to varying degrees in international survey rankings) as the service transformation agenda has become mired in a range of complex issues and challenges examined here.

1 INTRODUCTION

The emergence of the Internet as a mainstream venue for communications and commerce over the past decade has given rise to online delivery mechanisms as a centrepiece of both the public and private sector service strategies alike. With regards to the public sector, the e-government agenda has come to denote the broad application of new information and communication technologies (ICTs) to the public sector as a whole. In most countries, however, e-service delivery denotes the chronological starting point and the main strategic impetus for operationalizing the Internet for public sector usage.

Within such a digital context, the Government of Canada (GOC) provides unique insight into the challenges of online and multi-channel service delivery. Recognized by organizations such as the United Nations, the OECD and Accenture Consulting as a leading jurisdiction in online service capacities, Canada began its second major phase of service delivery transformation in 2005 with the creation of Service Canada. Building on prior efforts to move information and services online, Service Canada's mission is to expand integrated service delivery capacities (in terms of both service offerings and delivery channels) across government in order to realize more citizen-centric outcomes.

The purpose of this chapter is, therefore, to provide a critical assessment of both the Canadian federal government's experience to date and the prospects for Service Canada going forward. This article puts forward three variables that have been responsible for the decelerating progress of the Canadian public sector generally and Service Canada specifically since its early emergence and success, namely: (i) Process—structural and cultural challenges of internal governance in realizing more integrated and online service offerings; (ii) Place—accentuating the multi-channel puzzle is the tension between urban and rural environments and the multitude of service architectures in urban settings (combined with the dearth of such actors in rural and remote locations); and (iii) Politics—the IT literary of political leaders and the impacts of scandal and minority politics over the past decade.

The chapter is organized as follows. Section 2 contextualizes the Service Canada model by reviewing the main contours of electronic service delivery in the e-government era: it also sketches the Canadian context by describing the evolution of Service Canada. Section 3 then examines the four aforementioned variables shaping the Service Canada experience. Section 4 concludes the chapter with a summary of the present IT governance and service quagmire confronting the Government of Canada.

2   THE EVOLVING GOVERNANCE OF ELECTRONIC SERVICE DELIVERY[1]

The emergence of Web 2.0 has called into question for many how best governments should move into the networking and transformational era (Dutil et al., 2010). Up to this point, much of e-government's evolution has reflected something of a linear path examined in this note—with an emphasis on government-wide and public sector–wide strategies for interoperability and integration (leading to some elements of transformational outcomes). The challenge today is whether such a path can be aligned with the emergent networked realities taking shape outside of the public sector (facilitated by online social networking and cloud computing that empower users with a greater set of choices in terms of front end and back end architectures).

Prior to Web 2.0, within the realm of e-government and online service, such learning was relatively static—limited to user surveys of one sort or another (such as the example of Canada's much famed Citizen's First Surveys). With Web 2.0 emerging as a driver of more interactive and dynamic learning, consistent with a culture of mass collaboration (individually and organizationally), a much more collective engagement process is required.

Consequently, government must facilitate the widest possible set of dialogues across all stakeholders, while also acknowledging and leveraging the reality that many such dialogues will form outside of the purview of government as we have traditionally come to know it. Early public opinion data suggests that governments enjoy a level of support by the public to pursue the transformational potential of Web 2.0 for service and democratic renewal. Yet polls and surveys cannot be enough to gather the tacit knowledge of those citizens (or customers in the service realm) proving to be early adapters to new social networking platforms, mobile channels and the like (Dutil et al., 2010).

It is important to underscore how the urgency for governments may at times be both understated and overstated. In terms of the former, clearly any level of service satisfaction at present cannot be viewed as reason for inaction given the widening expansion of online communities and virtual channels. With regards to the latter, however, active Web 2.0 usage remains limited to a relatively small segment of the population, presenting an opportunity for public sector providers to not radically re-organize themselves to the whims of this early adapter group but instead to engage them as an important source of learning and knowledge. And it is here, once again, where demographics becomes so crucial since the dilemma for government is a relatively aging cadre of senior managers far removed from the realities of newer generations of workers growing up in an Internet and now Web 2.0 era (Tapscott & Williams, 2006).

In sum, Web 2.0 and collaborative innovations emerging through experimental processes are all the more likely to be poorly suited to central coordination. For many governments, embracing this sort of organic approach to mass collaboration and Web 2.0 innovation may not fit easily with the emphasis during the past decade on integrated portals and specialized service providers.

2.1 From GOL (1999) to Service Canada (2005) to Service Canada 2.0 (?)

The impetus for the major components of the federal e-government strategy arose from a broader effort, *Connecting Canadians* that was crafted in the late 1990s. Many early online services models floundered on overly optimistic projections for take-up levels, and the Government of Canada was criticized by the federal Auditor General for lacking a rigorous business plan to guide efforts. Most fundamentally perhaps, the vertical structures of separate departments serving individual Ministers largely translate into autonomy over interoperability: as one observer put it, 'silos continue to reign' (Coe, 2004, p. 18).

Such findings underscored the growing need for more rigorous collaborative mechanisms and performance frameworks to both facilitate shared action and gauge progress, particularly in service delivery agendas that transcend traditional reporting relationships (Roy, 2006a; 2006b). In recognition of the need for deeper reforms, the Government created a flagship service transformation vehicle, Modernizing Services for Canadians (MSC). In essence, MSC acknowledged not only the challenges confronting Government online (GOL) but it also recognizes that online service delivery must co-exist and align effectively with other service delivery channels, such as telephone and in-person facilities. Beginning with what was the largest department providing domestic programs and services to Canadians, Human Resources Development Canada (HRDC), MSC aimed to change the focus of HRDC from the business of conducting transactions to a new emphasis on building relationships with citizens: "it is transforming the current complex delivery network into a single integrated service delivery network that provides seamless, multi-channel service to Canadians."[2]

MSC became a vehicle to transform a set of services and programs amounting to over $70 billion annually (via an HRDC network of call centers, processing centers, kiosks, web sites and portals, government offices and third-party delivery agents) within a department that counted more than 25,000 employees. Building on this foundation, the 2005 creation of Service Canada sought to extend this concept and approach to a government-wide scale (in a manner that GOL was simply never able to do for the aforementioned reasons).

Accordingly, the underpinnings of the Service Canada concept were a "citizen-centered" business model that sought to focus on people not programs via four foundational elements to this new approach: (i) a focus on the citizen; (ii) one-stop government service; (iii) integrating citizen information; and iv) collaborate and partner (Roy, 2006a/b; Dutil et al., 2010).

Service Canada's mission was thus to apply these concepts in order to improve service, lower costs, and, above all, achieve better outcomes for citizens. There has been documented evidence of improvements in this regard—in terms of both the governance model underpinning a government-wide perspective on service organization and delivery and actual performance (Dutil et al., 2010). Most notable in this latter realm has been extensive surveys conducted by governments themselves to gauge and track over time the public's satisfaction levels with transactional processes led by Service Canada both online and offline. Though not without controversy and methodological debate (Dutil et al., 2010), Service Canada's early accolades and initial progress stem from its positioning as the centerpiece of what today might be thought of as the "Service 1.0" era of e-government: an era of the Internet's emergence when government's sought to remain firmly in control of online content and the delivery channels being deployed to provide information and services to citizens in new ways.

This is not to suggest that such an era is over—merely that it is increasingly under strain and challenged by the evolution of a more interactive, user-driven online universe simplistically denoted as web 2.0 (Roy 2010). Even those responsible for the creation of Service Canada have recognized the need and opportunities intertwined with today's evolving digital world and the new potential for more directly and innovatively engaging the public in not only evaluating the service experience (through post-transactional surveys and the like) but also contributing to the design and execution of service mechanisms and related policy frameworks. The former and founding administrative head of Service Canada, for example, offers the following depiction of what might be termed as a Service 2.0 approach: "Mass collaboration has the potential to transform most spheres of government, but public service delivery is an especially promising area: mass collaboration can help government and the citizenry develop better, more timely and personalized service at lower costs with better outcomes" (Flumian, 2009).

Despite this potential (sketched out by a former public servant outside looking in), and notwithstanding the very real progress that Service Canada has achieved as a single window of information on federal government programs and offerings, the entity has done little to embrace Web 2.0 capabilities beyond leveraging them to better communicate the presence and mission of Service Canada (i.e., a communications platform to market the Service 1.0 infrastructure). Moreover, Service Canada has regressed from its initial ambitions of becoming a single integrated provider of all Government of Canada services to one more focused on a subset of programs and services (albeit the largest bundle of such offerings to individuals provided from within the Human Resources and Skills Development Department). Lastly, following the 2011 federal election the newly constituted Conservative majority government announced the creation of a new federal agency, Shared Services Canada—its mission to focus on consolidating and refurbishing internal IT infrastructures across the Government of Canada. The appointment of the most recent administrative head of Service Canada to lead SCC suggests a diminishment of importance of external service delivery reform as a political priority relative to anticipated cost savings from internal restructuring.

3   DISSECTING RISING STATURE AND CURRENT PREDICAMENTS

This section explores and explains more fully this evolution and stagnation of Service Canada as well as the wider implications for the IT governance reform efforts of the Government of Canada.

The evolving institutional and governance challenges faced by Service Canada can be understood through three separate yet inter-related variables initially invoked at the outset of this chapter: process, place, and politics. Each of these variables will be examined in turn.

3.1   Process

The importance of process has already been recognized in the preceding section in terms of initial and ongoing challenges between the traditionally vertical lines of public sector organization and accountability and the increasingly horizontal and networked demands of integrated service delivery models. Whereas Service Canada provides a single informational window on Government of Canada service offerings, many critical programs and services remain largely under the realm of individual departments and agencies. Two of the most notable, large-scale examples include the payment and processing of tax returns (Canada Revenue Agency, or CRA) and the application, processing and production of Passports (Passport Canada, a special operating agency within the Department of Foreign Affairs). Despite largely separate administrative apparatuses between these entities, the online presence of government has enabled cross-listed web-links to better direct citizens, and limited forms of cooperation such as Service Canada acting as a receiving agent for passport applications in remote communities.

Yet one of the more interesting public administration questions arising from the Service Canada experience is to ask precisely what Service Canada is? Unlike the two aforementioned examples of CRA and Passport Canada—each legislatively constituted and thus accountable for both process and performance, Service Canada has never received any such legislative underpinnings. Perhaps this uncertainly explains why Service Canada has not published an annual report online since 2008–2009. More than imagery, the absence of such formalization has greatly inhibited Service Canada from being more assertive in partnering with other federal actors as well as other levels of government (Langford & Roy, 2008). Today, as will be explained further below (in Section 3.3 on politics), there is reason to believe that this quasi-existence has confirmed Service Canada's role as a service provider for a single department—which in and of itself may well be a more realistic assessment of its place and capabilities. With regards to the attitudes of other federal entities towards Service Canada, moreover, it is perhaps telling that a recent presentation of strategic priorities for the Passport Office (itself a legislatively constituted "special operating agency" within a department) invokes the need for new partnerships but makes no mention of Service Canada as a potential partner.[3]

In short, there have been no formal collaborative underpinnings in terms of organizational governance to enable Service Canada to become a catalyst for cross-governmental collaboration and deeper service integration on a government-wide scale.

3.2   Place

At present, any urban centre in Canada is home to a myriad of public sector service delivery operations. In Halifax, Nova Scotia, as just one typical example, this assortment would include but not be limited to the Municipality, the Provincial Access Nova Scotia offices, Service Canada and Passport Offices, plus a range of semi-public and private facilities such as Canada Post and its private competitors and financial institutions (with their own branches plus those embedded elsewhere such as in grocery stores). While certain incremental innovations such as BizPaL (a common informational portal for new business formation[4]) and integrated processes for birth registration and social insurance numbers have been undertaken, the more significant potential for intra- and inter-governmental collaborative arrangements lies in sorting out this multitude of costly and largely separate multi-channel systems (Langford & Roy, 2008; Dutil et al., 2010; Roy, 2010).

Yet it also bears noting that in an increasingly networked and participative environment depicted as Web 2.0, it becomes necessary to ask the question as to whether it is, in fact, for government to "sort it out" (at least in the traditional manner of devising strategy and delivering service in a linear manner). As interoperability and mobility heighten there is a much greater potential for new and old intermediaries to provide new ways to bundle and deliver services both online and in person. In Australia, for instance, it is Australia Post that delivers most services for state governments, also acting as a recipient for passport applications and other federal services: in 2010, the Australian federal government initiated a dialog on payment reform—with an eye to expanded usage of electronic systems via a wider assortment of public–private and multi-jurisdictional arrangements. Australia and Canada, both federations, also share the separate and jealously competing constitutional egos of federal and provincial (state) entities, along with subsumed municipalities which admittedly augments the inter-jurisdictional challenges relative to unitary countries such as Denmark (Chiara Ubaldi & Roy, 2010).

In many leading digital jurisdictions in Europe, by contrast, local governments are the front line point of access for the public sector as a whole (Chiara Ubaldi & Roy, 2010). Although much easier to accomplish in unitary countries, it nonetheless bears noting that even perpetually unstable and fragmented federated country such as Belgium has managed an integrated back office infrastructure that is now yielding electronic smart card innovations in service bundling across jurisdictional lines. Belgium, as with much of Europe, benefits from a much higher degree of digital literacy by elected officials than is the case in Canada at the moment. Herein lines the third determinant—politics, and the unwillingness of elected officials to tackle to hard questions of paper and place in a direct and collaborative and holistic manner.

3.3 Politics

One constant theme of e-government research since the inception of online activity and electronic services has been the importance of political leadership to support, drive and sustain the sorts of systemic changes implied by the presence and interaction of process, paper, and place considerations on public sector governance models (Roy 2006a, 2006b; Dutil et al., 2010). Although Canada benefited from such political engagement early on—leading to the creation of and widely noted online presence Service Canada, such political interest has waned in recent years, distracted by a massive federal spending scandal and the recent economic downturn (both of which were addressed within the context of several years of minority Parliaments).

As noted above, the formation of a majority government in 2011 has to some extent revived interest in digital matters—albeit seemingly in a way framed by concerns around federal spending and deficit reduction plans. In other words, IT and government are once again viewed as drivers of cost savings despite the limited success that governments have had in Canada or elsewhere at realizing significant savings in light of rapidly changing technological infrastructures and, in the case of Canada, well documented concerns about an aging and increasingly antiquated IT infrastructures in need of significant financial investments. Thus, the creation of Shared Services Canada suggests an inward focus consistent with pressures for efficiency and consolidation but ill-suited to adaptation and innovation to newly emerging challenges and potentials such as those identified by Flumian (above).

Additionally, and in line with the discussion of place based pressures, it bears noting that despite the many international accolades stemming from significant national visibility (itself stemming from the centralized structures of Canadian fiscal federalism), Service Canada was itself built upon preceding models crafted at the provincial level. Today, consistent with a longstanding North American tradition of public sector reform as a bottom-up movement of subnational experimentation leading to federal (i.e., national reforms), it is once again municipalities and provinces leading the charge on new innovations such as open data initiatives that seek to more directly engage citizens in service design processes.

Yet despite the existence of a federal-provincial Council of senior managers responsible for respective jurisdictional service efforts (i.e., Service Canada, Service Nova Scotia, Service Ontario etc.), itself an important vehicle for cross-learning, joint research, and incremental innovations, the shared view among most provincial officials is that Service Canada's attentions and resources are largely diverted inwardly toward federal government operations and priorities at the expense of significant cross-jurisdictional reform. The exclusion of municipalities from this body on the one hand, and the absence of any formal political mechanism to underpin the sorts of shared accountability relationships that would be required for a holistic public sector perspective further underscores the limitations of the status quo. The additional risk stemming from the inward focus of federal officials and politicians on government-wide consolidation and new developments such as cloud computing is an accentuation of this relative separation of federal, provincial, and municipal processes at the expense of planning for a more holistic public sector architecture capable of crafting innovation solutions to the challenges of process, paper, and place.

4 CONCLUSION—LOOKING AHEAD

Since its creation in 2005 Service Canada has proven to be partially successful. On the one hand, it is has facilitated both online via call centers and online via its portal a government-wide informational dimension that had not previously existed. On the other hand, the absence of more robust governance made it impossible for this entity (that is neither a department nor an agency in legislative terms) to extend much beyond its still consequential role as delivery agent for the basket of programs and services within the HRSDC portfolio. Yet this latter reality may well prove to be a mixed blessing for two reasons: first, it is questionable as to whether a single entity could administratively consolidate and deliver "all" federal government services; and second, and more recently, the more dispersed, distributed and participative era of Web 2.0 now fully challenges even the strategic rationale behind attempting to do so.

The present conundrum facing Service Canada and the public sector as a whole, then, remains the existence of many "single" windows of service providers: Service Canada, Service Nova Scotia (or most any province), municipal portals and 311 call centers, along with a growing myriad of collaborative endeavours linking private and public agents (and giving urgent rise to the need for a more robust identity management ecosystem to underpin such experimentation that effectively represents the struggle between democratization of service innovation and the centralized security apparatuses of governments at each level).

The present mindset and culture of centralization inherent within federal and provincial government models would thus suggest that Service Canada become the face for public sector service to citizens for all governments (or at the very least dictate the terms of any collaborative arrangements involving other government levels). Such an implicit stance looms large in explaining the current state of paralysis described above (since it is naturally enough a non-starter for provincial authorities—leading to the dearth of political collaboration required to underpin wider and deeper forms of concerted action). Conversely, a refashioned Service Canada—more autonomous with a corporate governance regime of shared governance encompassing federal, provincial and municipal representation, could instead focus on spurring the creation of a more open and shared backend infrastructure for the public sector as a whole. Yet the manner by which Service Canada has recently stalled and given way on the backend to the newly created Shared Services Canada suggests that the dearth of collaboration seems destined to continue for some time to come.

NOTES

1. Early parts of this section are drawn from the following article: Roy, J. (2006). E-Service delivery and new governance capacities: "Service Canada" as a case study. *International Journal of Services Technology and Management, 7*(3), 257–271.
2. These quoted captions are from internal MSC planning documents made available to the other by MSC managers. They have also been used as a basis for a case study focusing on the private sector's role in collaborating with the federal government's lead MSC department (then HRDC) responsible for MSC (Dutil, Langford, & 2005).
3. See http://www.ppt.gc.ca/consultations/articles/2010–05–20-csfi-eng.pdf.
4. See www.bizpal.ca.

REFERENCES

Chiara Ubaldi, B., & Roy, J. (2010). E-Government and Federalism in Italy and Canada—A Comparative Assessment. In C. Reddick (Ed.), *Comparative E-Government* (pp.183–199). New York: Springer.
Coe, A. (2004). *Government Online in Canada: Innovation and Accountability in 21st Century Government*. Cambridge, MA: Kennedy School of Government Graduate Research Paper.
Dutil, P., Howard, C., Langford, J.,& Roy, J. (2010). *The Service State—Rhetoric, Reality, and Promise*. Governance Series. Ottawa: University of Ottawa Press.
Flumian, M. (2009). *Citizens as Prosumers—The Next Frontier of Service Innovation*. Ottawa: Institute on Governance.
Government of Canada (2005). *Government Online 2005—From Vision to Reality and Beyond* (GOL Annual Report). Ottawa: Treasury Board Secretariat. Available at http://www.gol-ged.gc.ca.
Langford, J., & Roy, J. (2008). *Moving Towards Cross-Boundary Citizen-Centred Service Delivery: Challenges and Lessons from Canada and Around the World*. Washington, DC: IBM Center for the Business of Government.
Roy, J. (2006a). E-service delivery and new governance capacities: 'Service Canada' as a case study. *International Journal of Services Technology and Management, 7*(3), 257–271.
Roy, J. (2006b). *E-Government in Canada: Transformation for a Digital Age*. Ottawa: University of Ottawa Press.
Roy, J., (2010), Web 2.0 and Canada's public sector: Emerging opportunities and challenges. In B. W. Wirtz (Ed.), *EGovernment—Grundlagen, Instrumente, Strategien* (pp. 469–494). Wiesbaden: Gabler.
Tapscott, D., & Williams, A. (2006) *WIKINOMICS—How Mass Collaboration Changes Everything*. New York: Penguin Group.

4 Transformative E-Government and Public Service

Public Libraries in Times of Economic Hardship

John Carlo Bertot, Paul T. Jaeger, and Natalie N. Greene

CHAPTER OVERVIEW

Over the past decade, public libraries in the United States have become central to the delivery of e-government to the public. A recent evolution in library e-government activities has been the creation of partnerships between libraries, government agencies, and other institutions. Drawing from the results of several ongoing research projects, this chapter will examine these partnerships and their roles in transforming the ways government agencies can serve the public, services are delivered to the public, and members of the public can be included in government activities. Using both qualitative and quantitative data, this chapter will provide insights into a rapidly developing transformation of public libraries that is occurring because of the influence of e-government. The chapter will also discuss the ways in which the role of the library in the provision of e-government has been central to the transformation of government in the age of the Internet.

1 INTRODUCTION

The technologies and capabilities of e-government have increased the ways in which members of the public can reach and interact with governments and government information and services, but gaps in access and technological literacy result in many users needing assistance with e-government. The main place that members of the public in the United States turn to help is the public library. During the economic downturn, demands for e-government access and assistance in public libraries have increased as greater numbers of patrons are applying for unemployment and other social supports, seeking jobs, and otherwise dealing with economic hardships. Yet, in this period of increased usage, both the public libraries providing the e-government access and the local, state, and federal government agencies providing the e-government services have reduced capacity due to budget cuts.

E-government began to cause significant shifts in the uses of library technologies and the activities of librarians by 2005, as more government agencies moved services online, closed physical offices, and created new online-only services (Bertot et al., 2006a; 2006b). Through e-government, public libraries help patrons seek government support, enroll children in school, file taxes, take written driving tests, pursue continuing education, apply for licenses, pay fines, apply for government jobs, recover from emergencies, and innumerable other functions of local, state, and national government. In a few years, libraries have become the backbone of e-government information, communication, and services for all those who lack other means of access. Government agencies in the early 2000s began to direct citizens to the library for help in using the materials that the agencies had put online (Jaeger, 2008; Jaeger & Bertot, 2009). These significant new responsibilities of e-government access, training, and assistance have become major responsibilities of libraries at the same time that there are fewer community outlets where the public can seek help with government information and services (Jaeger & Bertot, 2011).

In between these pressures, public libraries and government agencies around the United States have created partnerships based on e-government to provide enhanced or entirely new services to members of the public, ranging from social service agencies and libraries streamlining the online process of applying for benefits across agencies to libraries serving as centers for immigration applications. These transformative e-government-based programs have evolved from a combination of economic hardship, shifting government services to online only availability, and the lack of Internet access and digital literacy skills by intended users of e-government services. A mismatch often exists between those individuals most likely to qualify for government services and benefits and the high percentage of those individuals lacking the required skills and access to use e-government services (Pew, 2010).

These e-government responsibilities have significantly transformed public libraries, necessitating changes in staff training, resource creation, collection development, and technological infrastructure. E-government brings large numbers of patrons to the library needing access to and assistance with e-government. To meet their needs, librarians must move from information intermediaries to information-based service intermediaries.

2   DATA COLLECTION

The *Public Libraries and the Internet* national surveys began tracking the growth of public library Internet connectivity and uses in 1994, just as public libraries began adopting Internet-based technologies (Bertot, 2011). Now part of the larger *Public Library Funding and Technology Access* study (http://www.ala.org/plinternetfunding), this survey remains the one source of detailed, longitudinal data about the relationships between the Internet and public libraries. The survey provides both national and state estimates regarding the public access technology infrastructure, services (e.g., training, employment, e-government), and resources (e.g., content and materials, particularly digital) that public libraries offer. The study also explores funding and support for public access technology, services, and resources, as well as obtaining data to conduct analysis using metropolitan status variables to show access and service availability in differing communities.

The survey uses a stratified "proportionate to size sample" to ensure a proportionate national sample. This sampling approach ensures high quality and generalizeable data within the states analyzed, nationally, and across and within the various strata. The study team uses the Institute of Museum and Library Services (IMLS) public library dataset to draw its sample. Respondents typically answer the survey between September and November of each survey year.

The survey consistently receives responses from one-third or more of the 16,672 public libraries, with response rates of sampled libraries above 70 percent. Weighted for both national and state level analysis, the high survey response rate and representativeness of responses demonstrate the high quality of the survey data and the ability to generalize to the public library population. Unless otherwise noted, the survey data in this chapter are from the 2010–2011 Public Library Funding and Technology Access Survey (Bertot et al., 2011). The study results over time are available at http://www.plinternetsurvey.org/.

Public library partnership data was obtained through a combination of site visits and interviews. During the period of April–September 2011, the authors visited nine library systems across the United States. Using a semistructured interview style, researchers discussed the programs with administrators, and in some cases, conducted observations of participants using the services. In many cases, discussions led to recommendations of other partnerships occurring across the country. In addition, the authors interviewed state library agency staff in five states to ascertain statewide issues and partnership initiatives. Interviews were also conducted with government agency representatives, including those from the Internal Revenue Service and the Government Printing Office, to provide insight into agency perspectives on current and future e-government services, as well as the needs that library partnerships are fulfilling—or could fulfill.

Partnership data was drawn from research currently in progress. Web searches and an extensive literature review led to the identification of many of the site visit locations and interview subjects. In particular, information gathered from the IMLS-funded grant, Libraries & E-Government: New Partnerships in Public Service, administered by the American Library Association and the Information Policy & Access Center at the University of Maryland, contributed much of the background research for the partnership section of this chapter (see http://ipac.umd.edu/our-work/egovernment-partnerships for more information).

3   TECHNOLOGY ACCESS AND USAGE

The extent of e-government transformations of public libraries is demonstrated in results from the 2010–2011 survey (Bertot et al., 2011):[1]

- 99.3 percent of public libraries offer public Internet access;
- 64.5 percent report that they are the only provider of free public computer and Internet access in their communities;
- 85.7 percent offer wireless (Wi-Fi) Internet access; and
- An average of 16.0 public access computers are available at each library.

Though communities may have cafés, coffee shops, or other establishments that provide free Wi-Fi, they do not by and large provide public access computers.

Libraries offer a range of information technology instruction: 38.0 percent offer formal training classes, 28.1 percent offer one-on-one training, 78.8 percent offer point-of-use assistance, and 29.5 percent offer online training materials (Bertot et al., 2011). Among libraries providing formal instruction, 92.9 percent offer general computer skill classes, 93.5 percent offer general Internet use classes, 81.9 percent offer general online searching classes, 79.5 percent offer general software use classes, and 54.5 percent offer online database classes. A primary use of the Internet in public libraries now is seeking information, communicating, applying for services, and accessing services from governments—89.7 percent of libraries help people understand and use government websites, 80.7 percent help people apply for services, and 67.8 percent help people complete forms (Bertot et al., 2011).

The rise of e-government as a core library function has coincided with a dramatic spike in patron needs related to a traditional library function— seeking help with employment. With high unemployment levels and increasing ubiquity of online-only job information and applications, 90.9 percent of libraries provide access to online job resources, 74.5 percent help people create resumes, and 71.9 percent help people apply for jobs online (Bertot *et al.*, 2011). In fact, 91.8 percent of library respondents ranked services to job seekers as one of their most important contributions to their communities (Bertot et al., 2011). To help job seekers, libraries provide point-of-use assistance (79 percent), formal training classes (38 percent), online training materials (29 percent), and one-on-one training (28 percent).

Libraries face several major challenges in providing sufficient Internet access to meet current demand (Bertot et al., 2011):

- 77.2 percent reported that space limitations prevent additional workstations, whereas 54.4 percent state that the lack of electrical outlets or sufficient cabling is a significant barrier to adding workstations or laptops.

- 76.2 percent reported having insufficient public access Internet workstations to meet patrons' needs during at least some part of a typical day.
- 44.9 percent reported that their Internet connection speed is insufficient to accommodate patron demand some or all of the time.

With increased usage, these added pressures on the network and infrastructure are occurring as library funding is being cut around the nation (Bertot & Jaeger, 2012; Sigler et al., 2012). A simple lack of access is not the only driver of this usage—the presence of a helpful, skilled librarian, who can assist those who lack the necessary information literacy skills required to fill out online forms or search for vital information draws patrons to the library (Jaeger, 2008; Jaeger & Bertot, 2009; Jaeger et al., 2012).

Recent economic events have sped the transformations created by e-government. Between 2006 and 2008, the number of Americans with library cards increased by 5 percent, in-person library visits increased by 10 percent, and library website visits increased by 17 percent, with 25 million people visiting the library more than 20 times in 2008 (Davis, 2011). The need to use technology to access social services is particularly acute; millions of people now rely on government-provided social services to meet basic needs that are available primarily or only online. With one in six Americans living in a household where there is difficulty feeding the household members and nearly half of older adults facing poverty, many Americans who have never previously applied for social services now find themselves seeking government support (Chen, 2010; Reuters, 2010). With libraries being the trusted social outlet for free public Internet access and assistance, people with no access, insufficient access, or insufficient digital literacy primarily turn to the library to apply for and access vital social services (Bertot, 2010; Bertot & Jaeger, 2011). Because public libraries are so well positioned to offer e-government services, use of public library computers for this purpose is high, especially among users who have no other access to the Internet outside of the library (Becker et al., 2010).

4 LIBRARY PARTNERSHIPS AND TRANSFORMATIVE E-GOVERNMENT

With the knowledge of this trust and usage, libraries have begun to use the Internet as a tool for reaching out into the community and creating partnerships with local and state government institutions. A prime example of this trend is the Baltimarket project—a "virtual supermarket" that enhances access to nutritious and affordable food in areas of the city that had little access to adequately stocked grocery stores—in Baltimore, Maryland. Established through collaborations by the libraries and the City Health Department with an area grocer, the Maryland Institute and College of Art, and the Baltimore City Enoch Pratt Free Library System, the program is truly a community effort. Essentially, the Virtual Supermarket allows residents to order their groceries online at their local library and then retrieve their food on the designated pick-up day, which takes place once a week for one hour. Program volunteers and workers reach out directly to schools, churches, and community associations to find participants. On pick-up days, information on nutrition and health is presented as a way to tie in government initiatives to the service.

Another innovative service is the New Immigrant Project in Austin, Texas. Through New Immigrant Centers eight library branches offer conversation clubs, dedicated computers with language programs installed, multilingual materials, and an extensive online presence with links to community organizations and government websites, this project is an example of a library and city government coalescing on a solution to a local problem. Austin is also home to a collaboration between the library and the Texas Workforce Center. This particular partnership offers employment services including job counseling, referrals, computer classes, and other necessary skills training. The Workforce Center also houses the Community Tax Center, which is open during tax season, but staffed year round with employees working on partnerships with community organizations and the IRS.

At the forefront of the e-government movement is the State Library and Archives of Florida, which has funded numerous library-related e-government projects. Among these is the "Florida Right Service, Right Now" Web portal that connects citizens to county services by linking problems (e.g., I need healthcare assistance; I need job assistance; etc) to county services that are populated by local libraries. Another site "Get Help Florida" offers an "Ask a librarian" feature in which users can text, chat, or email with a librarian to get help with government needs. Some of the services highlighted include income eligibility for certain government aid programs, locations of shelters listed by city, and places to get food across the state. These two sites show an understanding of the need for libraries to intercede on behalf of citizens with the government with regards to finding information.

In Hartford, Connecticut, the public library has formed partnerships with Catholic Charities Migration and Refugee Resettlement Services, the City of Hartford's Office of Human Relations, Everyday Democracy, and the University of Connecticut's School of Social Work in order to better serve the city's immigrant population through their The American Place initiative. The team offers training to new community residents who volunteer to connect new immigrants with community services. The library also provides extensive resources on immigration, including citizenship classes, a language laboratory, and immigration forums that cover a wide range of citizenship topics. Furthering the government connection, the library offers passport services on the library premises and even occasionally hosts citizenship swearing-in ceremonies.

The District of Columbia Public Library (DCPL) offers several access points to government services. When the DC Public School system lost its federal funding for adult literacy programs in 1995, the library established the Adult Literacy Resource Center, which works with over 70 adult literacy programs in the area. The Resource Center, physically located at the main branch of DCPL, offers materials for Graduate Record Examination (GRE) preparation, language learning, basic math and reading skills, and other necessary learning instructions. Local programs, as well as the learners themselves, can use these materials. DCPL also offers a robust computer training program, which is entirely staffed by volunteer instructors. Classes range from basic typing and word processing skills, to job searching strategies, to health literacy (a course sponsored by the National Library of Medicine of the National Institutes of Health and the District of Columbia Department of Health's HIV/AIDS Administration).

From small scale efforts such as a dedicated computer for filling out taxation forms, found at many libraries around the nation, to a larger initiative like Baltimarket, libraries are finding ways to leverage their access to the Internet and their central role in their communities. Underlying these services is the central theme of community transformation through the public library's e-government roles, especially when combined with government and other agency partnerships. At their core, each of these library initiatives is seeking to transform a community through the resolution of critical challenges. For example:

- The Baltimarket program is about building a healthy community through nutrition instruction, information, and access to healthy foods. This is in direct response to the lack of healthy food alternatives in the communities in which the program is run.
- The DCPL suite of programs reflect multiple challenges that the District of Columbia faces, including education, literacy, digital literacy, and health literacy, to name several.
- The Hartford Public Library's The American Place is a direct response to the diverse needs of immigrant populations that have migrated to the City of Hartford, and spans meeting the needs of immigrant children in schools, language barriers faced by new immigrants, immigration process challenges, and the need to link a range of literacies in order to participate in the immigration process.

E-government is an underlying critical aspect of each of these transformations; however, the transformative process is enhanced through the combination of the library's intermediated assistance that more fully integrates and meets the needs than a simple, and often stand-alone, e-government transaction. There are often more complexities to any given interaction than a single online form.

5   TRANSFORMATIONS, IMPLICATIONS, AND CONCLUSIONS

As much as e-government has transformed the nature of the public library and the ways in which it serves the community, the prolonged economic downturn and the impact of attendant cost-cutting approaches have transformed e-government usage in public libraries and the centrality of public libraries to e-government access. The combination of a prolonged economic downturn and ever-increasing range of e-government services means that public libraries now face several challenges in meeting these service needs:

- Many libraries struggle with infrastructure compression in areas of space, connectivity, and other supports to expand the number and capacity of computers available to patrons (Bertot et al., 2011; McClure, Jaeger, & Bertot, 2007).
- Libraries are increasingly the only access point in communities for free Internet and assistance using the Internet (Jaeger & Bertot, 2011).
- The Internet both has augmented existing library services and established new social roles, with e-government and job seeking being the most prominent and time-intensive of these new roles (Jaeger, 2008; Jaeger & Bertot, 2009).
- Many other types of outlets for government information and services that the public was able to previously rely on have moved primarily or exclusively online, driving people without other access points to the public library (Jaeger & Bertot, 2011).

These challenges are all tied inextricably to both the rise of e-government and the economic downturn. As a result of these new approaches to delivering government information, communication, and services in a means that relies on public library computers, access, and librarians, public libraries have been transformed in nature of the terms of their functions, their roles in their communities, and the expectations patrons and governments have of them.

Large numbers of patrons come to libraries specifically to use the computers to search for work and to use e-government. Most users are not coming to the library for pleasure reading, renting movies, and learning at their leisure. They are coming to the public library for information-laden e-government and employment services and resources, as well as the training and assistance of librarians in using these services and resources. For those who need assistance, have no access, or have insufficient access, going to the library is no longer a choice when there are no other outlets of free public Internet access.

These same changes are also a transformation of the traditional work of libraries. Just as e-government and the economic downturn have combined to shift patron reasons for using the library, these same changes have helped to redefine libraries away from their historical functions as curators of information. Instead, libraries perform different functions in the context of supporting connections between patrons and information, primarily through promoting digital literacy and serving in social work capacities to help patrons through major life needs, like applying for social services and seeking employment online.

Similarly, librarians are shifting from information intermediaries to information-based service intermediaries. This means they need to know more about the services than the information content itself, representing a transformation from the librarian as reference for information to the librarian as intermediary to online services. Helping patrons work with e-government websites and services and filling out online applications requires the ability to both impart digital skills and the knowledge of what content is necessary to fill the major life need and the ways to accomplish the necessary tasks. Public librarians now do not just provide information, they work the structure, content, and delivery mechanisms of information to best suit their communities and individual patrons. As information intermediaries, librarians take information and transform it to so that it contributes needed value to their communities.

The importance of intermediation represents a transformation of work of librarians. As part of the initial push for e-government by the federal government in late 1990s and early 2000s, a key part of the argument was that e-government would connect citizens directly to government without any need of an intermediary, what was commonly called "G-2-C" service. However, it is clear that intermediaries are still necessary for many citizens in many transactions, with users engaging government through a range of both technologies and service outlets staffed with people. And, in some cases, a librarian is serving as the intermediary.

Effective library/government partnerships, such as those detailed above, present another form of government transformation—building new community services and roles based on the Internet and e-government. Many of the partnerships present the delivery of services that neither libraries nor government agencies are capable of independently, and all of these partnerships meet specific needs in their surrounding communities. The Baltimarket program, using library computers to bring groceries into a food desert, acts to alleviate a major problem while also promoting digital literacy and empowerment with health information. The other examples discussed above, from immigration processes to social services, show similarly innovative approaches to bridging library and government agency resources and skills.

These partnerships not only are transforming what libraries and government agencies can provide to their communities, they are also transforming the relationships between libraries and other government agencies. Through these partnerships, government agencies benefit not only from the ability to provide services they would not otherwise be able to, they benefit from the association with public libraries. As public libraries are consistently rated as the most trusted government institution, e-government and partnerships have served to align other government agencies with public libraries in the minds of community members.

The relationship between public libraries and e-government has also served to transform government itself. Public libraries—by ensuring that members of the public have the access and training necessary to use e-government—have facilitated the growth of e-government. Without librarians being able and willing to serve as intermediaries between members of the public and e-government information, communication, and services, government agencies would not have been able to close so many physical offices and move so many services online.

A final transformation through the interaction between governments, libraries, and users, is the transformation of communities. E-government service roles of public libraries respond to community needs that can span broad societal issues such as literacy, nutrition, health, child and family welfare, and employment, for example. Thus, the transformations can extend to communities as libraries and governments work together through e-government services.

These transformations of public libraries demonstrate the many ways in which e-government has changed both social institutions and government. Public libraries have been an essential, if scarcely noticed, part of the expansion of e-government in the United States. In the process, their activities have been significantly changed, as have the expectations for libraries by patrons and governments and the jobs of librarians. While in most cases these changes have resulted in more responsibilities and less funding for libraries, they also have facilitated new ways to serve communities. However, public policy does not account for these transformations.

For all of their support in the growth and functioning of e-government, public libraries have not been rewarded through policy decisions. Public libraries are increasingly envisioned as part of the national infrastructure to promote connected and inclusive communities, an expectation made clear in the Federal Communication Commission's *The National Broadband Plan* (2010) that openly acknowledges the reliance of the federal government on public libraries for delivering e-government and teaching digital literacy. However, the funding sources for public libraries are almost entirely local, with less than 1 percent of funding for libraries coming from the federal government (Davis, 2011). As a result, the federal government is increasingly using libraries to deliver its information, communication, and services without contributing in any meaningful way to their funding. The concurrent defunding of public libraries at both the state and local levels creates even more pronounced disjunctions between the government expectations for libraries and the levels of government support of libraries. For public libraries to continue to meet these vital needs, policies at local, state, and federal levels must better account for the transformed roles that public libraries now play in society and reflect the enormous level of reliance by the federal government on libraries.

Public libraries can survive and thrive in these transformed roles, as the innovative partnerships to meet community needs demonstrate. However, if policy decisions simultaneously bleed libraries of their resources and continue to pile on additional social responsibilities, libraries will not be able to continue to operate, much less meet patron and government needs. As policy decisions are made related to libraries, it would serve policy-makers well to consider what the level of success of e-government and related public services would be without public libraries to guarantee access and assistance. Indeed, the success of some e-government services will likely depend on the ability of libraries and other intermediary institutions to serve as community-based providers of e-government services.

NOTES

1. More recently released public library e-government survey data are available at http://www.plinternetsurvey.org.

REFERENCES

Becker, S., Crandall, M. D., Fisher, K. E., Kinney, B., Landry, C., & Rocha, A. (2010). *Opportunity for all: How the American public benefits from Internet access at U.S. libraries*. Retrieved April 28, 2012 from http://tascha.washington.edu/usimpact

Bertot, J. C. (2011). Public libraries and the Internet: A retrospective, challenges, and issues moving forward. In J. C. Bertot, P. T. Jaeger, & C. R. McClure (Eds.), *Public libraries and the Internet: Roles, perspectives, and implications* (pp. 15–35). Westport, CT: Libraries Unlimited.

Bertot, J. C. (2010). Community-based e-government: Libraries as partners and providers. In M. A. Wimmer et al. (Eds.), *Proceedings of the 9th IFIP EGOV 2010 Conference* (pp. 121–131). New York: Springer.

Bertot, J. C., & Jaeger, P. T. (2011). Community-sourcing: Bridging resources, partnerships, and ICTs to promote transformative government. *Joint Proceedings of Ongoing Research and Projects of IFIPS EGOV and ePart 2011* (pp. 47–556). New York: Trauner Verlag.

Bertot, J. C., & Jaeger, P. T. (2012). Implementing and managing public library networks, connectivity, and partnerships to promote e-government access and education. In S. Aikins (Ed.), *Managing e-government projects: Concepts, issues and best practices* (pp. 183–199). Hershey, PA: IGI Global.

Bertot, J. C., Jaeger, P. T., Langa, L. A., & McClure, C. R. (2006a). Public access computing and Internet access in public libraries: The role of public libraries in e-government and emergency situations. *First Monday, 11*(9). Retrieved April 28, 2012 from http://www.firstmonday.org/issues/issue11_9/bertot/index.html.

Bertot, J. C., Jaeger, P. T., Langa, L. A., & McClure, C. R. (2006b). Drafted: I want you to deliver e-government. *Library Journal, 131*(13), 34–39.

Bertot, J. C., Sigler, K., DeCoster, E., McDermott, A., Katz, S. M., Langa, L. A., & Grimes, J. M. (2011). *2010–2011 Public library funding & technology access survey: Survey findings & report*. College Park, MD: Information Policy & Access Center, University of Maryland College Park. Retrieved April 28, 2012 from http://www.plinternetsurvey.org.

Chen, S. (2010). The new hungry: College-educated, middle-class cope with food insecurity. *CNN*. Retrieved April 28, 2012 from http://www.cnn.com/2010/LIVING/12/13/food.insecurities.holidays.middle.class/index.html.

Davis, D. M. (2011). Public library funding: An overview and discussion. In J. C. Bertot, P. T. Jaeger, & C. R. McClure (Eds.), *Public libraries and the Internet: Roles, perspectives, and implications* (pp. 193–214). Westport, CT: Libraries Unlimited.

FCC. (2010). *The national broadband plan: Connecting America*. Washington DC: Author. Retrieved April 28, 2012 from http://www.broadband.gov/

Jaeger, P. T. (2008). Building e-government into the Library & Information Science curriculum: The future of government information and services. *Journal of Education for Library and Information Science, 49*, 167–179.

Jaeger, P. T., & Bertot, J. C. (2009). E-government education in public libraries: New service roles and expanding social responsibilities. *Journal of Education for Library and Information Science, 50*, 40–50.

Jaeger, P. T., & Bertot, J. C. (2011). Responsibility rolls down: Public libraries and the social and policy obligations of ensuring access to e-government and government information. *Public Library Quarterly, 30*, 1–25.

Jaeger, P. T., Bertot, J. C., Shuler, J. A., & McGilvray, J. (2012). A new frontier for LIS programs: E-government education, library/government partnerships, and the preparation of future information professionals. *Education for Information, 29*, 39–52.

McClure, C. R., Jaeger, P. T., & Bertot, J. C. (2007). The looming infrastructure plateau?: Space, funding, connection speed, and the ability of public libraries to meet the demand for free Internet access. *First Monday, 12*(12). Retrieved from http://www.uic.edu/htbin/cgiwrap/bin/ojs/index.php/fm/article/view/2017/1907

Pew Internet. (2010). *Government online*. Retrieved April 28, 2012 from http://www.pewinternet.org/Reports/2010/Government-Online.aspx

Rueters. (2010). Nearly half of elderly in U.S. will face poverty. *MSNBC.com*. Retrieved April 28, 2012 from http://www.msnbc.com

Sigler, K. I., Jaeger, P. T., Bertot, J. C., DeCoster, E. J., McDermott, A. J., & Langa, L. A. (2012). Public libraries, the Internet, and economic uncertainty. In A. Woodsworth (Ed.), *Advances in librarianship, vol. 34: Librarianship in times of crisis* (pp. 19–35). London: Emerald.

5 A Green Revolution

Innovation and Transformation in the Use of ICT by the Irish Department of Agriculture

Frank Bannister, Regina Connolly, and Philip O'Reilly

CHAPTER OVERVIEW

In the late 1990s, the Irish Department of Agriculture's 30-year-old computer systems were in crisis. After a near disaster in 1998 the Department launched an ambitious 5-year strategic plan to completely modernize its information and communications technology (ICT). The plan called not only for a shift from the old mainframe technology to a modern distributed computing architecture but for a change in mindset; regarding technology as a vehicle for delivering direct benefits to farmers and agribusiness in the form of better services, new services, lower costs, and less paperwork. The multiple outcomes of this process have resulted in a transformation in the ways that farmers interact with the department and have led to a whole range of innovative services. This chapter describes the particular approach taken, the multiple benefits of this transformation and some of the lessons learned.

1 INTRODUCTION

Historiography is a small but growing area of interest in computer and information systems research (Mason et al., 1997a; 1997b; Bannister, 2002). A premise of historiography is that there are useful lessons than can be learned from the past. This chapter presents a historiographical study of the development of ICT in the Irish Department of Agriculture, Food and Fisheries (DAFF) over a period of 40 years. Reflecting the subject matter of this book, the emphasis will be on the last 15 years though events during the earlier period will be briefly outlined. The reason for this time frame is that in late 1998 the department was confronted by a number of crises that forced it to rethink its entire approach to its computer systems. The story of how this was done and what was learned from this experience provides the core of this chapter.

Historiography differs from conventional case study research both in the time frame and in the more limited nature of the evidence that is available. It can be approached from a theory generation perspective and from a purely narrative perspective. There are also many possible research questions a historical study might seek to answer. In this chapter two questions are addressed: what happened and what lessons for practice emerge from this?

In the 1990s, the DAFF experienced four major crises. The cause of each was different: two major changes in the common agricultural policy (CAP), an outbreak of bovine spongiform encephalopathy (BSE) and the discovery of serious failings in the department's accounting systems. A common thread running through each of these crises was the department's computer system, which during this period struggled to cope with the changes and demands being placed on it.

It should not have been thus. The department had been one of the first Irish departments of state to acquire a large computer in 1969. But poor management understanding of the potential of ICT and other priorities meant that by 1990 the department's systems were dated and inflexible whilst morale in the IT department was low. To make matters worse, the IT group had split into two hostile camps. Problems with the systems came to a head in 1998. Following a "systems review" of the department, senior management decided to act and for the first time in its history, the department commissioned a strategic information systems plan (SISP) and recruited a Chief Information Officer (CIO). The brief for the new CIO was a formidable one. The requirement was to turn the ship around by replacing and/or upgrading aging legacy systems, changing a top management culture which had long been dismissive of the value of IT, integrating two powerfully opposed IT groups into one, modifying a department wide culture which viewed IT as a problematic and underperforming operation and re-motivating a demoralised IT unit. The remainder of this chapter describes how this was done and the lessons learned from this experience.

2   BACKGROUND AND CONTEXT

Agribusiness, food and fisheries is Ireland's largest indigenous industry employing some 150,000 people with an annual output value of over €24 billion. Nearly 90 percent of Ireland's beef and dairy produce is exported to markets worldwide and many of the operations of the industry depend on real-time access to the ICT systems of the Irish Department of Agriculture, Fisheries and Food.[1]

The DAFF operates in a particularly challenging external environment due to the nature of the Common Agriculture Policy support schemes and the ever-present risk of animal health and food safety crises. CAP payment schemes are complex and have demanding implementation timelines with which all member states struggle to comply. Any shortcomings in terms of controls or timeliness can incur EU-imposed financial penalties that can potentially run to hundreds of millions of euro. Animal health crises cannot be predicted and they must be responded to without delay. Food safety incidents must likewise be dealt with decisively to protect human health and the reputation of Irish food and valuable export markets.

In addition to the above, the DAFF is responsible for smooth operation and delivery of approximately €3 billion per annum in financial supports to farmers and agribusinesses as well as for animal disease testing and the tracing of farm animal movement from birth through to entry to the food chain (or death). In Ireland there are two million bovine births and seven million bovine animal movements each year. In addition to all of the other challenges faced in 1999, the department was going to have to change its ICT architecture and essentially all of it business applications without any disruption to its on-going operations.

To further complicate matters, many people and organizations act as trusted agents of the department. These include private veterinary practices, livestock marts, meat/slaughter plants, major food processors and exporters, providers of farm management software packages, vendors of animal tags, outsourced animal movement bureau, forestry companies, farm planning providers that submit claims on behalf of farmers and the Irish Cattle Breeders' Federation. These groups need access to specific information. For example, approximately 15 million on-farm disease tests are carried out annually by approximately 600 private veterinary practices (PVPs) across Ireland. The results of these tests must be recorded against animal records in the department's animal health database. Each proposed movement or slaughtering for human consumption is then pre-checked against this database to determine if it is permissible. The extensive interaction between PVPs and the department was highly labor-intensive. To add to the problems, the system was based on dated county-by-county mini-computers and recorded exceptions only rather than all test results.

3   A PROGRAM OF PARALLEL STREAMS

Turning around ICT in the above circumstances required simultaneous action on several fronts. This chapter describes four important aspects of this process concentrating primarily on the years 2000–2004. These key fronts were technical, political, operational, and organizational, each of which is now discussed.

3.1   Technical Strategy

On the technical front there were several sub problems that needed to be addressed in parallel. These are illustrated in Table 5.1.

Table 5.1 Overview of Strategy

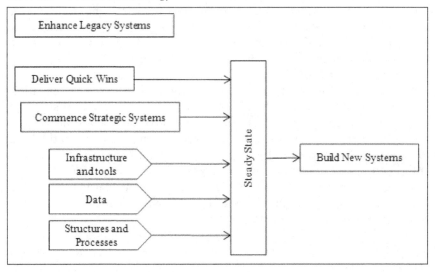

From the outset, a number of principles were agreed that underpinned all subsequent decision making about the technical aspects of the plan:

1. Existing operations could not be disrupted, even though temporary disruptions would have made implementation easier at several points.
2. The architecture was envisaged in a number of layers (Table 5.2). It was recognised that the data layer would be the most critical part of the new architecture as anything else could be fixed in retrospect much more easily than problems in the data structure, and it was essential that data could be re-used where it occurred across the various lines of business.

Table 5.2 Multilayer Architecture Used

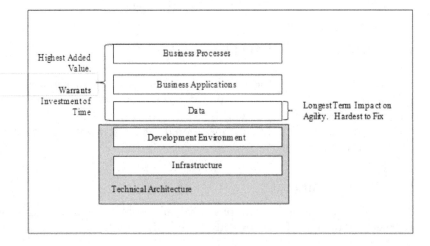

3. Consequently there would be one corporate data model and within this three key entities would be: *customer, animal*, and *land*. The legacy corporate data structure inherited at the start of the project was highly fragmented. Clearly, collecting data once, getting it right and re-using it as needed would yield major efficiencies and improve data integrity. It was therefore decided to develop a high-level corporate data model and let whichever application project first needed a key entity take responsibility to fully flesh out that aspect of the model while taking account of future corporate uses.

4. While legacy systems would be maintained for the time being, the department would move to emerging technologies for its new applications with a view to doing the same for legacy systems as each one needed a major re-write. Emerging technologies were monitored, and opportunities for each technology to deliver operational benefits were examined or trialed.

5. A policy known as "deep e-government," linking back office systems directly to customer systems where possible, would be adopted. This was in contrast to the front-end orientation of most e-government at the time.

6. The five layers of the architecture would be addressed on a phased basis. The top layer, that is the business process architecture, was not to be attempted at the outset and would be revisited. The overall architecture of the business applications, the second layer from the top, was only addressed to the extent that there would be a corporate customer system as a hub for all applications, and that there would be a single view of the customer, a single view of the land and a single view of the animal. It had been determined that the data layer would be key to the future and would be addressed first.

7. The technical environment would be procured on the basis of bundled solution incorporating the underlying infrastructure, operating system, and development environment. The department did not have the resources to dedicate to selecting and integrating best-of-breed components and would have found such an approach difficult to support.

8. All of the corporate business applications should be built using a three-tiered approach (user interface, application, and data) with a standard desktop browser providing access for internal users. Consistent style sheets would be developed for the user interfaces.

Beyond the above, the overall architecture of the complete portfolio of business applications was not specified in detail at this stage.

3.2 Political Strategy

Given the history of ICT in the department, achieving and improving internal morale in the ICT group and maintaining external credibility were going to be critical success factors from the outset. One way to deliver a quick win was on the desktop. This was done by installing a standard well-specified PC with a set of office products and a standard browser to front the corporate applications. Whereas there were as yet no new corporate systems, the PCs could be used to access legacy applications. More importantly, staff no longer had problems with e-mail or incompatible versions of office tools and the new LANs and WAN meant no interruptions in service. Coupled with the DAFF Intranet—*eZone*, and Internet access, all staff now had easy access to up-to-date information. The psychological impact of the new machines and the local tools were significant. ICT was delivering something that staff could see and use.

Other quick wins included Short Message Service (SMS) from the desktop and videoconferencing. As events unfolded, having these desktops and office servers, a newly architected network (WAN and LANs) and the SMS facility in place proved to be fortunate indeed when Foot and Mouth Disease arrived in Ireland in March 2001 (see Section 4). These successes and others built further confidence throughout the organization in ICTs judgment and ability to deliver working solutions for the business needs of DAFF reliably and on time.

3.3   OPERATIONAL STRATEGY

Conventional 1980s structured methodologies assume that the ICT application developers gather requirements from a line of business unit and translate those into detailed functional specifications that are signed off and then built (Gasson, 1995). The view taken in DAFF during this program was that conventional structured methods would be too slow and labor-intensive. Furthermore, with such an approach there is a considerable likelihood of looping-back at testing stage to correct misunderstood requirements leading to cost and time over-runs and sub-optimal application structures (Morris, 1990). Instead, teams were established which combined business specialization as well as ICT skills. Contrary to the prevailing view (see Ross and Weill, 2002), the lead ICT person was expected to understand fully current business requirements as well as possible future scenarios. By understanding the business, the ICT lead person could anticipate where flexibility would be likely to be required in the application and in particular the implications for the underpinning data structures that would have to support the business and application change into the future.

A good example of this approach in action was the *Corporate Customer System*. The 2000 strategy had included a proposal that all operational systems would share common customer data. In order to achieve this there would need to be a single system or set of functionalities to create records of all customers and all of their relationships. This should include a rich view of all the customer relationships with the organization and in the case of DAFF would extend to the relationships with herds or other entities with which the department dealt.

A decision was therefore taken early in the project to introduce a strategic program to deliver this type of functionality. Since this program would be long-term and the system would be central to the overall group of operational systems, it was decided that the project management, design, and build leadership would be carried out by in-house ICT staff with contracting restricted to the programming level. The outcome was a system which rapidly became a core component of the department's operations and which remains so to this day.

The deep e-government principle was applied to all major developments, streamlining the operational processes. During the development of the animal health computer system this principle eliminated the vast volumes of paper flowing between the DAFF and private veterinarians.

3.4 Organizational Strategy

An immediate problem that had to be faced was the shortage of internal resources. In 2001 there were two particularly large-scale application projects that needed to get underway (integrated mapping and payments system (iMAP) on the CAP area aid based payments and the animal health computer system (AHCS)) and there simply were not the skilled in-house resources to do these, so the outsourcing approach was the only feasible option.

For these initial projects, to try to ensure knowledge transfer and post-implementation control, in-house resources were deployed as members of the team. For subsequent projects, in-house resources were assigned to project management and technical lead positions on all high value tasks of strategic long-term importance.

In assigning ICT staff to various roles throughout the program, considerable attention was paid not just to their technical skills and experience, but also to their personality and work-style preferences. This approach in assignments resulted in a more productive workforce.

4 PAYBACK

In the period between 2000 and 2004 alone, several major crises/developments were to test the effectiveness of the new computer systems and the department's ICT capability. Four of these will be briefly considered.

By far the most significant, in national terms, was the outbreak in March 2001 of foot and mouth disease (FMD) that spread quickly throughout the United Kingdom. Ireland as a country has FMD clear status. Any loss of this would have had catastrophic consequences for the economy. FMD is airborne and highly contagious. With so much movement between the United

Kingdom and Ireland, an outbreak was inevitable, and this occurred on one farm on the northeast coast of Ireland. Reaction from the department was swift. Movements to and from the infected areas were traced and all herds within a chosen infection zone were visited, tested and culled where necessary. This enormous operation required the setting up of a Local Disease Control Center with access to all of the department's ICT systems including full customer information, herd profiles, and spatial mapping information. The successful confinement of FMD in Ireland reinforced the fact that ICT was central to the department's operations, and, secondly, its own in-house ICT department was capable of delivering under pressure.

A consequential development was a decision to tag sheep. Ireland had a world-class traceability system for bovines that underpinned the reputation of quality Irish beef. Sheep, on the other hand, were neither tagged nor traceable at this time. In the immediate aftermath of FMD, it was decided by the then minister that all eight million sheep in Ireland would be individually tagged enabling full tracing of sheep movements within a 2-month period.

Involving just four people—two ICT and two line-of-business staff—the business process and the design of the system was completed in 2 days, specified and built in 4 weeks, and rolled out in a further 4 weeks. The system, subsequently known as STAR (Sheep Tagging and Registration), went live on time and managed the issuing of five million tags in its first month of operation. In addition to consolidating the ICT division's reputation for delivery, it confirmed the value of deep e-government since the process fully integrated the business processes of the tag vendors with the DAFF systems.

A third example of the impact of the new regime was demonstrated when the EU committed to a mid-term review of the 2000 CAP reforms in 2004. The CAP reform offered member states a number of options and Ireland chose an option that was the most economically attractive. The government decided to implement this in 2005. Due to the flexible structured data model developed for the *Corporate Customer System* and the linkages that it allowed for recording all periods of ownership of holdings over time, it was possible to accurately calculate payments, thus positioning the Department as a leader among EU CAP paying agencies.

The final major unanticipated development during this period was an extension in the department's remit. During the delivery of single farm payment system, a cabinet reshuffle resulted in the responsibility for Forestry being transferred to the DAFF. The department from which it transferred had planned on embarking on a major project to integrate the management of Forestry supports, applications for afforestation, grant payments and on-going premia payments. Accurate mapping was a critical part of this as on-going payments are made in respect of specific areas. Mapping is also critical for determining the suitability of plantation areas. Consequently, many layers of spatial information are necessary against which applications must be checked before approval.

Given the overlap, the department was able to leverage the developments that were happening on the agriculture side and develop an integrated forestry system that used the same spatial database as the agriculture schemes, giving access to over thirty layers of spatial information. This was subsequently expanded to provide an online service to forestry companies, where they could prepare their maps using the department's mapping tool.

By 2004, as a direct consequence of all of these strategies and despite a shortfall in the resources available to it, the department had delivered on the 5-year program ahead of schedule and gone beyond what was envisaged in many areas. The capabilities of ICT had increased beyond recognition, and it had changed from being regarded as an overhead expense to a strategic tool.

5 DEVELOPMENTS POST 2004—APD

In 2004 an Operational Strategy Group, chaired by the CIO was set up to inform a new ICT Strategy facilitating identification of those processes that through re-modeling and ICT support would offer the greatest potential benefit across the organization.

This shift in focus prepared the ground for the much greater shift in 2006 when ICT, in conjunction with the veterinary inspectorate, proposed it would trial a new approach to develop generic agile business processes supported by generic, configurable ICT applications that could be used across vertical business units. This would be known as agile process development or APD. That top management was prepared to take this risk indicates how far ICT in the department had traveled in 5 years.

A third strategy document was prepared in 2007. In this APD was incorporated as the standard preferred approach to all new developments and indeed to reflect the shift in focus the name of the function was changed from ICT to IMT (Information Management and Technology). Table 5.3 illustrates the change in emphasis in the three plans.

Table 5.3   Principal Stages in Adding Value

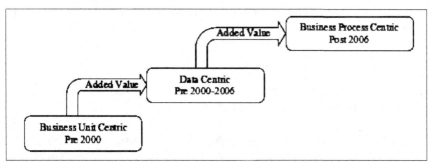

In any large organization there is a tendency for complexity to increase and with vertical business units this effect can be amplified resulting in inflexibility (Golden & Powell, 2000). By 2005 a strategy of avoiding large projects had been well established, in favor of phased releases with each subsequent release enriching the functionality as necessary. Indeed by this time, despite the myriad of applications that the department historically had and the 250 EU schemes being implemented, the application layer and the business process layers of the architecture were each being represented on a single A4-sized graphic that could be related to by all. Consequently, by the time it came to moving up the value chain to agile business processes and more flexible generic ICT applications, the ethos of simplicity was well embedded.

6   REFLECTIONS: THE TRANFORMATION OF ICT

6.1   A Decade of Achievement

By 2010 the department had an integrated set of information systems underpinning all of its operations based on a coherent base of corporate data with a single view of the customer, a single view of the land with its parcels uses and features and a single view of the animals with their movement history and health status.

The geographical information system displays more than thirty layers of information about land including its parcels or divisions, its usage, its conservation or habitat status and can immediately identify if it is acceptable for afforestation. Integrated information about all of the department's customers is available in real time. The reputation of the department's ICT function is today such that it has been approached by a number of other public service agencies to take on their ICT support.

The overall result of the strategy adopted in 2000 and subsequently is that DAFF is now seen as an exemplar of IT use. Well-architected business processes and ICT solutions mean that DAFF is particularly agile in its operations, something which is critical in this sector. By exploiting these capabilities, the department has reaped the financial dividends too in terms of public expenditure. It now delivers a wider range of services to a much higher standard of customer service, with almost one third fewer staff than just five years ago.

6.2   Some Lessons Learned

Some of the lessons that have emerged from this decade are unsurprising, whereas others conflict with accepted wisdom.

- *Ad hoc* initiatives, projects, or services will not deliver e-government transformation. Any organization seeking such e-transformation needs strategy, a coherent programme and adequate skilled resources (Weill &Vitale, 2001).

- A successful program needs a combined business and ICT perspective. It is therefore critical that the CIO is at management board level. If the CIO is not at "board" level, he or she may not have the ability to get the necessary attention focussed on e-government opportunities. The lower status of the head of IT pre-1998 was reflected in the systems the department had.
- For any CIO to achieve successful e-government transformation, he or she needs to have the appropriate focus, experience, credibility and authority.
- In a situation where ICT's reputation is poor, quick wins are important. Although they must not be allowed to derail the success of the long term plan, intelligent compromises between the ideal way of tackling a problem and immediate business and political needs must sometimes be found.
- Achieving early successes changes the morale of the ICT team and raises their credibility with their colleagues elsewhere in the organization. This increases the confidence and productivity of the ICT people and their willingness to be creative and ambitious. It likewise creates a confidence throughout the organization that they can successfully deliver on ambitious projects and an awareness of the scale of the operational gains of such projects.
- Large projects are best avoided. As projects get larger, risk tends to increase exponentially rather than linearly. The risks associated with very large projects are enormous (Hana, 2009). Furthermore, in the case of the DAFF organization, besides technology changes, the occurrence of significant operational change, beyond national control, would mean any long project could be "shooting at a moving target." Therefore, while a number of very large projects had to be completed at the start of this program (e.g., the animal health system) it was decided that large individual multi-year projects would be avoided. Instead, functionality would be built and delivered on a phased basis in line with the overall architecture.
- Early progress cannot be confined to easy projects and quick wins. The big tasks have to be progressed too. These are essential to build capability, to address big needs of the organization and are often the building blocks upon which future sustainable success can be delivered.
- While quick wins and the early delivery of large projects will build the reputation of an ICT over time, it is innovation that will sustain that reputation (Courtright & Smudde, 2007). As it builds, the ICT function can be more ambitious in what it proposes to do for the organization, and if it wants to deliver greatest results, then it needs to move up the value-chain.

- Organizations that have an in-house ICT function should fully exploit this. Just because the ICT function is centralized in an organization should not mean that it is separated from the business. It must be an integral part of the business and carry the responsibilities that go with that. In-house ICT and other business units should relate as equals within the business rather than reducing the relationship to that of a supplier-customer with Service Level Agreements (SLAs) or insourcing. The experience in the DAFF demonstrates the potential for a very creative symbiotic relationship.
- Whereas ICT people work a lot with technology, it is critical to remember that ICT staff are "human" resources. In assigning ICT staff to roles or projects, it is worth paying attention not just to the technical skills and experience, but to their own personality and work-style preferences (Morgeson et al., 2005). This will result in motivated staff and incomparable results.
- Government agencies are among organizations most likely to depend on bespoke software, given that their operating models are often unique and are driven by political and administrative structures and policies. To be capable of reacting to business changes or events with sufficient agility, there needs to be a mind shift in their in-house ICT. The in-house ICT function needs to think and act more like the producers of commercial off-the-shelf software—thinking not of today's needs for one "customer," but the needs of all its "customers" today and tomorrow. If it does this, it can design agile business processes and configurable ICT solutions.
- Whereas on the one hand the organization must push ahead with its coherent program, it should be alert for the unplanned opportunities along the way, be they new technological developments such as web services technology which emerged during the decade as a major enabler for the department new business challenges or crises that arise that create an opportunity for innovation and learning. A crisis, besides its pain, invariably presents and opportunity to progress the capabilities of the organization and to improve its performance (Lalonde, 2007).

There is an old and somewhat cynical saying that one should never waste a good crisis. Faced with a series of crises in the 1990s, DAFF took the opportunity to tackle a problem that they had failed to address for 30 years. While this account has focused on the ICT group, it must not be forgotten that it was the top management of the department that made the decision to commission the plan and appoint a new CIO at senior level. One unspoken lesson is that the willingness of top management to put its trust in its CIO and his team is also critical to success in ICT. The story of the DAFF from 2000 to 2011 illustrates that the most dysfunctional of ICT operations can be turned around and in a relatively short time. It requires leadership, commitment, courage, hard work, and a willingness to take some degree of risk. The latter is not always a characteristic found in public servants, but where sensible risk taking is combined with these other factors, the results can be remarkable.

NOTES

1. Like many Irish government departments, the Department of Agriculture has changed its name several times over the years. For simplicity the abbreviation DAFF will be used throughout this chapter.

REFERENCES

Bannister, F. (2002). The dimension of time: Historiography in information systems research, *Electronic Journal of Business Research Methods*, 1(1), 1–10.

Courtright, J. L., & Smudde, P. M. (2007). 'Leveraging Organizational Innovation for Strategic Reputation Management', *Proceedings of the 11th International Conference on Reputation, Brand, Identity and Competitiveness*, May 31–June 2, Oslo, Norway.

Gasson, S. (1995). The Role of Methodologies in IT-Related Organisational Change. *Proceedings of BCS Specialist Group on IS Methodologies, 3rd Annual Conference, The Application of Methodologies in Industrial and Business Change*, North East Wales Institute, Wrexham, U.K., September 4.

Golden, W., & Powell, P (2000). Towards a definition of flexibility: In search of the Holy Grail? *Omega, 28*(4), 373–384.

Hana, N. K. (2009). *e-Transformation: Enabling New Development Strategies.* Springer: New York.

Lalonde, C. (2007). Crisis management and organizational development: Towards the conception of a learning model in crisis management. Proceedings of the Organizational Learning, Knowledge and Capabilities Conference Ivey School of Business, London, Ontario, June 14–17, pp. 507–517.

Mason, R., J. McKenney, J., & Copeland, D. G. (1997a). An historical method for MIS research: Steps and assumptions. *MIS Quarterly, 21*(3), 307–320.

Mason, R., McKenney, J., & Copeland, D. G. (1997b). Developing an historical tradition in MIS research. *MIS Quarterly, 21*(3), 257–276.

Morgeson, F. P., Reider, M. H., & Campion, M. A. (2005). Selecting individuals in team settings: The importance of social skills, personality characteristics, and team work knowledge. Personnel Psychology, 58(3), 583–611.

Morris, S. (1990). Cost and time overruns in public sector projects. *Economic and Political Weekly, 25*(47), 154–168.

Ross, J. W., & Weill, P. (2002). Six IT decisions your IT people shouldn't make. *Harvard Business Review*, (November), 80 (1–11).

Weill, P., & Vitale, M. (2001). *Place to space—Migrating to eBusiness models.* Boston: Harvard Business School Press.

6 Bridging E-Government and Performance in the Italian Public Sector

Carlotta del Sordo, Rebecca Levy Orelli, Emanuele Padovani, and Enrico Deidda Gagliardo

CHAPTER OVERVIEW

The chapter presents an account of the likely consequences that performance monitoring systems have on public service transparency and accountability through e-government technology. The research draws upon a study on the Brunetta reform (from the name of the Ministry of Public Administration) to foster public sectorproductivity, whose key principles are efficiency, meritocracy, accountability, and transparency. Specifically we outline the rationale for introducing performance monitoring technologies in public central administrations (ministries), the use the central government made of the system and the ways in which central public administrations responded to such compulsory performance monitoring system.

1 INTRODUCTION

E-government is about a process of reform in the way governments work, share information, and deliver services to external and internal clients. Specifically, e-government harnesses information technologies (such as Wide Area Networks, the Internet, and mobile computing) to transform relations with citizens, businesses, and other arms of government. These technologies can improve public sector performance in a variety of ways: better delivery of government services to citizens, improved interactions with business and industry, citizen empowerment through access to information, or more efficient government management. The resulting benefits can be less corruption, increased transparency, greater convenience, revenue growth, and cost reduction.

The chapter presents an account of the likely consequences that performance monitoring systems have on public transparency and accountability through e-government technology. The research draws upon a study of the Brunetta reform (from the name of the Italian Ministry of Public Administration) to foster public sector productivity, whose key principles are efficiency, meritocracy, accountability, and transparency. One of its key elements is represented by its linkage to the Italian ongoing e-government strategy. Specifically we outline the rationale for introducing performance monitoring technologies in public central administrations (ministries), the use the central government made of the system and the ways in which central public administrations responded to such compulsory performance monitoring system.

The chapter is structured as follows. The next section provides the theoretical framework for performance and e-government in the public sector, whereas the third introduces the Italian answer to the EU request in terms of e-government implementation over the last four years. The fourth section provides an analysis of the Brunetta reform content that represents the starting point of a new path for performance measurement through e-government in Italy, whereas the fifth section measures the first implementation results. The last section draws some conclusions.

2 THE THEORETICAL FRAMEWORK FOR PERFORMANCE IN THE PUBLIC SECTOR

Despite the massive research on how to measure performance, to implement and use performance measurement systems, and to compare performance, there remains a surprising lack of clarity on the core notion of "performance" itself.

Performance measurement is set around the idea that each public organization formulates its own envisaged performance by defining specific performance indicators which are used to steer and control activities with the aim to get strategic goals (De Bruijn, 2002). Hatry defines performance measurement as the "measurement on a regular basis of the results (outcome) and efficiency of services or programs" (1999, p. 3). Bouckaert and Halligan (2008) consider performance as "not a unitary concept . . . [which] must be viewed as a set of information about achievements of varying significance to different stakeholders." This brings to the question of what are defined as "achievements." Achievements may be viewed as a synonym for results, which is the most typical view taken by many practitioners from the performance measurement movement.

An alternative route for a definition of performance may be to use classification or typology systems to understand different types of performance. In fact, the notion of multidimensional performance is widely accepted both in terms of span (i.e., its horizontal expansion of the results dimension) and depth (i.e., its micro, meso, and macro vertical dimensions) (Bouckaert & Halligan, 2008, pp. 14–34). Typically, in terms of span the classification of performance into different categories such as inputs, process, outputs, and outcomes is the most important distinction made in the field, but there are a considerable number of variants (for example, see Hatry, 1999; Anthony & Young, 2003; Poister, 2003). From these elementary performance components, two main concepts are created: efficiency, as the ability to minimize inputs given a certain level of outputs or maximize outputs given a certain amount of inputs, and effectiveness, as the ability to achieve the goals or standards provided.

Performance can also be defined at different levels in a governmental system. It may be defined at the organizational level or the bureaucratic system. Even at the organizational level, one may view performance from the standpoint of the bureaucracy or the political level. Alternatively, performance may be defined as the individual employee level which is perhaps more typical in the human relations management field (Talbot et al., 2005). This would be the case of individual performance appraisals. From an external perspective, the focus on the different dimension of performance is driven by the different stakeholders' interests.

Both the administrative and managerial sciences agree on the need to understand performance measurement, and thus the core notion of "performance" in the public sector in a dynamic or evolving context (Pollitt et al., 2007; De Bruijn, 2002). Thus, the challenge is to move in handling this dynamism. Pollitt (2007) posits that several factors may influence the change in a performance measurement system over time. One factor is the linkage between the performance measurement system and managerial or political activities. In explaining how and why the performance concept is volatile in the public sector, we can use the "performance regime" concept by Talbot and co-authors (Talbot et al., 2005; Talbot, 2006). They suggest that a multitude of actors, such as government departments, ministries, legislatures, audit, inspection, judicial, and regulatory bodies may be involved in defining the context within which a government may be engaged in developing and adopting a performance measurement system, thus in shaping the prevailing idea of performance that has to be accomplished.

Like any other program of government, performance measurement does not work by itself (Miller & Rose, 1990), but it requires "technologies" if it is to be made operable. Technologies are devices for intervening (Hacking, 1983), and they include notation, computation and calculation, procedures of examination and assessment, etc. Today they can be identified with information technologies (IT). More specifically, during the last 10 years web-based applications have given raise to what has been labeled as e-government. E-government has acted as the fundamental IT tool in public sector reform strategies (Reddick, 2010) and has proved to provide more efficient and effective public services (Biancucci et al., 2001; Palvia & Sharma, 2007), transparency (Cho and Byung-Dae,

2004) and interaction between government and its stakeholders (Palvia & Sharma, 2007).

The concepts presented above give raise to three dimensions that appear to be important when e-government applied to performance management is studied. These three dimensions shape the concept of e-performance (i.e., the set of dimensions of analysis that are to be considered when implementing e-government solutions for performance management). The first dimension deals with the "performance regime" and, more generally, the different stakeholders' interests' ideas and refers to the nature of the accountability relationship that represents the source of the "account giving" of a public organization in a broader system. The accountability literature has focused on the classifying the different types of frameworks in place by governments to control and provide justification for government actions. Romzek and Dubnick (1987; 1991) have conceptualized four types of accountability mechanisms, depending on the source of agency control—internal or external—and the degree of control over agency actions—high or low. When the relationship between the accountor and the accountee is hierarchical within the same organization and the degree of control—in terms both of range and depth of actions—is high, a bureaucratic accountability mechanism is in place. Legal systems are used as an accountability mechanism which is external but the level of control remains high. The professional accountability approach is used for specific reasons, usually associated with the degree of complexity or difficulty of a specific activity, public officials can rely upon experts of a specific field only who are hired to study specific problems (i.e., internal source of control). Finally, political accountability refers to the relationship between constituents and representatives, the latter being responsive to constituents, given their policy priorities and programmatic needs.

	Agency control: INTERNAL	Agency control: EXTERNAL
Degree of control over agency action: HIGH	1. Bureaucratic	2. Legal
Degree of control over agency action: LOW	3. Professional	4. Political

Figure 6.1 Types of accountability systems. Source: adaptation from Romzek and Dubnick (1987, p. 229).

Considering again the "performance regime" concept and the idea that the concept of performance is shaped dynamically by a multitude of perspective by stakeholders discussed above, the second dimension of e-performance concerns the level of government and types of external stakeholders involved. For example, different levels of government (i.e., state and local governments) may interact with the federal or central government to shape IT system deployment, or a government website may be developed involving groups of such users as entrepreneurs, educators, and teenagers.

The third dimension derives from the different dimensions in terms of span of performance and concerns the types of performance for which e-government is intended to accomplish. IT offers different services or information to citizens, other governments, contractors or internal managers. E-government information could include items such as how the government is structured, how laws are passed and other basic government information. Overall, e-government strategies may prevail one of the two main dimensions of performance, either efficiency or effectiveness (Hammers Specht, 2000; Worral, Remenyi, & Money, 2000; Heeks, 2001; Hammers Specht & Hoff, 2005).

3   TRANSFORMATION OF E-GOVERNMENT IN ITALY OVER TIME

Over the past several decades, there has been a significant evolution of the adoption and use of information technology systems in the public sector and the main attention of the European countries have been focused on e-government. E-government is typically defined as providing government services via the Internet or other technologies to citizens and businesses (Chen & Gant 2001). It is about using the tools and systems made possible by Information and Communication Technologies (ICTs) to provide better public services to citizens and businesses (Hood & Margetts, 2007).

In Europe, the idea of a European Information Society was introduced by the European Council in Copenhagen in 1993 (European Commission, 1993). Stimulated by increased global competition, at the end of the 1990s the Commission launched a new initiative entitled *eEurope: An Information Society for All* (European Commission, 1999). In 2000, the European Commission launched the *eEurope initiative* aimed to realize the potential benefits of better access for all citizens to the new services of the information age (European Commission, 2000). The present *eEurope* initiative, launched in 2010, is labeled *Information Society and eGovernment*. Within such document, the EU's main policy strategies in the e-government field are explained in the *e-government Action Plan 2011–2015*, designed to help governments to meet demands concerning the services they provide to citizens and businesses. It supports the transition from current e-government to a new generation of open, flexible and collaborative seamless e-government services at local, regional, national and European levels that will empower citizens and businesses (E-government factsheet European Union, Ed. 3.0).

If e-government services are to provide significant added value to citizens and business, then it is crucial that different government bodies, both within a country and in different EU Member States, are able to share information easily and co-operate in serving citizens. Moreover each country adapts the European strategies to its particular context. In the next section, the Italian choices in terms of e-government strategies over time are presented.

The Italian seven strategic objectives about e-government strategy were identified before the Brunetta reform. The policies were prevailingly oriented to growth the productivity, to reduce the administrative burden and to enhance public services (E-government factsheet Italy, Ed. 11.0).

During October 2009, the Italian Government approved the legislative decree n.150 implementing the Law n.15 of 4 March 2009 on civil service reform and for the efficiency and transparency of public administration (parr. 4–5). The reform gives more emphasis on performance measurement, while in the past management control was central. The legalistic tradition Italian public administration, focused on the control of inputs more than on evaluation of outputs, has made it quite difficult for the past 30 years to enact reforms based on the theories of new public management (NPM). NPM focuses on citizen as taxpayer and on various indicators of performance, hence on controlling outputs, in order to introduce management mechanisms patterned after the private sector and directed to efficiency.

The immediate objectives of the Brunetta reform on e-government are improving the organization of work, progressively raising the quality of government services to the public, and boosting both labor and total factor productivity in all sectors of the public administration (Table 6.1).

Table 6.1   Italy's E-Government Main Policy Strategies after Brunetta Reform

Strategy	Description
1.	A reinforced selection mechanism for economic and career incentives, with a view to reward the most worthy and skilled employees, encouraging commitment and deterring malpractices.
2.	A performance assessment system that help Public Administrations reorganizes their activities according to set targets and to an overall enhancement requirement. 'Customer satisfaction', transparency and merit rewarding are the milestones of such a system.
3.	Collective bargaining provisions will be aligned with those regulating the private sector. upplementary bargaining and additional remuneration will be conditional on the real attainment of planned results and management savings.
4.	Increased importance will be given to managers, entrusted with concrete tools and subject to economic sanctions in case of failure to comply with their obligations.
5.	Disciplinary proceedings have been simplified and a catalogue of particularly severe infractions leading to dismissal has been put in place.

Source: E-government factsheet Italy 14.0.

As to the timing, in March 2009 the Parliament delegated the government for the public sector reform to deliver a decree with the reform. In October 2009, the Brunetta reform Decree was issued; by the end of the same year the National Authority for Assessment, Transparency and Integrity (namely Civit) took over. In July 2010 performance measurement principles and in November 2010 Performance plan, transparency and individual performance measurement principles were issued by Civit. The reform is completely operative since January 2011.

4   THE BRUNETTA REFORM

The topic of performance measurement and e-government came to prominence in Italy following the approval of the Brunetta reform (from the name of the Ministry of Public Administration) with Law n. 15/2009 and the subsequent Legislative Decree 150/2009. The reform is aimed at fostering public sector productivity and represents the starting point of a new path for performance measurement through e-government.

The reform in fact uses e-government solutions in order to manage and measure public administration performances, so it is shaped on the concept of e-performance and its three dimension. The first dimension deals with the nature of the accountability relationship and the principle underlying the reform is "Transparency." It is understood as the total accessibility of all information about the organization, management trends, the use of resources for the pursuit of institutional functions and results, the measurement and evaluation activities, to permit widespread forms of control. It is a political accountability approach since the source of agency control is external (i.e., by the citizen) and the degree of control over agency actions is still low and without punishments.

The second dimension of e-performance concerns the level of government and types of external stakeholders involved. The Brunetta reform engages a wide span of stakeholders, since it is engineered around all citizens, in their role of stakeholders of the public services acting as drivers of the innovation. The central purpose of the decree is to resolve the fundamental problem of democracy, namely how to ensure that the state, in its political and administrative organization, answers to the citizens for what it does.

The third dimension concerns the two main measures of performance, efficiency and effectiveness. The reform is aimed at fostering faster economic growth by boosting the efficiency and productivity of the public sector, which responds to a vision of the public administration as a productive sector, a provider of services. This reform is also related to the financial situation of the Italian public sector that has greatly deteriorated over the last 5–6 years.

Transparency is one out of the three cornerstones of the reform, together with evaluation and merit. The measurement and evaluation of the performances are aimed at improving the quality of services offered by government. First, this evaluation needs to embrace the administrative organization as a whole, the individual organizational units, as well as the individual employees. Secondly, it must be transparent with regard to information about the measurement and evaluation of performance. In the middle of the performance evaluation criteria should be placed the satisfaction index about delivered services and therefore the citizen. Any monetary incentive related to the subject can be granted to public employees only on the basis of new criteria for performance evaluation.

The public administrations annually assess both organizational and individual performance. Performance evaluation is carried out at different level by the "Independent Evaluation Body" (namely OIV) of which every administration must adopt in order to assess the performance; the Commission for evaluation, transparency and integrity of government, for guidance and coordination of the evaluation of performance in all public authorities (namely Civit); and the individual heads of organizational units involved in the performance cycle. Moreover, the cycle of performance measurement should be regulated by a deliberation approved by each government and named "Measurement and Evaluation System" that identifies stages, timing, methods, subjects and responsibilities of the measurement and evaluation performance process.

The organizational performance measurement and evaluation system covers, among others, policies about satisfaction of the community needs, plans, programs, and measuring activities of level of implementation, degree of satisfaction of activities and services through interactive mode, qualitative and quantitative development of relations with citizens, stakeholders and users of services, efficient use of resources, quality and quantity of provided services, and promoting equal opportunities.

The measurement and evaluation of individual performance of managers and employees is connected to the performance indicators, the achievement of specific individual goals, the quality of the contribution to the overall performance of the structure, ensured through the professional and managerial skills demonstrated, and the ability to evaluate their own employees, demonstrated by different opinions.

5   FIRST IMPLEMENTATION OF THE BRUNETTA REFORM AT THE CENTRAL GOVERNMENT LEVEL

Every administration has an obligation to publish specific information on its institutional website in a special section of easy access and consultation, labeled "Transparency, evaluation and merit." The information or documents that are supposed to be published are the 3-year program for transparency and integrity and its state of implementation; the plan and report on performance; the total amount of rewards allocated and actually distributed to the performance; the analysis of data on the degree of differentiation in the use of rewarding both for managers and their employees; the names and curricula vitae of members of independent bodies responsible for evaluation and performance measurement functions; curricula of managers drawn up in accordance with the European model; the remuneration of managers, with specific evidence on the variable components of wage and related components to the result evaluation; curricula and wages of those who hold positions of political administration; assignments, paid and unpaid, granted to public employees and private subjects.

In terms of implementation, concerning ministries, all available documents requested by Brunetta reform, are compulsory published on line on the Civit website (section "Attuazione della Riforma—Ministeri e Enti Nazionali," Reform implementation—Ministries and Other Entities), that allows monitoring the state of the art. As shown in Figure 6.2, the Civit website provides a list of all documents which are available so far (for example, since the first performance management cycle has not been finished yet, the performance report is not available). They are Performance measurement and evaluation system (Sistema misurazione valutazione); Three-year plan for transparency and integrity (Programma trasparenza); Performance plan (Piano della performance); and Quality standards (Standard qualità).

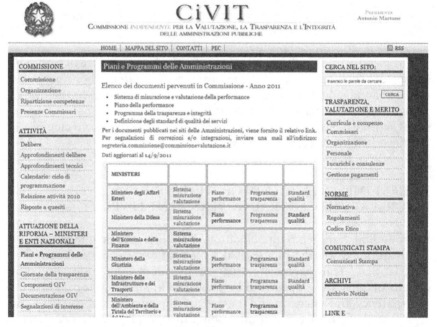

Figure 6.2   Civit website—reform implementation—ministries and other entities section. Source: www.civit.it (retrieved October 15, 2011).

The Performance measurement and evaluation system is part of the overall performance management cycle that consists of definition and assignment of goals, values expected, results and their indicators; link between objectives and resources; ongoing monitoring of exercise and activation of any corrective actions; performance measurement and evaluation, overall and individual; use of reward systems, according to merit criteria; reporting of results to the political-administrative bodies, the heads of governments and appropriate external bodies, citizens, stakeholders, users and recipients of services. Objectives are programmed over 3 years before the beginning of the year and defined by the political-administrative bodies, after having consulted the heads of the administration that, in turn, consult the managers or heads of organizational units. The objectives are defined in accordance with the budget and their achievement is a condition for the grant of proposed incentives.

Every administration adopts the 3-year program for transparency and integrity, to be updated annually, which indicates the initiatives planned to ensure an adequate level of transparency and legality and the development of integrity culture. The public administrations guarantee maximum transparency in every phase of the described cycle of performance management. In the t3-year program for transparency and integrity timing, resources and tools dedicated to the effectiveness of initiatives are specified. In case of non-adoption of the 3-year program for transparency and integrity, or non-fulfillment of the requirements for publication on the website, payments of salaries for managers responsible for the result are suspended.

The last document is the performance plan. Performance measurement is at the heart of the reform: what, how and when to measure? The reform gives more emphasis on performance measurement, while in the past management control was central. Performance plan is a 3-year planning document that identifies strategic and operational objectives and defines indicators for measuring and evaluating the performance of the administration and objectives and related indicators assigned to managers. Report on performance shows, in the final balance, the organizational and individual results achieved in relation to individual objectives and planned resources, with variance analysis, and gender budgeting and it must be adopted by June 30. The report on the validation of the performance is mandatory condition for access to tools to reward merit. Both the plan and the report must be immediately transmitted to the Civit and the Ministry of Economy and Finance.

As Figure 6.2 shows, on the Civit website there are different levels of the Brunetta reform implementation concerning e-government effect. Each ministry should prepare, approve, and upload on its websites the Brunetta reform package and send it to Civit in order to comply with the transparency rules. When Civit receives a document, it verifies the content and uploads it on its website, with the upload date. Sometimes ministries draw up the requested material, but they are not ready to publish it on the websites yet. This is the reason why the color used for the document is different on the Civit website (blue for documents with link and black for documents without link).

Even if the reform started on January 2011, at present almost all ministries (11 out of 13, see Table 6.2) show both the Performance measurement and evaluation system and the Performance plan, according to the reform rules. The complete online state will be reached quite soon, considering that the remaining documents have been already approved, except for the Ministry of Economy and Finance Performance plan.

The 3-year plan for transparency and integrity needs to be revised annually given its 3-year horizon, and this is the reason why we have a lower degree of implementation of e-government tools. Lastly, the Quality Standards seems to be less in use, but it should be considered that its core content is part of the Performance Plan. Consequently, often Ministries do not split in to two documents the Performance Plan, but leave the quality standards as part of its presentation. The presence of a Quality standard should be assessed considering jointly the contents of Performance Plan and Quality Standards.

Table 6.2   Ministries: Status of Brunetta Reform Implementation through E-Government

Ministry of	Performance Measurement and Evaluation System	Performance Plan	Three-year plan for transparency and integrity	Quality Standards
1. Foreign affairs	x	x	x	x
2. Defense	x	x	x	x
3. Economy and finance	x			
4. Justice	x	x	x	x
5. Infrastructure and transport	x	x	x	x
6. Environment, Territory and See	x	x	x	
7. Interior affairs	x	x		x
8. Education, university and scientific research	x	x		
9. Employment and welfare	x	x	x	
10. Agricultural, alimentary and forest policies	x	x	x	x
11. Health	x	x	x	
12. Economic development	x	x	x	
13. Cultural heritage	x	x	x	x
Total on line documents	11	11	9	4

Source: www.civit.it (retrieved October 15, 2011).

The Brunetta reform acts also on the merit cornerstone. On the Civit homepage, there is the Transparency, evaluation and merit section ("Trasparenza, Valutazione e Merito," see Figure 6.2, on the right) that allows citizens to know about people involved in different projects, money paid and results achieved. That should be of help in evaluating the use of public resources and their effectiveness.

6 CONCLUSIONS

The case of Italy highlights a central government case where the first step of e-performance implementation has taken place almost homogeneously in all ministries. Whereas a content analysis is needed to fully understand whether the substance of the published documents match at least with compulsory contents, it can be stated that the mechanisms provided by law have been able to assist policy makers to fulfill the e-performance strategic goal, at least in its first move. Noticeably, the Civit commission has been able to support ministry's managers and the OIVs to publish the first two key documents of e-performance, namely Performance Measurement and Evaluation System and Performance Plan. In fact, the reform gives more emphasis on performance measurement, whereas in the past management control was central.

The reform has been a success, at least in the first initial stages, and e-government appeared to be a strong mean for implementing the goals of the reform Nevertheless, since the Brunetta reform is newly implemented, it is too early to determine the extent of success and its implications. Moreover, being only at the first round, it is too early to make meaningful evaluation or assessment of the success of the reform as a whole. Further development of the research may involve the comparison with other European countries, because it will be more useful once the Brunetta reform will be concluded and its effect in terms of success measured.

The reform has been carried out not only by publishing guidelines, but also by supplying further comments on guidelines, closer technical examinations for specific purposes, plenary meeting sessions, one-to-one meetings, and FAQ sessions online. *De facto*, the Civit has worked for and with the key actors of the e-performance reform. This can be considered as the key success factor, since this commission has been the crucial difference between this and previous public management reforms. At the same time, all ministries had already implemented e-government solutions, as shown by Overall On line Sophistication (OOS) values (that places Italy at the tenth position (European Commission, 2007) among the European countries (del Sordo et. al., 2012). OOS in fact provides an indication of the extent to which the online provision of services is based on new models of front and back-offices integration, the reuse of available data and to what degree the idea of pro-active service delivery is embedded.

Therefore any advance from performance measurement and management solutions to what we have called e-performance have been possible with any particular difficulties.

REFERENCES

Anthony, R. N., & Young, D. W. (2003). *Management Control in Nonprofit Organizations* 7th edition. Burr Ridge, IL: McGraw-Hill/Irwin.

Biancucci, R. J., Goode, L. J., Hunter, P. A., Owings, K., Tucker, A., & Willett, R. B. (2001). CFO survey—A preview: Electronic government. *Journal of Government Financial Management*, 2, 36–39.

Bouckaert, G., & Halligan, J. (2008). *Managing Performance, International Comparisons*. Routledge: London.

Chen, Y., & Gant, J. (2001). Transforming local e-government services: the use of application service providers. *Government Information Quarterly*, 18(4), 343–355.

Cho, Y. H., & Byung-Dae, C. (2004). E-government to combat corruption: The case of Seoul metropolitan government. *International Journal of Public Administration*, 10, 719–735.

De Bruijn, H. 2002. *Managing Performance in the Public Sector*. London: Routledge.

Del Sordo, C., Orelli, R. and Padovani, E. (2012). E-government challenges in European countries. In K. J. Bwalya & S. Zulu (Eds.), *Handbook of research on e-government in emerging economies: Adoption, e-participation, and legal frameworks*. Usa: IGI-Global.

European Commission. (1993). *Growth, competitiveness and employment: The challenges and courses for entering into the XXIst century*. White Paper: com. Retrieved from http://europa.eu/documentation/official-docs/white-papers, accessed on May 2012.

European Commission. (1999). eEurope: An Information Society for Us All. Retrieved from http://europa.eu, accessed on May 2012.

European Commission. (2000). eEurope Action Plan. Retrieved from http://ec.europa.eu/information_society/eeurope/2002/index_en.htm, accessed on May 2012.

European Commission. (2007). *The user challenge benchmarking the supply of online public services*. Belgium: Capgemini.

Hacking, I. (1983). *Representing and intervening*. Cambridge: Cambridge University Press.

Hammers Specht, P. (2000). The impact of IT on organization performance in the public sector. In G. D. Gaarson (Ed.), *Handbook of public information systems*, pp. 141–151. New York: Marcel Dekker.

Hammers Specht, P., & Hoff, G. (2005). Information technology investment and organizational performance in the public sector. In G. D. Garson (Ed.), *Handbook of Public Information Systems*, pp. 127–142. New York, London: CRC Press.

Hatry, P. H. (1999). *Performance Measurement. Getting Results*. Washington, DC: The Urban Institute Press.

Heeks, R. (2001). Understanding e-governance for development. IDPM i-Government Working Paper 11.

Hood, C., & Margetts, H. (2007). *The tools of government in the digital age*. New York: Palgrave Macmillan.

Miller, P., & Rose, N. (1990). Governing economic life. *Economy and Society*, 19(1), 1–31.

Palvia, S. C., & Sharma, S. (2007). *E-government and e-governance: Definitions/domain framework and status around the world.* Foundations of E-government. Hyderabad, India: IECG.

Poister, T. H. (2003). *Measuring Performance in Public and Nonprofit Organizations.* San Francisco: Jossey-Bass.

Pollitt, C., Van Thiel, S., & Homburg, V. (Eds.). (2007). The New Public Management in Europe: Adaptation and Alternatives: Palgrave MacMillan.

Reddick, C. G. (2010). *Comparative e-government.* New York: Springer..

Romzek, B. S., & Dubnick, M. J. (1987). Accountability in the public sector: Lessons from the Challenger tragedy. *Public Administration Review, 47*(3), 227–238.

Romzek, B. S., & Dubnick, M. J. (1991). *American public administration: Politics and the management of expectations.* Nerw York: Macmillan.

Talbot, C. (2006). *Performance regimes and institutional context: Comparing Japan, UK and USA.* Tokyo: International Symposium on Policy Evaluation,.

Talbot, C., Wiggan, J., & and C. Johnson. 2005. *Exploring performance regimes: A new approach to understanding public sector performance.* Report for the National Audit Office. Nottingham Policy Papers no. 4.

Worral, L., Remenyi, D., & Money, A. (2000). A methodology for evaluating the effectiveness of delivery of IT services. A comparative study of six British local authorities. In D. Garson (Ed.), *Handbook of public information systems,* pp. 501–520. New York: Marcel Dekker.

7 Identifying Core Capabilities for Transformational Local Digital Government
A Preliminary Conceptual Model

Luis Felipe Luna-Reyes and
J. Ramon Gil-Garcia

CHAPTER OVERVIEW

Using information technologies to transform government organizations has been an important component in public sector reform efforts around the world. However, benefits from such strategies often remain only a promise, not a reality. In order to better understand the reasons for digital government success and failure, many researchers have explored the problem following one of two approaches: (1) identifying a list of success factors or (2) developing a better understanding of the problem through process models. In this chapter, following the process tradition, we propose the use of a resource-based view of the organization to explore core capabilities of local governments for transformational digital government. Based on the perspectives of thirty-four municipal Chief Information Officers (CIOs) from different regions in Mexico, who participated in three workshops in June 2010, we propose a preliminary conceptual model of the core capabilities and resources necessary for a successful transformational digital government strategy.

1 INTRODUCTION

In the last two decades, governments around the world have increased the use of information technologies (IT) as key components of their administrative reform efforts. This particular strategy has been commonly named digital government, and consists of the use of IT in government operations, services, and democracy. The inclusion of digital government strategies responds to the promise of IT to transform government activities, creating value for citizens, businesses, and other stakeholders. Some of these promises include increases in tax collection, efficiencies and savings in government operations, greater transparency, and improved accountability (Gil-Garcia & Helbig, 2006). However, there is little evidence of such transformation (Feller, Finnegan, & Nilsson, 2011; Scholl, 2005). Generally, benefits from IT investments do not automatically result from the introduction of new technologies, but from a coordinated series of efforts aligned with the main strategy of the organization, such as process improvements, staff training, and better organizational standards (Feller et al., 2011). Moreover, and particularly important in the public sector, organizational activities are also constrained by institutional arrangements (Fountain, 2009; Stafford & Turan, 2011). In this way, benefits from digital government are to a large extent still a promise for many government organizations.

Local governments are not an exception, and they face particular challenges. Local government IT departments have limited influence on the municipality development plans and policies, and they often do not have the appropriate organizational structure, trained staff, or budget to manage a digital government strategy. Local CIOs also perceive local laws and regulations as important challenges to digital government. In particular, the 3-year term of a mayor in Mexico is perceived as a major challenge for two reasons: any strategy needs to be implemented in a short period of time and frequently the next mayor does not carry on with the main strategies and objectives. The general lack of resources available to local governments and their municipal CIOs is a problem not only in Mexico, but also around the world (Holden, Norris, & Fletcher, 2003). As a result of these particular challenges, local governments often fail to achieve the lofty objectives of digital government.

There are two main perspectives to explain the limited transformational impacts of digital government initiatives. The first of these two perspectives has focused on the search for key success factors (see, for example, Gil-Garcia & Pardo, 2005). These studies usually involve statistical testing of the impact of factors, such as the size of projects or high-level management support in the success of digital government initiatives. In contrast, a second approach consists of the detailed study of the development process for a particular project (see, for example, Luna-Reyes, Zhang, Gil-Garcia, & Cresswell, 2005). This approach usually relies on case data and process models to explain project success. Following this later tradition and enriching it with key concepts from the resource-based view of the organization, this chapter proposes that there is a set of intertwined core capabilities required to successfully implement a truly transformational digital government strategy. The main question guiding our research is which core capabilities and resources are necessary to develop a transformational local digital government program?

The chapter is organized in six sections, including the foregoing introduction. Section 2 presents a review of previous studies focusing on local digital government and the resource-based view of the organization. This view suggests that there are some core capabilities that allow organizations to performing certain actions in a better way. These capabilities are intertwined and, therefore, they cannot be studied in isolation. Section 3 describes the research design and methods used for this study. This chapter is mainly based on three workshops with thirty-four Mexican local government CIOs. Section 4 highlights core capabilities and resources identified in the workshops. Section 5 proposes an initial conceptual model and describes each of its main components. Finally, Section 6 provides some final comments and suggests areas for future research in this topic.

2   LOCAL DIGITAL GOVERNMENTS AND CORE CAPABILITIES

This section introduces two areas of research that are relevant to our work. The first subsection includes a review of recent studies about digital government at the local level. The second subsection constitutes a review of the resource-based view of the organization. We think that this view could potentially contribute to a better understanding of digital government as a transformational phenomenon.

2.1   Digital Government at the Local Level

The most significant disparities in taking advantage of the transformational potential of digital government take place at the local level. Several local governments have seized the opportunities offered by digital government and have not only become leaders in digital transactions, but have reached an advanced stage of digital government in which citizen participation is an essential component (Fagan, 2006). Unfortunately, other localities are facing constraints in terms of budget, human capabilities, infrastructure, and know-how (Holden et al., 2003). Some of the most important areas of opportunity for digital government at the local level are providing information, offering digital government forms and online transaction processing, improving urban services, strengthening tax collection capabilities, improving strategic planning processes, and facilitating the creation and implementation of partnerships with other authorities (Beynon-Davies & Williams, 2003). Digital government is a powerful tool for mayors to listen to citizens' needs, enabling them to act quickly and efficiently (Reddick & Frank, 2007). Moreover, local governments with greater presence in the network are able to offer various applications such as electronic commerce, transactions, customer service, geographic information systems, and citizen participation (Kaylor, Deshazo, & Eck, 2001). Areas of particular interest for transformational government are those related to citizen services, where technology offers opportunities for personalization, access through multiple channels, or even service co-creation by government and citizens (King & Cotterill, 2007).

Similar to other levels of government, the adoption of digital government at the local level is the result of organizational factors (features and capabilities of the government's IT department) and contextual factors (external influences such as population size and citizen demands) (Gil-Garcia & Pardo, 2005; Reddick, 2004). Among the main determinants of the success of digital government strategies are an appropriate infrastructure (Holden et al., 2003); the existence of digital citizens (Asgarkhani, 2007); the provision of interactive services; and the inclusion of citizens in order to more precisely understand the problems and opportunities in the community (King & Cotterill, 2007). Increased citizen participation allows local governments to obtain more information, thereby giving them the opportunity to offer a wider range of services that better meet the population's needs. A municipality's size and type of government are also determining factors in the implementation and development of digital government (Moon, 2002).

Other factors that impede the advancement of digital government are limitations in the technological infrastructure, cultural and educational paradigms, appropriate software acquisition, the large investment necessary to begin digital government programs, security and privacy, complications that may unexpectedly arise in the implementation and monitoring phase, and doubts about the return on investment from building a website to provide services to the population. A major disadvantage, especially in developing countries, is the advancement of public education, because if the population does not have the necessary knowledge, online access of municipalities will be very small and, consequently, the benefit to citizens will be limited (Evans-Cowley & Conroy, 2006). Organizational and institutional innovations have proven to be effective ways to overcome some of these challenges. Four configurations have been identified in the literature: aggregation (joining municipal efforts), syndication (sharing services), consumption (citizens, universities and other stakeholders as consultants), and co-creation (Feller et al., 2011).

2.2   Resource-Based View of the Organization

A potentially useful strategic view to transformational digital government is provided by the Resource-Based View of the firm (RBV). One of the first contributions to the study of the RBV was conducted by Penrose (Rugman & Verbeke, 2002). However, it wasn't until 1984 that the study of resources as a key component of a firm's performance became important (Wernerfelt, 1995). Barney (1991) noted that competitive advantages are the result of capacities and resources that companies control, which are valuable, rare, imperfectly imitable, and not substitutable. Such resources and capabilities can be seen as bundles of the tangible and intangible; for example, management skills, organizational routines and processes, and information and knowledge (Barney, 2001). The dynamic capabilities approach allows for identifying the firm's core capabilities and how combinations of expertise and resources could be developed, deployed, and protected (Teece, Pisano, & Shuen, 1997). The importance of dynamic capabilities lies in their ability to create, integrate, recombine, and release resources, thus modifying the original resource base. In the long term, a competitive advantage lies in using dynamic capabilities sooner, more astutely, or more fortuitously than the competitors to create an advantageous resource configuration.

RBV has been incorporated into the analysis of the role that information systems and information technologies play in organizational performance. RBV provides an analytical framework for assessing the strategic value of information systems, as well as a guide for differentiating between various types of information systems and evaluating their impact on performance of the organization (Wade & Hulland, 2004). In fact, empirical research has found a positive relationship between superior IT capability and superior firm performance (Bharadwaj, 2000). Some empirical studies have shown that managerial IT skills, capital requirements, proprietary technology, and technical IT skills are core attributes to provide sustainability and better performance. Moreover, the quality of IT business expertise and the relationship infrastructure (competitive capabilities) have been found to significantly affect competitive advantage and the intensity of organizational learning (a dynamic capability) was significantly related to all of the capabilities (Bhatt & Grover, 2005).

RBV has already been applied to public sector organizations through identifying internal dynamic capabilities and establishing levels of trust to enable uses of these capabilities. Reflecting over the experience, managers involved in the project concluded that "during the planning phase, where the environmental climate was imperative, the focal capability was the capability to be innovative. During the developing phase, where the environmental climate was commutative, the focal capability was the capability to be adaptive. Finally, during the operating phase, where the environmental climate was propulsive, the focal capability was the capability to be responsive" (Chan & Pan, 2006, p. 492). Therefore, we propose that the RBV of the organization could be useful to understand the transformational aspects of digital government at the local level.

3   RESEARCH DESIGN AND METHODS

The research reported in this chapter is part of a 2-year project to develop a model for local digital government in Mexico. The model is conceptualized as a set of strategic guidelines to help local governments in making transformational investments in information technologies and systems to create public value. The project involved four main components: (1) an exploration of current practices and models of digital government at the local level; (2) a national survey of citizens in Mexico about local government services; (3) three workshops with municipal CIOs; and (4) three case studies of local governments in Mexico. This chapter reports on the third component of the project.

The main purpose of the workshops was to gather views and experiences on the perception and implementation of digital government strategies in Mexican local governments. To select workshop participants, we divided the 2,441 Mexican Municipalities in four strata according to the Mexican Senate classification: rural (less than 10,000 inhabitants), semi-urban (between 10,000 and 149,000 inhabitants), urban (between 150,000 and 600,000 inhabitants), and metropolitan (more than 600,000 inhabitants) municipalities. We had the participation of thirteen CIOs from metropolitan municipalities, thirteen from urban municipalities, and eight from semi-urban municipalities. All participants received travel-related expenses, but no other financial compensation. The workshops took place between June 29 and July 6, 2010, two days each. The agenda included discussions related to strategic components of a transformational digital government strategy at the local level, such as vision, mission, objectives, core capabilities, and key challenges. As mentioned before, a total of thirty-four CIOs from local governments within different states in Mexico participated in the workshops and they were evenly distributed across the country's main regions (see Figure 7.1).

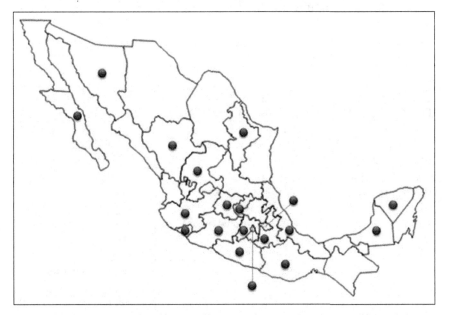

Figure 7.1 Geographic distribution of municipalities participating in the workshops.

To summarize and discuss the main conversations on core capabilities from the workshops, we use the grammar of system dynamics. The method helps to obtain a better understanding of verbal theories, with the potential to inform or improve the activities of both theorists and empirical analysts (Patrick, 1995). Although the method includes the mathematical formalization of conceptual models and simulation, in this chapter we only introduce and discuss the conceptual qualitative model, which is a commonly used approach to understand structural relationships among key accumulations in systems (Wolstenholme, 1999). Such accumulations could be understood as core dynamic capabilities (Warren, 2002).

4   CORE CAPABILITIES FOR LOCAL DIGITAL GOVERNMENT

In this section of the document, we will describe the main conversations related to core capabilities that took place during the three workshops with local CIOs. Before describing the main results of the conversations, and as a way of providing context for such results, we want to share one of the vision statements, collectively developed during the workshop with the metropolitan CIOs. From their point of view, digital government at the local level consists of "using information technologies to support in an effective, coordinated, efficient, transparent, and participative way the implementation of public programs and policies that contribute to significantly improve both citizen's quality of life and the level of competitiveness of the municipality." Guided by this transformational vision

Table 7.1   Core Financial Capabilities from the Perspectives of Local CIOs

Semi-urban		Urban		Metropolitan	
IT area with enough budget	14	Special budget for IT infrastructure	8	Special budget for IT department	0
Financial plans to acquire and maintain infrastructure	11	Financial support to accomplish goals	0	More financial resources for technology investments	7
Managerial methods to allocate budget	11	Adequate and responsible investment in technology	2	Short and long term budget plan	0
		Well-allocated budget to support high-priority projects	1	Budget to government areas to pay for IT services	0
				Budget for technology investments	0
				Budget for new projects	0

and other similar ones in the other two workshops, CIOs participated in a brainstorm exercise to answer the question: What are the core capabilities (human, financial, technical, organizational, etc.) that a municipal government should have in order to accomplish the digital government vision that we have developed?

Once the three workshops were completed, the research team revisited the capabilities elicited during the brainstorm exercise, re-clustering those with similar meaning. Table 7.1, for example, presents one of these new clusters, core financial capabilities, as described in each of the three workshops. The table shows an English translation of the labels used in each workshop, as well as the number of votes that each of the groups assigned to the capability. Grayscales represent the importance of each capability relative to others in each workshop. These tables are useful for comparison purposes. For instance, the three groups recognized having an IT area with an adequate budget as an important capability. Semi-urban municipalities found this capability to be extremely important because most participants in this workshop were struggling to create the municipality's IT area. The capability was perceived as less important relative to others for the urban CIOs, but definitively much less important for metropolitan CIOs. Capabilities listed also show that the smaller municipalities were more concerned with basic needs, while larger municipalities were more concerned about long-term investment plans and new projects.

Following this procedure, the research team created twelve clusters in the six categories presented in Figure 7.2. This conceptual framework used for categorization of core capabilities is an adaptation of previous work at the Center for Technology in Government (Gil-Garcia, Pardo, & Baker, 2007). There were only three clusters associated with the three more general categories (Context, Institutional Framework, and Interorganizational Collaboration and Networks), one for each category. There was also one cluster for each of the more technical categories, Technology and Information and Data. In contrast, seven clusters were related to Organizational Structures and Processes, including human resources, financial procedures, processes and standards, and training among others. Unfortunately, because of space limitations, we cannot include in this chapter the full set of clusters. Interested readers can find the full list in the project workshop report (Luna-Reyes, Gil-García, & Celorio-Mansi, 2010).

In terms of technology, participants in the workshops paid special attention to infrastructure. Smaller municipalities even included appropriate electrical infrastructure as a basic need. Other CIOs in bigger municipalities included servers, networks, and personal computing in the conversation. Other identified capabilities were related to the need for technical standards for data and development, as well as the optimal use of hardware and software. Data and information was a category with less importance

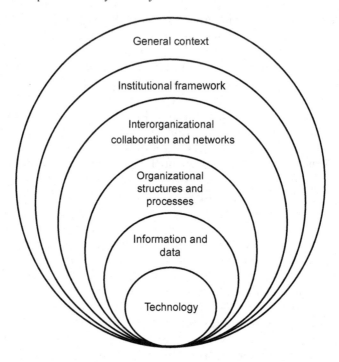

Figure 7.2   Main categories of core capabilities. [Translated from Luna-Reyes, Gil-García, & Celorio-Mansi (2010)]

from the point of view of workshop participants. The only reference to this category was made in terms of data and information security plans.

As mentioned before, the category of organizational structures and processes had the most ideas derived from the workshops. Workshop participants discussed the importance of having enough personnel with the proper credentials, certifications, and experience, as well as the capability of continuous learning through formal training programs for all employees in the municipality, not just the IT personnel. Financial resources and budgeting processes were other important core capabilities included in the conversation. Another cluster of core capabilities the local CIOs identified in the workshops were related to standard processes and IT methodologies. First, they discussed the importance of having effective, and even ISO certified, business processes in the municipality and formal programs of process improvement. On the other hand, they referred to specific IT methodologies, such as ITIL (Information Technology Infrastructure Library), as important capabilities to develop, as well as having multiple channels for service delivery. Top-management support and an appropriate organizational structure for the IT area were also included as important capabilities in the organizational category. Finally, planning and project management were the last clusters identified by workshop participants in the area of organizational processes and structures.

Table 7.2 Top Fifteen Capabilities in Terms of Importance

Capability	Votes S-Urb		Votes Urban		Votes Metro		Total Votes
1. Well-trained human resources	Y	9	Y	14	Y	7	30
2. Laws and regulations for IT in government	Y	6	Y	9	Y	10	25
3. Special budget for IT department	Y	14	Y	8	Y	0	22
4. Adequate infrastructure	Y	7	Y	11	Y	3	21
5. Commitment from public servants	Y	8	N	0	Y	12	20
6. Budget for technology investments	Y	11	Y	2	Y	0	13
7. Resource managerial methods to allocate budget	Y	11	Y	1	N	0	12
8. Senior management support	N	0	N	0	Y	11	11
9. Project continuity	Y	10	N	0	Y	0	10
10. Well-allocated budget to support high-priority projects	Y	8	Y	2	N	0	10
11. Paradigm change	Y	9	N	0	N	0	9
12. Corporate information security plan	N	0	Y	9	Y	0	9
13. Long term vision	N	0	N	0	Y	8	8
14. IT decision capacity	N	0	Y	0	Y	8	8
15. Smart innovation according to trends and needs	Y	8	N	0	N	0	8

In terms of interorganizational collaboration and networks, municipal CIOs mainly discussed the importance of relationships with all ministries and areas of the municipal government to facilitate collaboration in project development and implementation, but also the idea of exchanging technologies and applications among municipalities emerged in the conversation several times. In terms of institutional capabilities, local CIOs talked about the creation of an organizational culture of innovation, as well as having a proper set of laws and regulations to guide digital government plans and activities. All CIOs mentioned as an important institutional enabler the fact that the Municipal Development Plan explicitly includes a strategic component on information technologies. Some CIOs also mentioned governance structures and citizen councils as core capabilities for success. Finally, in terms of the general context, CIOs included the availability of research on current IT trends and needs in terms of information technologies and the development of an informatics culture among the public as core capabilities.

Additionally, the whole list of ideas was organized in terms of votes and perceived level of development. Both the labels and descriptions of the ideas were taken into consideration to make a final list of 91 different capabilities. Table 7.2 shows the top fifteen capabilities in terms of the number of votes that they obtained in all workshops. The list of the top fifteen mainly includes capabilities in the organizational category, with a couple of capabilities in the institutional and technology categories. Several of these top-ranked capabilities belong to the financial cluster, as well as personnel experience and commitment. Project continuity and a long-term vision are also core capabilities in this top list. However, the most important capabilities in terms of votes were not necessarily the best developed from the perception of participants (see Table 7.3). Only two of the items listed in the top fifteen were also considered best-developed capabilities. It is important to note that long-term vision and laws and regulations are particularly low in the table, as well as a set of capabilities related to financial resources. Although infrastructure is ranked nineteenth in terms of level of development, it gets an average of 7.4 on a 10-point scale, which describes a situation in which there is plenty of room for improvement.

Table 7.3   Assessment of Current Development of the Top Fifteen Capabilities

*Capability**		Avg. S-urb		Avg. Urban		Avg. Metro	Avg. Total
2.	Senior management support	N	N/A	N	N/A	Y	8.5	8.5
14.	IT decision capacity	N	N/A	Y	7.5	Y	7.8	7.7
19.	Adequate infrastructure	Y	7.8	Y	7.8	Y	6.5	7.4
25.	Corporate information security plan	N	N/A	Y	6.9	Y	7.2	7.1
35.	Well-trained human resources	Y	7.3	Y	6.8	Y	6.4	6.8
37.	Project continuity	Y	5.9	N	N/A	Y	7.4	6.6
41.	Well-allocated budget to support high-priority projects	Y	5.6	Y	7.5	N	N/A	6.5
46.	Smart innovation according to trends and needs	Y	6.4	N	N/A	N	N/A	6.4
60.	Budget for technology investments	Y	4.9	Y	6.5	Y	6.3	5.9
60.	Resource managerial methods to allocate budget	Y	4.9	Y	6.9	N	N/A	5.9
65.	Paradigm change	Y	5.8	N	N/A	N	N/A	5.8
67.	Special budget for IT department	Y	4.5	Y	5.7	Y	6.8	5.7
68.	Commitment from public servants	Y	5.1	N	N/A	Y	6.1	5.6
69.	Long term vision	N	N/A	N	N/A	Y	5.5	5.5
77.	Laws and regulations for IT in government	Y	5.1	Y	5.5	Y	5.5	5.3

* The number represents the place of the capability according to the average development considering the 91 capabilities

5 A PRELIMINARY DYNAMIC MODEL OF CORE CAPABILITIES

Table 7.3 shows a conceptual model, which is based on the comments from the thirty-four local CIOs described in the previous section. Using the grammar of System Dynamics, the model includes key activities, accumulations, and feedback loops; it is intended to serve as a guide for developing an effective digital government strategy at the local level in Mexico. This initial dynamic model includes twelve key accumulations or core resources and competencies for local governments. These core competencies and resources are associated with the main categories and clusters identified during the workshops. In the current model, not all flows (activities) are shown explicitly, with the purpose of making the diagram simpler.

The main technical resources are all represented in the stocks inside the rectangle on the right side of the figure. These four stocks are all built through effort in work and the quality or efficiency of this work. Effort in work is conceptualized as a result of financial or human resources in the IT department in the municipal government, and quality and productivity of this work results from IT staff expertise and the clear articulation of plans

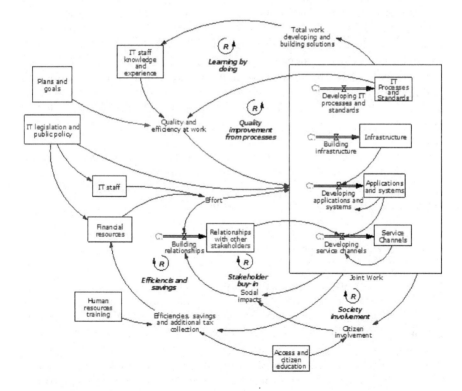

Figure 7.3 Preliminary dynamic conceptual model of core capabilities.

and objectives inside the IT department. Public policies and other legislation also have an effect on these activities, either constraining or enabling them. In addition, all these resources constrain or enable the development of other resources and important outputs. For instance, the development of infrastructure, IT processes and methods, systems, applications, and delivery channels all promote the development of benefits such as efficiencies, increases in tax collection, citizen participation, and other important social impacts. However, these benefits are not only the result of technology use, but other organizational and contextual factors, such as IT training of government employees or citizens' access to technology.

Our conceptualization includes five main reinforcing loops. All of these loops have the potential to promote the development of a digital government strategy, but all of them can also work as traps when capabilities and resources are not well developed. The first of these loops represents learning and expertise accumulation from the IT staff in developing infrastructure and applications. Again, although this loop can be seen as a virtuous cycle, when IT staff members have limited expertise, they are not productive enough to progress in the development of technical resources, and in turn have a low learning rate. This loop then implies a challenge for many local governments that lack sufficient IT expertise.

The second feedback loop shows the impact of IT methods and standards on productivity, suggesting that this technical capability may have an investment priority when compared to other resources. The loop named "efficiencies and savings" suggests that one way of acquiring additional resources to increase effort is through savings and efficiencies that result from digital government projects and applications. Finally, two more important feedback loops included in the initial conceptualization represent public involvement and buy-in of key stakeholders. These processes are, from our point of view, closely related to the social impact of digital government strategies. All these loops are reinforcing in nature, as we have previously established. In this way, they all represent potential traps in the initial stages of a strategy implementation.

6   FINAL COMMENTS

This chapter presents a preliminary model and more research is clearly needed. We are in the process of formalizing this model in order to explore the transformational impact of several investment strategies. We envision having a series of accumulations describing core resources and capabilities, all of them depending on investment priorities and a limited budget. In this way, we will compare investment strategies for infrastructure, as opposed to strategies with a focus on processes, standards, or systems development. We believe that such experiments have the potential to provide insights about the interrelations and relative importance of different core capabilities and resources, and get a better understanding of their relationships and impacts on transformational digital government. Future research should explore some of the specific capabilities and resources in order to disentangle their potential effects on other capabilities and resources, as well as their relative impact on the outputs and outcomes of the digital government strategy in local governments.

ACKNOWLEDGMENTS

The study reported here is the result of research and innovation projects in collaboration with "Fondo de Información y Documentación para la Industria—INFOTEC" in Mexico.

REFERENCES

Asgarkhani, M. (2007). The reality of social inclusion through digital government. *Journal of Technology in Human Services, 25*(1/2), 127–146.

Barney, J. B. (2001). Is the resource-based theory a useful perspective for strategic management research? Yes. *Academy of Management Review, 26*(1), 41–56.

Beynon-Davies, P., & Williams, M. D. (2003). Evaluating electronic local government in the UK. *Journal of Information Technology, 18*(2), 137.

Bharadwaj, A. S. (2000). A resource-based perspective on information technology capability and firm performance: An empirical investigation. *MIS Quarterly, 24*(1), 169–196.

Bhatt, G. D., & Grover, V. (2005). Types of Information technology capabilities and their role in competitive advantage: An empirical study. *Journal of Management Information Systems, 22*(2), 253–277.

Chan, C., & Pan, S. (2006). *Resource enactment in e-government systems implementation: A case study on the e-file system in Singapore.* Paper presented at the ICIS 2006 Proceedings, Milwaukee, Wisconsin, December 10–13.

Evans-Cowley, J., & Conroy, M. M. (2006). The growth of e-government in municipal planning. *Journal of Urban Technology, 13*(1), 81–107.

Fagan, M. H. (2006). Exploring city, county and state e-government initiatives: An East Texas perspective. *Business Process Management Journal, 12*(1), 101–112.

Feller, J., Finnegan, P., & Nilsson, O. (2011). Open innovation and public administration: Transformational typologies and business model impacts. *European Journal of Information Systems, 20*(3), 358–374.

Fountain, J. E. (2009). Bureaucratic reform and e-government in the United States: An institutional perspective. In A. Chadwick & P. N. Howard (Eds.), *Routledge handbook of Internet politics* (pp. 99–113). New York: Taylor & Francis Group.

Gil-Garcia, J. R., & Helbig, N. (2006). Exploring e-government benefits and success factors. In A.-V. Anttiroiko & M. Malkia (Eds.), *Encyclopedia of digital government.* Hershey, PA: Idea Group.

Gil-Garcia, J. R., & Pardo, T. A. (2005). E-government success factors: Mapping practical tools to theoretical foundations. *Government Information Quarterly, 22*(2), 187–216.

Gil-Garcia, J. R., Pardo, T. A., & Baker, A. (2007). *Understanding context through a comprehensive prototyping experience: A testbed research strategy for emerging technologies*. Paper presented at the 40th Hawaii International Conference on System Sciences, Waikoloa, January 3–6.

Holden, S. H., Norris, D. F., & Fletcher, P. D. (2003). Electronic government at the local level. *Public Performance & Management Review, 26*(4), 325–344.

Kaylor, C., Deshazo, R., & Eck, D. V. (2001). Gauging e-government: A report on implementing services among American cities. *Government Information Quarterly, 18*(4), 293.

King, S., & Cotterill, S. (2007). Transformational Government? The role of information technology in delivering citizen-centric local public services. [Article]. *Local Government Studies, 33*(3), 333–354.

Luna-Reyes, L. F., Gil-García, J. R., & Celorio-Mansi, J. A. (2010). *Hacia un Modelo de Gobierno Electrónico a Nivel Municipal para México: Reporte de Resultados de Talleres con Directores de Informática Municipales*. Cholula: Universidad de las Américas Puebla-INFOTEC.

Luna-Reyes, L. F., Zhang, J., Gil-Garcia, J. R., & Cresswell, A. M. (2005). Information systems development as emergent socio-technical change: A practice approach. *European Journal of Information Systems, 14*(1), 93–105.

Moon, M. J. (2002). The evolution of e-government among municipalities: Rhetoric or *reality? Public Administration Review, 62*(4), 424–433.

Patrick, S. (1995). The dynamic simulation of control and compliance processes in material organizations. *Sociological Perspectives, 38*(4), 497–518.

Reddick, C. G. (2004). Empirical models of e-government growth in local governments. *e-Service Journal, 3*(2), 59–74.

Reddick, C. G., & Frank, H. A. (2007). E-government and its influence on managerial effectiveness: A survey of Florida and Texas city managers. *Financial Accountability & Management, 23*(1), 1–26.

Rugman, A. M., & Verbeke, A. (2002). Edith Penrose's contribution to the resource-based views of strategic management. *Strategic Management Journal, 23*(8), 769–780.

Scholl, H. J. (2005). Organizational transformation through e-government: myth or reality? In M. Wimmer (Ed.), *Lecture Notes in Computer Science* (Vol. 3591, pp. 1–11). Berlin: Springer-Verlag.

Stafford, T. F., & Turan, A. H. (2011). Online tax payment systems as an emergent aspect of governmental transformation. *European Journal of Information Systems, 20*(3), 343–357.

Teece, D., Pisano, G., & Shuen, A. (1997). Dynamic capabilities and strategic management. *Strategic Management Journal, 18*(7), 509–533.

Wade, M., & Hulland, J. (2004). The Resource-based view and information systems research: Review, extension, and suggestions for future research. *MIS Quarterly, 28*(1), 107–142.

Warren, K. (2002). *Competitive strategy dynamics*. Chichester: John Wiley & Sons.

Wernerfelt, B. (1995). The resource-based view of the firm: Ten years after. *Strategic Management Journal 16*(3), 171–174.

Wolstenholme, E. F. (1999). Qualitative vs. quantitative modelling: The evolving balance. *Journal of the Operational Research Society, 50*(4), 422–428.

Part II

Benefits and Barriers to Transformation

8 Examining Successful Public Sector Electronic Services in Finland

Tommi Inkinen

CHAPTER OVERVIEW

This chapter provides an account of public sector electronic services from Finland. I focus on three specially awarded projects that aim to enhance electronic government. I frame the results with the contemporary literature on e-government. The three specific cases indicate elements of successful electronic services targeted at citizens. The results of the study are comparable to other countries advancing their electronic government and public sector e-services. Finland makes a good platform for case data: it has been regarded as one of the leading countries in technology development (e.g., WEF, 2010) but ranks lower in electronic government measures (e.g., UN, 2010). I conclude by addressing theoretical notions underlying Internet services and the significance of citizen-government relations in contemporary society.

1 INTRODUCTION

Political structure and the conduct of the democratic process involve the Internet in terms of electronic government (in detail Reddick, 2010), which entails flexible service production, higher civic participation, and efficiency gains. This chapter brings together two processes, namely, technology integration in public sector service production (Löfgren, 2007; Chadwick & Howard, 2008), and the management process and subcontracting (Hood, 1995; Dunleavy et al., 2006). This chapter presents three selected electronic services as denominators of how to create a successful electronic public sector service (Thomas & Strieb, 2003; Reddick, 2004; Saxena, 2005; Taylor, Lips, & Organ, 2007; Lean et al., 2009).

There are two main principles to implement new electronic services for public sector: a top-down approach or bottom-up one (Baqir & Iyer, 2010; Brown & Brudney, 2004). These are ideal opposites and in practice the implementation process includes elements from both of them. However, in practice project designs often follow one or other main principle. This division is identifiable among the studied three cases. They are projects (full list in Appendix 8.1) that have been awarded by the "Finnish Government Information Society Policy Program."[1] The chapter addresses two main questions: why have the selected cases been successful? and what common elements do these cases share?

Electronic government and governance involve a recognition of democracy, transparency in administration, public policy development, and participation in and improvement of public services (e.g. European Commission, 2010). Extensive research on electronic government has produced a number of classifications that segment public sector operations in terms of technological platforms (Grant & Derek, 2005). Carter and Bélanger (2005, p. 12) identified several key relations for the end-user to engage electronic services including trustworthiness (both technology and government), user friendliness, and the positive user experience (also Bélanger & Hiller, 2006).

Cases presented are considered according to their functionality and operation process. There are three main components, each of which is relevant for electronic government and governance including (1) provision logic (solution and responsibility), (2) customer potential and target group, and (3) technology interface, including the functionality (particularly user interface, data security and reliability) and potential of technology transfer to other locations.

2 ELEMENTS FOR SERVICE DEVELOPMENT

2.1 Provision Solution and Responsibility

The production of public electronic services involves four alternatives: public sector in-house; cross-administrative collaboration; public–private partnerships (PPPs); and fully outsourced private sector productions. These mechanisms are the main means to enhance public sector operations. West (2004, p. 25) analyzed the importance of sectoral co-operation within the government to create more user-friendly online services. Issues of citizen trust in government (e.g., Carter & Bélanger, 2005) and the potential that e-government has to increase the service functionality and citizen activity in participating public affairs are closely linked to provision arrangements as outsourcing has resulted in some cases in a jurisdiction debate about the use of public power by private companies.

Close collaboration between the private sector and public organizations is identifiable in the three cases. This is a functional division in order to understand public sector electronic services. For example, PPP service production is a common alternative (Yescombe, 2007). Thus, the organizing of the provision of public services involves profit-seeking private companies and public sector involvement in planning and managing the service in question. Companies that are owned by public sector entities (such as cities) and non-profit organizations are included in service provision (see Heintze & Bretscheinder, 2000). Thus, electronic public sector services are rarely a pure "public" issue in organizational terms. The subcontracting (provision arrangement) and production of the actual service almost always include segments created or produced by a private or publicly owned company.

Provision responsibility signifies the interrelations between and within public organs and refers to the service requirements identified in Finnish law for public entities: the organizational responsibilities differ greatly in the service production (implementation solutions differ according to legislations) of the military, the police, the rescue services, and the health services as well as the maintenance and development of the transport infrastructure. The distinction between public and private sector responsibilities in the production of these services has been under discussion for decades (e.g., Osborne, 1993; Bryson, 2004; Reddick, 2010). The changing mode in service production responsibilities involves a theoretical connection to the widely debated issue of "new public management" (e.g., Hood, 1995; Martins, 1995; Dunleavy et al., 2006; Williams & Lewis, 2008). The definition evidently extends beyond that of traditional government organizations: public sector services also include services that are fundamentally linked to societal structures including private contractors and non-governmental organizations (Kooiman, 2005; Bang, 2007).

For example, public transport (and electronic information concerning it) is considered here as a "public service." National variations are considerable in this regard: In Finland and in the Helsinki Metropolitan Area (HMA), public transport is organized by a local transport authority. Thus, public sector involvement is extensive, but the majority of transport is provided by private companies as subcontractors (compare to the U.K. railroad act of 1993 and privatization: Yvrande-Billon & M´enard, 2004). The overall HMA transport systems also involve local train services that are currently under the monopoly of a stated owned corporation (VR). Production responsibility is therefore relevant when considering the actualization of the services offered and their functionality.

2.2 Customer Potential and Target Group

Lean et al. (2009) and Carter and Bélanger (2005) have empirically tested factors leading to higher e-government adoption. Their analyses indicate that a service's usefulness, need, and trustworthiness are the most important user-point-of-view elements resulting in higher adoption levels. Therefore, this case based study includes the number of users is estimated in order to give an indication of the extent of the service potential. The user friendliness and the actual customer need, together with customer potential, are the main building blocks to develop a successful new service. The recognition of customer potential is extensively present in the identified case services. Separation into business-to-government (B2G) services and citizen services is needed. Private individuals interact less with the government than business organizations.

The role of the end-user, considered either as a citizen (Lean et al., 2009) or a consumer (Felix & Sutherland, 2004) is therefore essential: how has the service provider taken the user (adoption) potential into consideration in the service process? and how is the created service expected to change or modify the end-user experience and the provision efficiency for the producer including aspects of lower costs, higher service quality (i.e., shorter total or response time), or smaller number of transactions?

The issue of trust is elemental in the consideration of the willingness to use and interact with public sector organizations. Considering service interfaces, Tolbert and Mossberger (2006) studied the essential aspect of trust in the e-government process through a survey analysis of websites. Their results suggested that technical reliability and provision responsibility (local or national government) are elemental if trust building is to lead to a functional service. A key technological element is the identification process and reliability of secure information exchange between the client and the service provider.

2.3   Technology Interface and Transferability

Implementations of electronic services requires an efficient physical network structure (hardware), user-friendly service design (software developments), and also non-technological dimensions, for example, networking tools and other collaboration models that aim to bring together professionals and developers in order to collaborate and work together (see Bryson, 2004). Hardware solutions including the provision of physical (e.g. computer kiosks or screens) or WLAN access points are just as essential as the more common software based services. They are significant in creating universal and transferable technologies that will increase service quality. This is particularly noticeable in Finland, where cities (e.g., Oulu and Turku) are providing free of charge WLAN city networks to residents and visitors (Inkinen, 2011). Standards and interoperability are common notions in technology-society integration but several problems concerning technical reliability and interoperability still exist particularly in software development.

Finally, the potential for the technology transfer (universality) of the service is considered. Technology transfer is to a large extent dependent on technology platform as well as national arrangements of private–public sector relations. Chan and Chow (2007) discussed the particularities of public management policies in China and elaborated on the problematic of national contexts and generalizations based on national cases. National governments and their functions have significance in the "sphere" of the Internet. The specific national context signifies for the extent and content of online information. The mixture and intertwinement of provision responsibilities, competition legislation, and customer adoption (based on national and local cultures) together with the available and viable technology platforms together determine the potential of technology transfer to other countries and locations.

In a universal sense, we may consider the enablement of technology transfer, direct or indirect, and the flows of material or immaterial resources. In addition, contextual foci relate to computer and Internet skills concerning citizenship and the politics of rights in terms of egalitarian opportunities to live in a contemporary information society. This form of digital divide (Graham, 2002; James, 2008; Dobransky & Hargittai, 2006) incorporates a socio-economic structure and end-user needs/capabilities into the challenge of electronic service design and their transferability.

As a summary, the studied cases are applied as illustrative examples of public sector-service provision. Arguably, the politics of building a service provision structure have relevance for electronic government and public sector online service provision. National legislation matters as electronic services are always produced in a spatial context (Kellerman, 2002; Chan & Chow, 2007; Lean et al., 2009). They are designed to meet customer needs together with adequate quality requirements. Therefore they have a predetermined purpose within the administrative process, which fundamentally aims to increase efficiency and reduce costs. The automation of data management is targeted at enhancing data security (both in terms of individuals as well as organizations), reliability, and efficiency (time) in services provision (Wimmer & Traunmuller, 2000; Gauld, Graya, & McComba, 2009).

3 CASE STUDIES EXPLORED

3.1 Case Selection

I present three selected cases to clarify and "open up" different types of projects and efforts that were awarded by the Finnish Information Society Program. Innovative projects were awarded on two occasions (years 2004 and 2006) based on open call applications. In total the Policy Program rewarded 281 projects from various fields of technology–society integration on the recommendation of experts (for quantitative analysis, see Inkinen, 2012). Thirteen of them (excluding three special mentions) received a "prime minister's award" identifying them as the best of the best (Appendix 8.1). Three of these projects have been selected for closer analysis: An online Journey Planner; a short message service (SMS) ticketing for public transport; and the palkka.fi financial online service for small and medium-sized companies (SMEs) provided by the Ministry of Finance.

The decision to use these selected cases is based on the extensiveness of the available project information focusing on electronic service development. The data source is, as far as Finland is concerned, unique and provides an extensive overview of the variety of development projects in this field. The data are nationally bound, but their provision logic and technology implementations are repeatable in other locations (for qualitative methods, see Miles & Huberman, 1994; Coffey & Atkinson, 1996). Therefore, the cases have international relevance and provide an insight into operational and successful services. The data are considered the best available collection of project descriptions including information concerning their provision. The cases are from the years 2004 and 2006, but they are still relevant today in terms of their functionality and high user adoption. In addition, they have embedded themselves as integral parts of the overall service provision. Thus, the electronic (virtual) services contribute to physical (material) activities. These services are therefore complements and not substitutes for physical services.

3.2   SMS Ticketing for Public Transport

The first case "SMS Tickets in Public Transport" was the first in the world to offer the opportunity to buy metro and tram tickets via SMS. The service was launched in 2003, and it is still active. It represents an interesting combination of mobile phone technology with daily routines and business logic. The SMS ticketing service is for the Helsinki Metropolitan Area's public transport. The production logic follows the traditional PPP model in which a public sector authority outsources and collaboratively produces the end-service with a private sector company (see Langford & Roy, 2009). Approximately over 2,875,000 SMS tickets are sold annually, which amounts to a daily total of 8,800 tickets (HSL, 2010).

The provision arrangement behind the SMS ticketing service is a traditional combination of networks: local public transport is organized by the Helsinki Regional Transport Authority (HSL), which is responsible for the metropolitan area's transport including the municipalities of Helsinki, Espoo, Vantaa, and Kauniainen. HSL organizes the actual transport through contracts with carrier companies. The SMS ticketing also involves the collaboration of telephone operators indicating the second business network structure behind the service. Thus, the service is operator bound but in practice all the major mobile telephone operators participate in the service. The service is designed to be as easy to use as possible. The ticket requires one sent SMS message with a certain code and in return a ticket SMS is automatically sent in response. The service process is visualized in Figure 8.1.

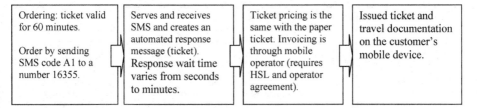

| Ordering: ticket valid for 60 minutes. Order by sending SMS code A1 to a number 16355. | Serves and receives SMS and creates an automated response message (ticket). Response wait time varies from seconds to minutes. | Ticket pricing is the same with the paper ticket. Invoicing is through mobile operator (requires HSL and operator agreement). | Issued ticket and travel documentation on the customer's mobile device. |

Figure 8.1   SMS ticketing process.

The technical solution is provided by a private company (plusdial. com), and the target customers are individuals. The service may be considered transferable to other locations if the public transport organization, as the local contextual arrangement, is suitable. The service has a problem with multi-channel ticket provision: the SMS tickets are valid only within the city of Helsinki, and there are some carriers that do not accept it, thus it is not fully equivalent to a paper ticket. Such limitations are found in particular bus connections, causing confusion. This is also one of the reasons why the English language information (for tourists) is limited—it would cause confusions and problems for people not familiar with the "common practices" of the city transport.

3.3   Getting There: An Interactive Online Journey Planner

The second awarded service is the "Journey Planner" (Figure 8.2), also steered by the HSL. The service provides "door-to-door" information on how to plan your trip. It estimates walking times to the nearest (time distance) bus or train stop, calculates the scheduled travel times and provides a total distance in time and in kilometers (and meters). Thus, it provides information on the best (fastest and/or shortest) public transport connections within the Helsinki region at any specified time. The service was launched in 2001 and is still active, indicating the demand and durability of the service. This journey planner is constantly up-dated and has become the most important information channel concerning public transport in HMA. It is a PPP solution ordered by HSL and operationalized by Logica Finland.

The service is provided with four languages (Finnish, Swedish, English, and Russian) and includes current changes and exceptions taking place in public transport. The journey planner may be considered a successful electronic service. It is used by tens of thousands of HMA citizens and tourists daily, and is one of the most widely used e-services in Finland (Ministry of Finance, 2009). The journey planner applies street addresses or "commonly known" locations as potential start and end points. Moreover, one innovative software addition is the GIS-service allowing the customer to indicate the start and end locations on a map.

Initial travel information input	Results for routes	Results on maps:

- Origin → destination
- Street address
- Map identification
- Specific locations (e.g., market square)
- Time and date
- Selection of:
  o Means of transport
  o Preferred exchange time
  o Accessibility choices
  o Ticket zones
  o Estimations for walking speed between transport stops for exchange
	- Shortest time or distance
	- Shortest walking distance
	- Total amounts of
	  o Walking
	  o Time
	  o Route distance
	- Combined travel information
	  o Includes all modes of transport (busses, metro, tramlines)
	  o Three suggestions per screen
	  o Earlier choices ←→ later choices
	  o CO_2 emissions for each route selection (based on used means of transport)
		- Indicates the start and end locations
		- If connections are needed, displays the connection zones and walking guidelines
		- Indicates time intervals for each mean of transport during the journey
		- Produces list of stops (stop name and street address)
		- Indicates right stop to step out

Figure 8.2   Journey planner user interface steps.

Figure 8.2 indicates that the HSL service has similar elements to those available in the map services of transnational Internet companies. This brings up an important question of scale: to what extent is it desirable for a small city organization to "compete" in its service provision with global corporations? The notion also involves the definition of virtual space ownership. An example here is Google's "streetview" service and the separation to "public roads" (accessible) "private roads" (not accessible). The question of privacy was also raised concerning identifiable faces on the service to which Google responded by digitally erasing facial characteristics identifiable in the views. Several larger cities in Finland provide their own municipal map services and thus they are "competing" with international companies. So far only Google has managed to produce a service so extensive that it has become a global "routine" option for location-bound information search.

3.4   Free Salary Accounting for SMEs

The third and final project concerns electronic government service for SMEs. "Palkka.fi" is a free of charge electronic management service targeted at small employers and households. It allows them to manage and calculate salaries and wages. The service also includes social security contribution shares and other legislated non-wage payroll costs. The service provides a free to use demo version for potential new users.

The service is available only in the two official languages of Finland (Finnish and Swedish). The service includes segments for calculating payments, taxation, and social security together with insurance costs and insurance applications. The service is provided by the Ministry of Finance in co-operation with private insurance companies and may be seen as a competitive public sector product for private sector finance management solutions such as provided by SAP, which commonly are too expensive and

Employer basic information	Selection of employee
- Company name, type, identification number, language	- Basic information (personal and employment contract)
- Address and contact	- Taxation information
- Bank account	- Insurance information
Taxation information	- Labor union information
- Frequency of notifications	- Credit liability information
Insurance information	- Absences from work
- Types of insurances (accidents, pensions)	**Calculation of salaries**
- Insurance company details (agreement identification numbers, ending dates)	- Salaries and benefits (cross)
	- Taxation
	- Vacations
	- Deductions
	- Other information

Printouts and summaries
- Salaries and accounting for each employee, employee groups and total
- Archives of past month/year salaries and employee costs
- Full salary payments and account details

Links to other organizations
- Bank contacts (home pages)
- Value-added and other tax notifications/accounts (Ministry of Finance)
- The Social Security Institution of Finland notifications (KELA)

Figure 8.3   A concise schematic of palkka.fi online user interface. All segments are interlinked and are usable from the main tool bar.

complicated for SMEs. The service is active and provides cost reductions for small businesses and NGOs.

Figure 8.3 portrays the user interface structure. The simplicity of the visualization stresses the importance of an easy-to-use philosophy in service production. Importantly, palkka.fi also provides direct links to other public sector services relevant for SMEs including taxation and banking. The interconnectedness of the services increases the usability of the design. Overall, the collaboration model involves a different version of the PPP arrangement compared to the two previous cases: collaboration between Finnish ministries and private sector banks has a long tradition concerning the identification process. In Finland practically all identification processes in electronic services are done with private online banking codes. Figure 8.3 shows that salary calculations involves social security information, insurance details, and agreements together with bank accounts. The use of service requires a high level of trust in the cloud service and its information security. Therefore, the collaboration in the identification and insurance/banking processes may be considered as a value-adding element provided by the service.

3.5   Discussion of Commonalities among the Cases

The first question of the chapter concerned the factors that are required for successful service implementation (compare Heeks, 2003). These commonalities are essential in a universal sense, and relevant elements have been statistically analysed concerning end-user adoption (Welch, Hinnant, & Moon, 2005; Carter & Bélanger, 2005; Lean et al., 2009). All services are considered to involve the following main principles:

1. They serve extensive and well-defined target (user) groups.
2. They are highly convenient and easy to use regardless of the OS platforms.
3. They are free of charge (the application use) except the SMS ticketing service in which the ticket naturally is normally priced. However, the application itself is free of charge (means of payment).
4. They are embedded into a service provision structure (they have existed long enough to establish themselves as a "known" alternative to other competing means of conducting the business in question).
5. They may be seen as transferable to other locations (universal). However, local business arrangements may cause difficulties if the business environments are fragmented.

All studied services are functioning today. Five of the listed services in Appendix 8.1 have terminated. This brings forth a problem of continuity: how to create a lasting service after the initial project period. This problem relates to consortium structures, because the private sector's role in electronic government is realized mainly through subcontracting. Ownership relations matter because national government and large cities own several of the companies creating e-solutions for them. Thus subcontracting between the public sector and the private sector is a blurred issue if ownership relations are considered.

The cases are successful due to their practical significance and customer potential. Key elements of a successful e-service require the durability and long-term commitment of the providing organization(s) to update and develop the service. The presented cases have high number of active users (realized customer potential). The technical end-user interfaces are easy to use and the customer is aware of the organization that they are dealing with. In other words, the services are produced by well-known organizations and they are easily approachable if the transaction fails (e.g., SMS tickets) or provides false information (e.g., journey planner).

As argued, the Internet, with the services provided online, is an efficient tool for modifying citizens' interaction with the public sector. The empirical challenge is to find out how citizens perceive themselves as customers and how they perceive service reliability and trustworthiness (see Heeks & Bailur, 2007). Administrative and political studies recognize this significance: how are services produced? who is allowed or expected to use them? and what type of governance does it support? Internet services are to a large extent substitutes for physical entities, in which services are realized through immaterial transactions, for example, selling SMS tickets. Virtual representations modify knowledge pertaining to their physical counterparts (e.g., Graham, 1998). In this process, the issue of assessing information reliability and critical content reading, which are required of the reader, becomes paramount.

4   FUTURE RESEARCH CHALLENGES

The public sector has traditionally produced the majority of its services in-house in Finland. This is gradually changing towards the adoption of collaborative solutions. A broader discussion of electronic service development expands beyond the presented locally and nationally created services. It relates to technology integration into a societal structure and market economy (West, 2005). What actually public services are and how they should be produced? A key problem in thinking of citizen-government relations is the ever-increasing complexity of society. This may be seen as a result of societal change in which technological solutions have an embedded role. This however, also brings several new challenges: an understanding of computer and technology structures in terms of privacy, security, and responsibility is becoming more important daily. The process is reflected in the business economy through technology transfer. Significant efforts are conducted from country to country in search of a one-solution-fits-all idea, with varying outcomes in terms of success.

There are both theoretical and empirical research challenges including how global flows of finance and information interlink, what political conditions underlie success in informational development, and how nation states support innovative e-service production. The question concerns information distribution, demand, and significance. A critical understanding of the rhetoric and representation used in the marketing of new services requires further attention. These research challenges are arguably embedded in societal development and technology integration: who presents public sector information and how does citizen interaction with the public sector change via electronic services? What is provided as a service and what is not? Potential research themes combine online service development and the administrative (political) realm including power structures between political decisions, and transparency and policies guiding the integration of technology into society.

APPENDIX

Table 8.1   Specially Awarded Electronic Services by the Finnish Information
Society Policy Program in the Years 2004 and 2006

Reward category and year	*Service and short description*	*Current condition*
New innovations category, 2006 (reward year)	Consumer Gadget: Allows to check the ethical background of a consumer item. The Consumer Gadget was designed for use in mobile-phone handsets. It uses the EAN barcodes of products facts.	Service no longer available
New innovations category, 2006	Palkka.fi: Provides a free internet service to small employers to calculate and pay the salaries and wages of their employees as well as the social security contributions and other non-wage payroll costs.	www.palkka.fi Service is active
Effectiveness and productivity category, 2006	The precompleted income tax return form: The taxpayer only needs to check the information entered by the Tax Administration.	www.vero.fi/veroilmoitus Service is active
Effectiveness and productivity category, 2006	Penguins in school – Now: Computer education: a school network using an open source software and LTSP technology increasing the use and effectiveness of computers with greatly reduced costs.	www.antarktis.fi Project no longer existing
Application and promotion of data security category, 2006	The SME Risk Management (PK-RH®) toolkit: Offers concrete tools for comprehensive risk management. It is backed by more than ten years of research and development carried out by research institutions and SMEs.	http://www.pk-rh.fi Project thematic active
Application and promotion of data security category, 2006	Citizens' computer support: The service maintains a list of local computer businesses to which customers can refer the customer if needed. The most common problems include starting up and viruses and other computer malware. The Citizen's computer support provides its customers with a diagnosis form.	http://www.kansal-aisenmikrotuki.fi Service is active
Special award (general), 2006	AddictionLink: Has grown from an information source into the most popular service on substance abuse in Finland. The service reaches a large segment of substance users. The idea underlying AddictionLink is to provide a set of services that support citizens and complement each other.	http://www.paihdelinkki.fi Service is active
Information society in everyday life, 2004	SMS Tickets in the Public Transport: The first in the world to offer the opportunity to buy metro and tram tickets via SMS.	http://www.plusdial.com Service is active

(continued)

Table 8.1   (continued)

Reward category and year	Service and short description	Current condition
Education and Learning, 2004	Virtual craft and design classes: A nationwide network community that connects pupils, students, teachers and researchers. The website distributes connects pupils, students, teachers and researchers. The website distributes	Service no longer available
eWork, 2004	New businesses and jobs through strategic development: Long term development area. Has created in six different call centres or customer service centres. www.naturepolis.fi Project has ended, thematic continues	
Cooperation projects, 2004	Journey Planner: The Helsinki Regional Transport Authority (HSL) door-to-door Journey Planner provides information on the best public transport connection within the Helsinki region at any specified time.	www.reittiopas.fi Service is active
eBusiness, 2004	ProCountor: An online financial administration service that makes it possible for all financial and accounting activities to be carried out at any time and anywhere.	www.procountor. com Service is active

NOTES

1. The policy programs were organized as attempts to overcome problems in sector government structures that often led to competition and collisions between ministries on cross-administrative issues. For example, the ministries of labour and industry may share development issues that overlap each other. The policy programs concerned important topics that were considered elemental in society. The first four original programs were labeled the "information society" (lead by the prime minister), "labour" (lead by the minister of employment), "entrepreneurship" (lead by the minister of industry and trade) and "citizen participation" (lead by the minister of justice) policy programs. Thus, information society was considered of major importance in the Finnish administration. These policy programs functioned during 2003–2007. The policy programs were redesigned in 2008–2011 to include only three programs, with the "information society" program being discontinued. (Finnish Government, 2011).

REFERENCES

Bang, H. (2007). Governing the governance. *Public Administration, 85*(1), 227–231.

Baqir, M. N. & Iyer, L. (2010). E-government maturity over 10 years: A comparative analysis of e-government maturity in select countries around the world. In

Reddick, C.G. (Ed.), *Comparative e-government*, Integrated Series in Information Systems 25 (pp. 3–22). New York: Springer.

Bélanger, F. & Hiller, J. S. (2006). A framework for e-government: Privacy implications. *Business Process Management Journal, 12*(1), 48–60.

Brown, M. M., & Brudney, J. L. (2004). Achieving advanced electronic government services: Opposing environmental constraints. *Public Performance & Management Review, 28*(1), 96–114.

Bryson, J. M. (2004). What to do when stakeholders matter: Stakeholder identification and analysis techniques. *Public Management Review, 6*(1), 21–53.

Carter, L., & Bélanger, F. (2005). The utilization of e-government services: citizen trust, innovation and acceptance factors. *Information Systems Journal, 15*(1), 5–25.

Chadwick, A. & Howard, P. (Eds.). (2008). *Routledge handbook of Internet politics*. New York: Routledge.

Chan, H. S., & Chow, K. W. (2007). Public management policy and practice in Western China: Metapolicy, tacit knowledge, and implications for management innovation transfer. *American Review of Public Administration, 37*(4), 479–497.

Coffey, A., & Atkinson, P. (1996). *Making sense of qualitative data: Complementary research strategies*. Sage: Thousand Oaks.

Dobransky, K. & Hargittai, E. (2006). The disability divide in Internet access and use. *Information, Communication and Society, 9*(3), 313–334.

Dunleavy, P., Margetts, H., Bastow, S., & Tinkler, J. (2006). New public management is dead-long live digital-era governance. *Journal of Public Administration Research and Theory, 16*(3), 467–494.

European Commission (2010). The European eGovernment action plan 2011–2015. Harnessing ICT to promote smart, sustainable & innovative Government. Brussels: European Commission. Retrieved August 19, 2011, from http://ec.europa.eu/information_society/activities/egovernment/ action_plan_2011_2015/docs/action_plan_en_act_part1_v2.pdf

Felix, B. T., & Sutherland, P. (2004). Online consumer trust: A multi-dimensional model. *Journal of Electronic Commerce in Organizations, 2*(3), 40–58.

Finnish Government (2011). Government Policy Programs. Retrieved December 23, 2011, from www.valtioneuvosto.fi/tietoarkisto/politiikkaohjelmat-2007–2011/en.jsp

Gauld, R., Graya, A., & McComba, S. (2009). How responsive is e-government? Evidence from Australia and New Zealand. *Government Information Quarterly, 26*(1), 69–74.

Graham, S. (1998). The end of geography or the explosion of place? Conceptualizing space, place and information technology. *Progress in Human Geography, 22*(2), 165–185.

Graham, S. (2002). Bridging urban digital divides? Urban Polarisation and information and communications technologies (ICTs). *Urban Studies, 39*(1), 33–56.

Grant, G., & Derek, C. (2005). Developing a generic framework for e-government. *Journal of Global Information Management, 13*(1), 1–30.

Heeks, R. (2003). Achieving success/avoiding failure in e-Government projects. IDPM, University of Manchester. Retrieved August 16, 2011, from http://www.egov4dev.org/success/sfdefinitions.shtml

Heeks, R., & Bailur, S. (2007). Analyzing e-government research: Perspectives, philosophies, theories, methods, and practice. *Government Information Quarterly, 24*(2), 243–265.

Heintze, T., & Bretscheinder, S. (2000). Information technology and restructuring in public organizations: Does adoption of information technology affect organizational structures, communications and decision making. *Journal of Public Administration Research & Theory, 10*(4), 778–812.

Hood, C. (1995). The new public management in the 1980s: Variations on a theme. *Accounting, Organizations and Society, 20*(2), 93–109.

HSL (2010). Ticket sales in different types of transportation. [In Finnish.] Retrieved August 9, 2011, from http://www.hsl.fi/FI/mikaonhsl/julkaisut/Documents/2010/Matkalippujen_myynti_liikennevalineissa_34_2010.pdf

Inkinen, T. (2011). The Internet in three Finnish cities: Accessing global networks. In Brunn, S. (Ed.), *Engineering earth. The impacts of megaengineering projects* (pp. 131–143). New York: Springer.

Inkinen, T. (2012). Best Practices of the Finnish Government Information Society Policy Programme: Technology, provision, and impact scale. *Transforming Government. People, Process and Policy, 6*(2), 167–187.

James, J. (2008). Digital divide complacency: Misconceptions and dangers. *Information Society, 24*(1), 54–61.

Kellerman, A. (2002). *Internet on earth. A geography of information.* London: Wiley.

Kooiman, J. (2005). *Governing as governance.* London: Sage.

Langford, J., & Roy, J. (2009). Building shared accountability into service transformation partnerships. *International Journal of Public Policy, 4*(3/4), 232–250.

Lean, O., Zailani, K., Ramayah, S. & Fernando, Y. (2009). Factors influencing intention to use e-government services among citizens in Malaysia. *International Journal of Information Management, 29*(6), 458–475.

Löfgren, K. (2007). The Governance of e-government: A governance perspective on the Swedish e-government strategy. *Public Policy and Administration, 22*(3), 335–352.

Martins, M. R. (1995). Size of municipalities, efficiency, and citizens' participation: A cross-European perspective. *Environment and Planning C: Government and Policy, 13*(4), 441–458.

Miles, M. B., & Huberman, A. M. (1994). *Qualitative data analysis: An expanded sourcebook.* Thousand Oaks, CA: Sage.

Ministry of Finance. (2009). SADe Services and Project Report 2009. [In Finnish.] Retrieved August 10, 2011, from http://www.vm.fi/vm/fi/04_julkaisut_ja_asiakirjat/01_julkaisut/04_hallinnon_kehittaminen/20100107SADepa/SADe_palvelu-_ja_hankeselvitys_2009.pdf

Osborne, D. (1993). Reinventing government. *Public Productivity and Management Review, 16*(4), 349–356.

Reddick, C. G. (2004). A two stages model of e-government growth: Theories and empirical evidence for U.S. cities. *Government Information Quarterly, 21*(1), 51–64.

Reddick, C. G. (Eds.). (2010*). Comparative e-government.* Integrated Series in Information Systems 25. New York: Springer.

Saxena, K. B. C. (2005). Towards excellence in e-governance. *International Journal of Public Sector Management, 18*(6), 498–513.

Taylor, J., Lips, M., & Organ, J. (2007). Information-intensive government and the layering and sorting of citizenship. *Public Money and Management, 27*(2), 161–164.

Thomas, J. C., & Streib, G. (2003). The new face of government: Citizen-initiated contacts in the era of e-government. *Journal of Public Administration Research and Theory, 13*(1), 83–102.

Tolbert, C. J. & Mossberger, K. (2006). The effects of e-government on trust and confidence in government. *Public Administration Review, 66*(3), 354–369.

UN (2010). E-Government Survey 2010. *Leveraging e-government at a time of financial and economic crisis.* New York: United Nations.

WEF (2010). *The global competitiveness report 2010–2011.* Geneva: World Economic Forum.

Welch, E. W., Hinnant, C., & Moon, M. J. (2005). Linking citizen satisfaction with e-government and trust in government. *Journal of Public Administration Research and Theory, 15*(3), 371–391.

West, D. M. (2004). E-government and the transformation of service delivery and citizen attitudes. *Public Administration Review, 64*(1), 15–27.

West, D. M. (2005). *Digital government: Technology and public sector performance.* Princeton: Princeton University Press.

Williams, W., & Lewis, D. (2008). Strategic management tools and public sector management. *Public Management Review, 10*(5), 653–671.

Wimmer, M., & Traunmuller, R. (2000). *Trends in electronic government: Managing distributed knowledge.* New York: Springer.

Yescombe, E. R. (2007). *Public-private partnerships. Principles of policy and finance.* Oxford: Butterworth-Heinemann.

Yvrande-Billon, A., & M´enard, C. (2004). Institutional constraints and organizational changes: The case of the British rail reform. *Journal of Economic Behavior & Organization, 56*(4), 675–699.

9 Identifying Online Citizens
Understanding the Trust Problem

Ruth Halperin and James Backhouse

CHAPTER OVERVIEW

The chapter begins by showing why online identity and identification are essential to the future development of e-government. With a focus on the European Union context, it highlights the ways in which combining and sharing new types of personal data afford new forms of e-government provision. The chapter then shows the current problem of the lack of citizens' trust in those public authorities responsible for online identification. We report on an empirical research that examined citizens' perceptions on the rollout of electronic identity systems in Europe. Drawing on grounded research using open coding content analysis, the authors examine over 700 respondents from Germany and the United Kingdom. The analysis suggests that the hostile attitudes of citizens derive specifically from perceived negative past experiences at the hands of the public authorities. The study relates three emerging themes in particular: IT failures, function creep, and political history of oppression to three aspects of the trustworthiness of public authorities, namely competence, integrity, and benevolence. Stressing the need to remedy the situation, the authors discuss how governments might set about repairing and enhancing institutional trust. Suggestions are made on how improved governance and regard for transparency in respect of public sector identity management systems can address the negative perceptions and pave the way for greater public acceptance of e-ID.

1 E-IDENTIFICATION, INTEROPERABILITY, AND E-GOVERNMENT

An important characteristic of e-government applications is their dependence on technologies for managing identity. For e-government to succeed means must be provided for citizens and businesses to engage electronically with government via secure networks that maximize user confidence and respect data protection standards. A system of authentication of electronic documents must also be planned and developed (Saxby, 2006, p. 1).

Identity management is, therefore, the *sine qua non* of e-government, where projects involve large-scale sharing of personal data and requiring the identification of citizens as they interact with the state. Major plans for digital identity management are being developed as part of the future development of e-government around the world. This research focuses specifically on the electronic ID (eID) plans in Europe (Kubicek & Noack, 2010) . In 2005 the eEurope Action Plan called on the European Commission to issue an agreed interoperability framework to support the delivery of pan-European e-government services to citizens and enterprises (IDABC, 2005). This plan of action encompassed an abundance of services aiming to harmonize tax, social security systems, educational systems, jurisdiction for divorce and family law, driving risks and benefit and welfare regimes across Europe (Kinder, 2003). The i2010 Strategic Plan highlighted interoperability as one of its four main challenges for the creation of a single European information space and essential for ICT-enabled public services. As part of the plan, the Interoperability Solution for Public Administration proposed a pragmatic approach to identity management and refers explicitly to the idea of an EU-wide eID system.[1] Along the same lines, the EU Digital Agenda 2020 defined interoperability as one of its key initiatives.[2]

While the interoperability agenda for Europe smacks of transformative promise, a number of challenges clearly emerge. First, technical challenges relating to data homogeneity and system interoperability for proper and efficient metadata exchange (Recordon & Reed, 2006). Second, challenges within the policy realm of the creation, communication and diffusion of commonly accepted standards[3] (Otjacques, Hitzelberger, & Feltz, 2007). Third, that challenges interact with these two: politics, culture and behaviour (Scholl, 2005). A crucial aspect of the third challenge involves citizens and their perceptions in relation to the adoption of interoperable identity management systems (IdMS) (Backhouse & Halperin, 2009). The notion of citizen-centric e-government (Reddick, 2010) however draws attention to this aspect of the emerging systems, an aspect that may vitally affect whether or not such systems win public acceptance.

2   RESEARCHING THE PERCEPTIONS OF CITIZENS TOWARDS EID

The study reported in this chapter addressed the gap in EU research on eID perceptions (Lusoli & Miltgen, 2009; Seltsikas & O'Keefe, 2010). It was designed to generate and analyse qualitative data so as to achieve a deeper understanding of citizens' perceptions on eID, and to reveal the reasoning underlying the prevailing views. The methodology adopted in this study drew on grounded theory (Glaser & Strauss, 1967) because it offers a research method that seeks to develop accounts grounded in the data and uses the analytical technique of open coding (Strauss & Corbin, 1990).

Data were collected using a web survey to explore the perspectives of European citizens toward the new interoperable systems planned by the European Union. A brief description was provided of the proposed EU scheme and of the introduction of a Europe-wide eID card, which would allow shared use for all governmental services across all European countries.

In order to generate qualitative data, the survey contained an open-ended question inviting respondents to comment freely on any aspect of eIDs. This method generated data in the form of free text. Although responses came back from several EU countries, the national representation of the data used in the present study was restricted to just two countries, Germany (N = 360) and the United Kingdom (N = 377), a high response rate that lent itself to rigorous content analysis.

Citizens were also asked to respond to demographic questions. The results indicated that the survey respondents is dominated by a relatively young population, with a mean of 34 years of age, a minimum age of 15 and maximum age of 77. In terms of gender, male respondents are heavily over-represented in the survey (female 17 percent, male 83 percent). Finally, on the question of political views, results indicated a mean of 4.53 on a 10 number scale with 1 indicating farthest left and 10 farthest right.

We recognize the limitation of web surveys as self-selected samples, but interviews would not have provided the rich, diverse and anonymous responses obtained through the web survey. We emphasise that our findings do not seek to represent the U.K. and German populations in a statistical sense. Instead, the validity of qualitative research stems from the plausibility and the cogency of the logical reasoning used in describing the results from the cases, and in drawing conclusions from them (Agerfalk, 2004). This study lays claim to analytical generalizability (Yin, 1984), in particular to the common type of generalizing from data to descriptions (Lee & Baskerville, 2003).

We used content analysis where the data are read and categorized into concepts that are suggested by the data themselves rather than imposed from outside (Agar, 1980). Units for analysis define units of meaning (Henri, 1992) whereby each response is partitioned into text segments representing ideas in the text. This method of open coding relies on an analytical technique of identifying possible categories, their properties and dimensions (Kelle, 2007).

Systematic content analysis of the dataset revealed ***trust*** as a major issue:

> *Governments cannot be **trusted** to maintain identity information on the citizen's behalf.*
> *The main problem is not the data that is stored on the ID-card, but the lack of **trust** in the authorities that handle the data.*

The salience of similar statements and, as we shall show later on, the logic of justification associated with them, led us to focus on trust-related beliefs.

3   ANALYZING TRUST-RELATED PERCEPTIONS

In this chapter we present the findings that emerged from the analysis focusing on trust-related perceptions. We illustrate them using the data that created trust perception categories, and further consult the literature to reconceptualise the data-driven categories, drawing from trust models and trust taxonomies.

3.1   The Distinctive Themes: Competence and Integrity

> *I believe the authorities will attempt to be honest and secure but ultimately will be unsuccessful in maintaining the confidentiality of my data.* (United Kingdom)

This quote from a U.K. respondent is chosen to illustrate a fundamental distinction arising from the analysis concerned with issues of trust and public authorities. The focus on honesty in the first part of the statement implies an assessment of the *integrity* of government. The second part of the statement however addresses the ability of the government to deliver a proper system, questioning its *competence*. These twin themes of competence and integrity emerged from the analysis as distinctive and independent categories. In the statement above, integrity of public authorities is assessed positively while the judgment for competence is negative.

In many cases, however, the responses reflected negative perceptions of trust in both the competence and integrity of public authorities:

> *Governments cannot be trusted to maintain identity information on the citizen's behalf, and once such information is under the control of governments, its abuse will necessarily follow—either by government itself, or by criminals who infiltrate government systems.* (Germany)

In this example the suggestion is that the abuse of personal data under public custodianship is inevitable—"*either by government itself,*" thus implying lack of integrity on the part of the government, "*or by criminals who infiltrate government systems*"—suggesting the inability of the government to secure the data from criminal attack.

The distinction between competence and integrity was therefore apparent in the grounded analysis process. We explore further these two themes.

I am not against ID cards in principle, but have grave doubts about the competence of those running the system. Human error is probably a bigger risk than IT. (U.K.)

The theme of competence was raised repeatedly with statements addressing the ability of the U.K. state to secure and manage personal data. Negative judgments of the technical proficiency of public authority was also found in the German responses:

Theoretically the electronic identity card is a smasher; unfortunately politicians tend to be technically insufficient at implementation causing significantly more harm than potential benefits to the citizens. (Germany)

It is implied that, given the sensitivity of the data, the lack of technical competence required for operating an interoperable IdMS could lead to harmful outcomes.

In the literature on trust relations, we discovered constructs similar to that of competence in our grounded analysis. In their integrated model of organizational trust, Mayer, Davis, and Schoorman (1995) propose the notion of ability (i.e., the ability of the trustee to do what the truster needs). Renn suggests that perceived competence is a component of institutional trust, defined as the degree of technical expertise in meeting an institutional mandate (Renn, 2008, p. 223). Clustering types of trusting beliefs, McKnight, Choudhury, and Kacmar (2002) identify in the literature a total of fifteen constructs. Among them are constructs related to competence, which include expertise, dynamism, ability, capability and good judgment. Studying trust relationship in the context of Business to Consumer (B2C) ecommerce, the McKnight et al. model configures competence as an attribute of trustworthiness.

Trust is often studied in the arena of ecommerce (cf. Gefen, Benbasat, & Pavlou, 2008; Sen, 2010), such as when a consumer is inclined to trust a vendor not previously known to him—*initial trust* (McKnight et al., 2008). By contrast, the public sector context represents a situation in which the service provider, the government, is already known to its "clients," the citizens. Indeed, the familiarity of citizens with governmental authorities found clear and frequent expression in our data:

We also already have all the evidence we need to know that massive governmental IT projects are massive disasters, since every single one in the past twenty years has been. (United Kingdom)

Evident in the data was the connection made to past experiences as a way of justifying the perception of incompetence:

Unfortunately the authorities have shown in the past their incompetence in realizing IT-projects. (Germany)

To summarize, our findings point to negative perceptions regarding the ability of government to operate a secure, interoperable IdMS. The responses testify to the low level of trust in public authorities, and the concern of citizens that governments will ultimately prove incompetent and therefore *"fail to deliver a working system."* A pattern was further identified in the justification logic of the respondents, relying on past experience: the perceived inability of the government to manage large-scale IT projects rests on a reputation for failure.

Our analysis found judgments concerned with government ethics ranging from moderate to extreme statements, such as viewing all public authority as corrupt. The notion of integrity, as well as similar concepts such as fairness, is found in research on trust-related perceptions (cf. Renn, 2008). Going beyond general judgments of integrity however, further analysis revealed that the major issue of integrity revolved around handling of personal data. More specifically, a key concern for the eID context was the potential for opportunistic behavior by public institutions:

> *I don't have the confidence that authorities can resist the temptation to use all available information to solve their acute problems e.g. "terrorism" or crime.* (Germany)

> *States cannot be trusted to restrict their use of citizenship data to what they promised in different circumstances.* (United Kingdom)

What emerge from the responses are scenarios often referred to as *mission creep*, where information collected for one limited purpose is eventually used for other purposes for which the data subjects have not approved. Some responses drew attention to particular third parties gaining access to identity information:

> *I am afraid that personal biometric data are combined with different databases and will be used for other purposes than the one originally determined. These "other" uses are for example—criminal prosecution, marketing, health insurance.* (Germany)

Here, this respondent proposes a number of potential "other uses" of personal data, including law enforcement—personal data shared between different public sector authorities, and marketing and insurance—personal data is passed on from government to private sector organisations.

Having once identified the centrality of the integrity issue, specifically with regard to information passing to third party, we devised a coding scheme to provide a more detailed picture of citizens' perception in this regard. The results of the analysis are summarised in Table 9.1.

Table 9.1   Mission Creep Categories in Rank Order

Rank	Mission creep categories	Proportion of statements referring to each category (%)
1	Criminal persecution	70
2	General	50
3	Commercial	20

Table 9.1 shows the percentage of statements made by respondents regarding general fear of mission creep as well as to specific kinds of mission creep. The concern most frequently addressed was the use of personally identifiable information for criminal persecution purposes, for example:

> *if a technology is once introduced, it will one day be used for criminal prosecution and the like by the authorities, even if that was excluded at the time of introduction.* (Germany).

Less frequently discussed but still important was the issue of sharing personal information with commercial organizations: "*I have a severe lack of faith in the ability and willingness of the authorities to protect personal data from being passed on to businesses*" (United Kingdom). Whereas citizens fear the possibility of ID data sharing between government and business, they are less concerned about the potential abuse of their information by the private sector than by the public sector: "*The abuse done by corporations is less problematic than the one by governments*" (United Kingdom). Private sector motives may usually be seen simply in terms of profit maximization, whereas public sector agendas may be less clear.

An often-cited example was the transfer of EU citizens' passenger data to the U.S. government:

> *EU authorities, inter alia, with the transmission of flight passenger data to the US already shown clearly that data protection doesn't play an important role. Why should I now rely on the same institutions?* (United Kingdom)

4.   BENEVOLENCE

> *It's not about easy access for citizens to authorities. The reason for ID systems is to establish surveillance measures. And this is communicated to me as an advantage for the citizen??* (Germany)

This statement encapsulates the third grounded theme that emerged and questions the *motives* behind government eID initiatives. Comments such as *electronic ID-cards are targeted specifically to record and analyze individuals and all their actions,* or the recurring use of the metaphors *"1984"* (mostly by British respondents) and *"Glassy Citizens"* (mostly by German respondents) were all taken to represent a negative perception of intrusive governmental surveillance. Attempting to conceptualize this emerging category within a trust relationship context, we explored the congruence between this data-driven theme and the theoretical concept of *benevolence* (Mayer et al., 1995). Benevolence refers to the expectation of goodwill and benign intent from a trusted party (Yamagishi & Yamagishi, 1994). It is a construct found in a number of trust models, often seen as a trustworthiness attribute, a trusting belief, or a type of trust perception (McKnight et. al., 2002). The concept of benevolence is akin to that of integrity in that both concepts reflect ethical traits, making them appear less distinct and independent of each other (compared to the trustworthiness attribute of competence). Mayer et al. (1995) have suggested, however, that benevolence refers to trustee motives and is based on altruism, whereas integrity refers to keeping commitments and not telling lies, traits that may be manifested for pragmatic rather than altruistic reasons.

As before, respondents justify their beliefs by reference to the past:

Such systems/approaches have been implemented in Germany between 1933 and 1945 with deadly outcome for some of the citizens. (Germany)

ID systems are for Nazi Germany and Soviet Russia and other Police States and Dictatorships. They are completely incompatible with a free, democratic society. (United Kingdom)

Evident in these quotes is the strong historical reference to totalitarian regimes. Respondents are suggesting that since governments have abused data in the past they are capable of doing so in the future.

The findings point to three discrete dimensions of trust beliefs about public sector institutions responsible for IdMS: trust in the *competence* of the authorities, in the *integrity* of the authorities, and in the *benevolence* of the authorities. The trust perceptions categories that emerged from our grounded analysis were compared with similar constructs found in trust models and taxonomies from the trust literature and this strengthens the view of these emerging themes as generic types of trust perceptions. Drawing on this literature further provided for a reconceptualization of the grounded categories in terms of trustworthiness attributes, particularly so in the case of benevolence.

While findings in all three categories reiterate the negative perceptions of citizen, suggesting an overall lack of trust in public authority, differences were observed when measured by the frequency of statements made with respect to each attribute. This is shown in Table 9.2.

Table 9.2 Trustworthiness Attributes in Rank Order

Rank	Trustworthiness attribute	Proportion of statements referring to each attribute (%)
1	Benevolence	70
2	Integrity	55
3	Competence	20

Table 9.2 indicates the proportion of responses pertaining to each of the three trustworthiness attributes of competence, integrity, and benevolence. The majority of the statements were coded within the benevolence category (70 percent). Integrity-related statements counted for 55 percent, and the least frequent category was competence, under which 20 percent of the statements were coded.

Moving beyond the generic typology however, the findings direct attention to specific trust-related issues associated with public sector IdMS, which are summarised in Table 9.3.

The competence theme points to perceived inability to operate securely a mission-critical system that stores sensitive personal data. The key issue represented by integrity was the use of personal information for purposes not originally declared and the passing of personal information to third

Table 9.3 Summary of Trust Perceptions Related to eID

Trust perception categories	ID-related issues	Justifications
Competence Extent to which public institutions will demonstrate ability to do what the citizens need	Inability to operate securely a mission-critical system that is storing and managing large amounts of sensitive personal data	Records of IT failures in public sector
Integrity Extent to which public institutions will demonstrate honesty in handling personal information of citizens	Passing personal information to third parties	Mission creep cases (autobahn toll collect data, passenger data)
Benevolence Extent to which public institutions will act in the citizens' best interests	Use of personal data as a means of overly intrusive surveillance	Political history (abuse of personal information in totalitarian regimes, mainly Nazi Germany)

party without approval. Judgment of government motives, whether benevolent or not, focused on the use of personal data for intrusive surveillance.

A pattern apparent in the findings concerns the way in which respondents rely on their knowledge and interpretation of prior events as a way of justifying and substantiating their perceptions. In the case of competence, the past record of IT failures in public sector was repeatedly mentioned. Lack of trust in the integrity of the government was explained by reference to past examples of mission creep. Finally, abuse of personal information by totalitarian regimes in the past was seen to lay the ground for similar behaviour in the future, should the opportunity arise.

Before considering some of the implications arising from our study, we draw attention to the evident similarity between findings in the United Kingdom and Germany. National differences in the data and analysis were marginal and very few were detected. As the analysis scaled up through the process of grouping higher-level categories into broader themes (Urquhart, Lehmann, & Myers, 2010), the national differences between the United Kingdom and Germany appeared even less significant, such that the refined analytical framework consistently represented both countries.

5   IMPLICATIONS AND CONCLUSION

A crucial issue raised by our research is the citizens' low trust in governments responsible for personal data. Seltsikas and O'Keefe (2010) explore the role of trust in the context identity management systems and eID, and find that government stakeholders believe that IdMS can be used to shore up the shortfall of trust. By contrast, our study finds that the technology adds to the risks they face.

Avgerou and Ganzaroli (2009) find that there are common assumptions in respect of developing countries about the potential of e-government to restore trust in government institutions. However in their study in Brazil, the researchers discover that the production of trust in government services mediated by information and communication technology depends on citizens' perceptions: the e-voting system is believed to be trustworthy only as long as the public authority responsible is seen not to be abusing its power. The problem centers on the institutions and not the technology. However Lippert and Ojumu (2008) in a study on e-voting find that innovators and early adopters are more likely to trust the technology and expressed an intention in this case to use e-voting systems.

Given the negative attitudes reported in our study, an obvious question would be how trust can be repaired? Part of the problem is that the low level of trust in government springs from perceived shortcomings in both integrity and competence (Rousseau and Sitkin, 1998). This double failure renders the recovery task much more difficult: research on trust repair suggests that remedies for integrity violations are at odds with those for competence violations. Kim and Dirk (2006) find that a full apology is more successful for a competence-based violation whereas for an integrity-based violation what works better is to mitigate the blame with external attribution, or indeed deny the fault outright.

So if the answer lies neither in technology nor in appropriate speech acts, such as denial or apology, what steps should governments take in order to retrieve the situation? Showing more transparency in personal data storage and processing might ultimately cast governments in a more benevolent light. There was a clear distinction in our data between the benevolence aspect of trustworthiness, with the forceful use of emotive expressions and rhetoric, and the competence and integrity aspects, which respondents tended to express in more rationalistic terms. Recent research based on neurological analysis showed a clear distinction in the brain areas associated with the dimensions of trust and distrust, with credibility and non-credibility being mostly associated with the brain's more cognitive areas, while benevolence and malevolence are mostly associated with the brain's more emotional areas (Benbasat, Gefen, & Pavlou, 2010). Benevolence appears to have potential for restoring trust; perhaps because it speaks to the emotional rather than the rational side, it offers a more direct route to the perceptions of citizens. Future research could explore this further and also examine the ethical considerations involved.

This study focused on data collected in just two European Member States and its relevance is in the analytical rather than the statistical generalizations that have emerged. However further studies in other Member States should be encouraged in order to widen the basis and strength of the generalizations found here. This research has thrown into sharp focus some issues of real importance to public authorities in their present quest to move towards citizen-centric e-government. There is keenly felt shortfall of trust demonstrated by citizens' negative attitudes. This deficiency can only threaten the success of the new systems, hinder their acceptance and put into jeopardy their eventual institutionalization. Our analysis of the negative attitudes expressed found three recurrent themes in the discourse of our respondents: IT failures and data leaks, mission creep and political history. These themes echo three established aspects of trustworthiness found in the literature and in our data: integrity, competence, and benevolence. The aspect most commonly referred to in our data is the last one, although much previous research has tended to focus on the first two. Integrity and competence are aspects of trust that are difficult to recover from when found lacking, although apologies have featured in the responses of public authorities. Benevolence however remains an aspect of trustworthiness that public authorities might reasonably examine further and policy makers in this area should consider changes that demonstrate more goodwill toward citizens. Citizens are more reassured by instrumental acts rather than by speech acts: deeds not words.

NOTES

1. http://ec.europa.eu/idabc/servlets/Doc?id=25286
2. http://europa.eu/rapid/pressReleasesAction.do?reference=MEMO/10/200&
   format=HTML&aged=0&language=EN&guiLanguage=en
3. http://www.ccbe.eu/fileadmin/user_upload/NTCdocument/en_annex_technical_s1_1192451405.pdf

REFERENCES

Agar, M. H. (1980). *The professional stranger: An informal introduction to ethnography.* New York: Academic Press.

Ågerfalk, P. J. (2004). Grounding through operationalization: Constructing tangible theory in IS research. Paper presented at the European Conference on Information Systems, Turku, Finland.

Avgerou, C., & Ganzaroli, A. (2009). Interpreting the trustworthiness of government mediated by information and communication technology: Lessons from electronic voting in Brazil. *Information Technology for Development, 15*(2), 133–148.

Backhouse, J., & Halperin, R. (2009). Approaching interoperability for identity management systems. In K. Rannenberg (Ed.), *Identity in the information society: Challenges and opportunities* (pp. 245–268). Berlin/Heidelberg: Springer.

Benbasat, I., Gefen, D., & Pavlou, P. A. (2010). Introduction: Novel perspectives on trust. *MIS Quarterly, 34*(2), 367–372.

Gefen, D., Benbasat, I., & Pavlou, P. A. (2008). A research agenda for trust in online environments. *Journal of Management Information Systems, 24*(4), 275–286.

Glaser, B. G., & Strauss, A. L. (1967). *The discovery of grounded theory: Strategies for qualitative research.* New York: Aldine.

Henri, F. (1992). Computer conferencing and content analysis. In A. Kaye (Ed.), *Collaborative learning through computer conferencing* (pp. 117–136). Berlin: Springer-Verlag.

IDABC. (2005). European Interoperability Framework for Pan-European eGovernment Services, V 1.0.

Kelle, U. (2007). The development of categories: different approaches in grounded theory. In A. Bryant & K. Charmaz (Eds.), *The Sage handbook of grounded theory* (pp. 191–213). London: Sage.

Kim, P. H., & Dirks, K T. (2006). When more blame is better than less: The implications of internal vs. external attributions for the repair of trust after a competence- vs. integrity-based trust violation. *Organizational Behavior and Human Decision Processes 99*(1), 49–65.

Kinder, T. (2003). Mrs Miller moves house: The interoperability of local public services in Europe. *Journal of European Social Policy, 13*(2), 141–157.

Kubicek, H., & Noack, T. (2010) Different countries–different paths extended comparison of the introduction of eIDs in eight European countries. *Identity in the Information Society, 3*(1), 235–245.

Lee, A. S., & Baskerville, R. L. (2003). Generalizing Generalizibility in Information Systems Research. *Information Systems Research, 14*(3), 221–243.

Lippert, S. K., & Ojumu, E. B. (2008). Thinking Outside of the Ballot Box: Examining Public Trust in E-Voting Technology. *Journal of Organizational & End User Computing 20*(3), 57–80.

Lusoli, W., & Miltgen, C. (2009). *Young people and emerging digital services. An exploratory survey on motivations, perceptions and acceptance of risks.* Retrieved from http://ftp.jrc.es/EURdoc/JRC50089.pdf access date: 1.5.2012

Mayer, R. C., Davis, J. H., & Schoorman, F. D. (1995). An integrative model of organizational trust. *Academy of Management Review, 20*(3), 709–734.

McKnight, D. H., Choudhury, V., & Kacmar, C. (2002). Developing and validating trust measures for e-commerce: an integrative typology. *Information Systems Research, 13*(3), 334–359.

McKnight, D. H., Cummings, L. L., & Chervany, N. L. (2008). Initial trust formation in new organizational relationships. In R. Bachmann & A. Zaheer (Eds.), *Landmark papers on trust.* Cheltenham, UK: Edward Elgar.

Otjacques, B., Hitzelberger, P., & Feltz, F. (2007). Interoperability of E-government information systems: Issues of identification and data sharing. *Journal of Management Information Systems, 23*(4), 29–51.

Recordon, D., & Reed, D. (2006). *OpenID 2.0: A platform for user-centric identity management.* Paper presented at the ACM workshop on Digital identity management. Alexandria, VA, USA , October, 2006.

Reddick, C. G. (2010). Citizen-centric E-government. In Reddick, C. (Ed.), *Homeland security preparedness and information systems: Strategies for Managing Public Policy.* 45–75.

Renn, O. (2008). *Risk governance.* London: Earthscan.

Rousseau, D. M., & Sitkin, S. B. (1998). Not so different after all: A cross-discipline view of trust. *Academy of Management Review, 23*(3), 393–404.

Saxby, S. (2006). eGovernment is dead: Long live transformation. *Computer Law & Security Report, 22*, 1–2.

Scholl, H. J. (2005). Interoperability in e-government: More than just smart middleware. Paper presented at the HICSS. *Proceedings of the 38th Annual Hawaii International Conference on System Sciences.* Hawaii.

Seltsikas, P., & O'Keefe, R. M. (2010). Expectations and outcomes in electronic identity management: The role of trust and public value. *European Journal of Information Systems 19*(1), 93–103.

Sen, H. (2010). Sellers' trust and continued use of online marketplaces. *Journal of the Association for Information Systems 11*(4), 182–211.

Strauss, A., & Corbin, J. (1990). *Basics of qualitative research: grounded theory, procedures, and techniques.* Newbury Park, CA Sage.

Urquhart, C., Lehmann, H., & Myers, M. D. (2010). Putting the 'theory' back into grounded theory: Guidelines for grounded theory studies in information systems. *Information Systems Journal, 20*, 357–381.

Yamagishi, T., & Yamagishi, M. (1994). Trust and commitment in the United States and Japan. *Motivation and Emotion, 18*(2), 129–166.

Yin, R. K. (1984). *Case study research: Design and methods.* Thousand Oaks, CA: Sage.

10 Profiling E-Participation Research in Europe and North America

A Bibliometric Analysis about Articles Published

*Manuel Pedro Rodríguez Bolívar,
Laura Alcaide Muñoz, and Antonio M.
López Hernández*

CHAPTER OVERVIEW

Web technology, particularly Web 2.0 and social networks, has changed the nature of political and public dialog, encouraging participation of citizens, allowing a greater involvement of citizens in public affairs and promoting public managers to use them in order to create more affordable, participatory and transparent public sector management models. Nonetheless, despite the relevance of the e-participation process in public administrations, prior research on the e-participation field of research has highlighted because of their low maturity and heterogeneity.

In this chapter, we perform a critical integrative review of prior literature on this field in order to profile e-participation research between 2000 and 2010. In this regard, the objective of the chapter is to compare and to identify tendencies in terms of research and the methodology used about e-participation in Europe and North America, offering a framework to help public administrators and researchers evaluate the field on e-participation and providing an overview of the current state of the art, highlighting potential opportunities for future research.

1 INTRODUCTION

In recent years, Web 2.0 technologies have introduced new ways for government to interact with citizens, such as emails, chats, online meetings and discussion forums, online transactions, blogs, e-voting systems, e-petitions, online polls or the citizen input box (Jiang & Xu, 2009), allowing citizens greater involvement in public affairs and encouraging public managers to use these possibilities to create more affordable, participatory and transparent public sector management models (McMillan, Medd, & Hughes, 2008). Web 2.0 also promotes an informed citizenry vis-à-vis voting decisions and improves information transparency (Osimo, 2008), trying to achieve an increase public confidence in government (Klijn, Edelebons, & Steijn, 2010), monitoring the behavior of public managers and politicians (Hui & Hayllar, 2010), and promoting the democratic process by offering debate and discussion on important issues of public concern (Jaeger, 2005). In addition, it allows citizens to participate in online lobbies (Quintelier & Vissers, 2009), to become involved in public sector management and to be informed about laws, regulations, policies and services (Osimo, 2008).

Elected politicians and candidates also see Web 2.0 as an opportunity to communicate with the public, giving citizens a more active advisory role in public affairs (Hui & Hayllar, 2010). Social networks like MySpace and Facebook, multimedia services such as YouTube, and personal microblogs and blogs like Twitter and Blogger have become essential tools for this process, allowing direct contact with voters (Johnston & Stewart-Weeks, 2007).

Nonetheless, despite the significance of the e-participation process in public administrations, research in this field has highlighted its immaturity and heterogeneity (Saebo, Rose, & Flak, 2008). Therefore, in the belief that scientific evidence results from the aggregation and accumulation of knowledge derived from prior research (Rodríguez et al., 2010), we consider it necessary to perform a critical integrative review of the literature in this field. Accordingly, our aim is to identify research trends and methodologies concerning e-participation in Europe and the United States, and to assist researchers in the development and direction of future analyses in this respect. In short, we hope to offer scholars a more profound understanding of the scope and significance of this field.

The remainder of this chapter is organized as follows. The next section presents a review about bibliometric studies in public administration, e-government and e-participation. In Section 3, the research methodology used is outlined, after which the results obtained from our empirical research are analyzed. Finally, our main conclusions are summarized and some questions on future trends in this area are highlighted for discussion.

2   LITERATURE REVIEW ABOUT BIBLIOMETRIC STUDIES

The academic literature in the field of public administration contains many studies that have set out to analyze theoretical developments and to provide a better understanding of methodological approaches (Bingham & Bowen, 1994), making a comparative examination of the research topics addressed in different publications (Bowman & Hajjar, 1978), or analyzing doctoral dissertations in order to evaluate the usefulness of the main approaches and concepts used (McCurdy & Cleary, 1984).

In the field of e-government, and until recently, very few bibliometric studies had been carried out. Yildiz (2007) discusses the limitations of prior research in this area and points out the need for empirical studies which would lead to new theoretical arguments, together with new concepts and categories. Heeks and Bailur (2007) focus their analysis on perspectives regarding e-government, research philosophy and the use of theory. Recently, Rodríguez Bolívar, Alcaide Muñoz, and López Hernández (2010) offer a view of e-government, providing a deeper understanding of the methodological scope available, analyzing the contributions made and indicating possible directions for future analyses in this field.

Regard e-participation, although there are several definitions of this term, the generally accepted term refers to ICT-supported participation in processes involved in government and governance; processes may concern administration, service delivery, decision making and policy making (Rose, Grönlund, & Andersen, 2008). Its broad definition has given place to wider e-participation research topics and to structure e-participation into ten key dimensions (Macintosh, 2004)–see Tables 10.1 and 10.2 in Appendix 10.1. As for the bibliometric analysis performed in the field of e-participation, the studies by Saebo et al. (2008) and Sanford and Rose (2007) provided a starting point in the field of e-participation, through an analysis that identified the main research topics and established a basis for inquiries into the model and the literature currently available. However, this research was carried out in 2006 and does not provide a comparison between research interests in the United States and Europe. Therefore, we intend to go further, performing a thorough review, in the hope that researchers may make use of our results to establish relationships and further develop this topic, and also exploit possible synergies.

3   EMPIRICAL ANALYSIS OF E-PARTICIPATION RESEARCH

The e-participation represents the expansion, transformation and greater involvement of citizens in public life and consultation processes (Robbins, Simonsen, & Feldman, 2008), increasing transparency, enhancing accountability and limiting the scope for arbitrary decisions and abuse of power (Osimo, 2008). In fact, e-participation would be useful if it was used as a transformative tool of democracy, making institutions work better (Pratchett, 2007) and improving the relationship between government and citizens (Coursey & Norris, 2008; Scholl, 2010). Nevertheless, research into this topic remains at an incipient, dispersed stage, lacking a clear literature base or research approach. A study of different e-participation experiences in the United States and Europe could enhance our understanding of the instruments used to promote the participation of citizens in public affairs and thus facilitate a resolution of democratic deficits (Nabatchi, 2010), improving the efficiency, acceptance and legitimacy of political processes.

3.1 Sample Selection

In compiling the substantial body of academic studies carried out in this field of research, we analyzed English-language academic and/or professional journals with major international impact (Braadbaart & Yusnandarshah, 2008), because journals provide a filter, establishing the nature and scope of the ideas presented to the academic community (Forrester & Watson, 1994) and are a valid indicator of the quality of academic productivity (Legge & Devore, 1987).

Following Lan & Anders (2002), the present study excludes the analysis of editorials, brief communications, letters to the editor, symposiums, articles of a professional nature, and book reviews, as they offer a limited view of the subject addressed. Nevertheless, we have taken into account articles included in special editions of journals, since these reflect more extensive research in certain subjects and the need to study them further.

Regarding the selection of articles, a two-phase search was carried out: in the first of these, a systematic search was made of the ABI/INFORM, ScienceDirect, Scopus, EmeraldInsight, Springerlink, and Business Source Premier databases, using descriptors and keywords such as *e-democracy, e-participation, electronic democracy, electronic participation, e-governance and participation,* and *digital democracy* (Sandford & Rose, 2007; Saebo et al., 2008). This initial search indicated that the main body of e-participation research articles had been published in journals listed in the multidisciplinary fields of information science and library science, public administration, and communication.

In the second phase, a search was performed of e-participation studies included in leading world journals listed in connection with these subjects. Unlike Wright, Manigualt, and Black (2004), we reviewed all the articles in each of the journals listed for these subjects. To do this, the title and the abstract (Lan & Anders, 2000), the keywords (Hartley & Kostoff, 2003) and the introduction of the articles setting out the research goals were taken as relevant factors. In the few cases in which the application of these discrimination criteria was not enough, we read the entire article. This exhaustive selection procedure was conducted separately by the three authors, to check the reliability of the coding (Lan & Anders, 2000). After selecting all articles, each author did his own cataloguing separately; the authors then met on several occasions to discuss the results, and to reach an agreement where discrepancies arose.

As a consequence of this somewhat laborious process, from a database initially composed of 13,247 articles published in thirty-six periodical publications listed in JCR in the fields of information science and library science (ten), public administration (eighteen), and communication (eight) during the period January 2000–December 2010, 189 met the selection criteria established, and focused on e-participation in the three fields analyzed–*Information Science and Library Science, Communication and Public Administration*-, with fifty-two articles in information science journals, sixty-three articles in public administration journals, and seventy-four articles in communication journals. Fifty-two articles were excluded as they dealt with e-participation in other countries or constituted generic literature reviews. In the two groups of results analyzed below (i.e., research into e-participation in the United States and Europe), four of the articles take into account data for both geographic areas. Therefore, we review seventy-seven articles examining e-participation in the United States and sixty-four articles examining this question from the standpoint of Europe (see Table 10.3 in Appendix 10.1).

3.2   Research Methodology

Articles included in the database were classified, using MS Excel, by year of publication, journal title, the authors' institutional affiliation (departments and universities), the main subject addressed, and the principal methodology used. When the articles examined multiple methods, double counting was avoided by focusing exclusively on the main methodology used. To ensure the efficacy of this approach, it was essential to identify the main aim of the paper. In addition, to determine the number of departments and universities of origin, each article was considered as a single unit, and divided among the number of authors.

To determine the subjects addressed and methodologies applied, the authors conducted a content analysis of each article separately, which provides a relatively systemic and comprehensive summary or overview of the dataset as a whole (Wilkinson, 1997). The categories were selected from those previously used in e-participation by Sanford and Rose (2007), and an exploratory qualitative analysis was performed, in which the issues discussed in academic papers were identified and catalogued. When articles dealt with several research topics, double counting was performed because it could give a wider overview of the state of the art in this field of knowledge. During this phase, QSR Nvivo 8 software was used to automate item coding. This empirical work provided a basis for the development and advancement of knowledge, through a careful synthesis of and reflection upon the contributions made in this interdisciplinary academic field.

4   DISCUSSION OF THE RESULTS

4.1   Comparative Analysis of Results from E-Participation Research in United States vs. Europe

The great interest on the use of different online tools for citizen participation is reflected in a gradual increase in the amount of research carried out in the field of e-participation in recent years (see Figure 10.1), especially regarding e-democracy (37.50 percent), e-deliberation (31.25 percent), e-decision making (28.13 percent), and e-campaigning (26.04 percent) (see Table 10.4 in Appendix 10.1). Although the general tendency in the publication of research studies is similar in the United States and Europe, growth has been slightly stronger among studies focusing on the United States, published since 2008.

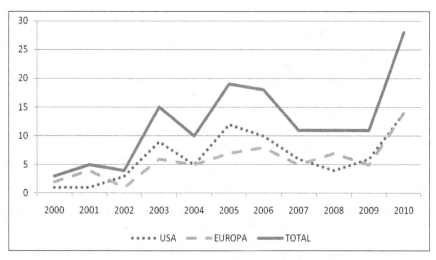

Figure 10.1   Time sequence for articles on e-participation (2000–2010).

Figure 10.1 shows there was a reduction in the number of articles published during 2005 but was followed by a sharp rise in 2010. This increase was probably due to the interest in determining how greater use is made of social networks in the course of political campaigns (Lattimer, 2009), together with the current need felt by citizens to present their concerns about policy proposals, creating online groups enabling interaction among members with views in common, thus producing exchanges of opinion and understanding (Klijn et al., 2010).

On the chronological evolution of research topics (Table 10.4 in Appendix 10.1), the area of electronic deliberation in the United States shows a clear upward trend in recent years, mainly due to the potential shown by e-deliberative processes to engage citizens in a modern, collaborative governmental structure (Nabatchi, 2010). This trend can also be seen in studies of advances in electronic decision making in Europe since 2008. In addition, since 2004 researchers have shown particular interest in the use made by politicians of interactive tools and social networking to achieve greater involvement by citizens in election campaigns, both in the United States and in Europe. However, less attention has been paid to e-voting, although this system could play an important role in revitalizing the electorate, and arouses many concerns (Kenski, 2005).

On the other hand, numerous articles dealing with e-democracy and e-governance have been published since 2003, although in the last 4 years the rate has tended to decrease, probably due to the greater focus on specific aspects of e-participation. In addition, there are issues that have been somewhat neglected, such as e-activism (1.04 percent), specialized forms of participation in support of a particular proposition or e-petition (2.08 percent), participation in party and group political processes (5.21 percent), and electronic surveys of opinion using sampling techniques (1.04 percent).

Nevertheless, the presence of e-participation research is still scarce, only making up 1.42 percent of all published articles in JCR-listed journals (see Table 10.3 in Appendix 10.1). In this regard, whereas there is a clear preference for three journals in the field of communication to publish this type of research, with 71.23 percent of the articles being published in *New Media and Society, Journal of Communication,* and *Media Culture and Society,* in the field of public administration there is a preference for four journals, *Public Administration Review, Administration and Society, American Review of Public Administration,* and *Public Administration,* which together account for 63.46 percent of the articles published. In the case of information science and library sciences journals, 79.03 percent of the articles published were found in journals such as *Social Science Computer Review, Aslib Proceedings, Government Information Quarterly,* and *Information and Society.*

With respect to analyses of e-participation in the USA, half of the articles are published in journals in the fields of public administration (*Public Administration Review* and *Administration and Society*), and communication (*New Media and Society* and *Journal of Communication*), while almost half of the articles dealing with e-participation in Europe are published in journals focusing on public administration (*Public Administration* and *Local Government Studies)* and information science (*Social Computer Review* and *Aslib Proceedings*).

4.2   Methodologies Used, Areas of Knowledge and Journal Preferences

In the United States, the percentage of empirical studies (88.73 percent; 63/71), is lower than that corresponding to European studies (93.7 percent; 60/64) (see Table 10.5 in Appendix 10.1). However, the opposite occurs concerning e-participation studies; in the United States, 52.52 percent of published articles used quantitative methods, whereas in Europe, 75 percent of the methods used were qualitative. In addition, the prevailing methodology used in the United States changed in 2002, while in Europe such a change did not seem to take place until 2008.

As shown in Table 10.6 in Appendix 10.1, in European studies, the research topics of e-community (40 percent), e-democracy (42.86 percent), e-decision making (69.23 percent), e-governance (66.67 percent), and e-deliberation (66.67 percent) are the most frequently analyzed and discussed, with case studies being used as the qualitative methodology. However, in the case of U.S. studies, the methodologies used were seen to be of a quantitative type, specifically regression analysis, especially with respect to e-campaigning (41.67 percent), e-community (63.63 percent), e-consultation (50 percent), and e-deliberation (55.56 percent). In both Europe and the United States, other methods were rarely used. In summary, European investigators tend to make more use of qualitative than of quantitative methodologies, although there was seen to be a relative change in 2008, while from 2002 U.S. researchers increasingly used quantitative methodologies in their analysis and research. In general, it seems clear that quantitative statistical methodologies are being applied ever more frequently.

In addition, the papers analyzed are mostly authored (61.83 percent; n = 131) by two or more colleagues, usually from the same university (68.70 percent; n = 131), although it is not unusual to see collaboration among members of different universities, and also among universities in different countries. The authors are mostly men, with just 24.27 percent of the authors in the field of e-participation being women (83 women vs. 259 men).

Also there is a specialized domain for authors in the fields of communication (27.65 percent), public and policy science (26.11 percent), and public administration (19.63 percent) (see Figure 10.2), although we observed the existence of heterogeneous knowledge areas such as computer science, information science and library science. Moreover, the contribution of practitioners in this area of research is almost testimonial (5.85 percent),

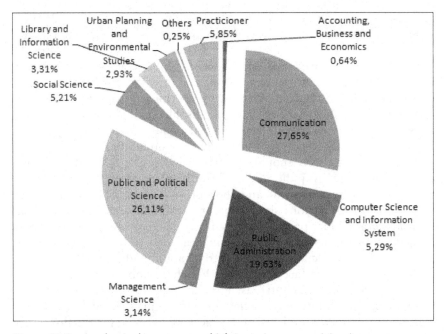

Figure 10.2 Academic departments which investigate e-participation.

with only eight articles, despite their practical vision and first-hand knowledge of the situation of many governmental agencies.

With respect to the subject preferences of leading journals, those focusing on public administration are particularly interested in articles about the use of decision-making tools to facilitate participation in the politician decision-making process and about participative consideration of a political topic through reasoned discussion online. Communication-oriented journals tend to highlight articles on the use of interactive tools in political campaigns (see Table 10.7 in Appendix 10.1). In information science and library science journals, on the other hand, the subject matter is more diverse: the *Social Science Computer Review* is particularly interested in articles on improving the shape of societal democracy with respect to participation, while the *Aslib Proceedings* and *Information and Society* contains articles on e-campaigning and e-deliberation, respectively.

5   CONCLUSIONS

E-participation has become the main issue addressed by some journals (Raadschelders & Lee, 2010). Articles, using interactive tools based on Web 2.0, seek to establish a framework for citizens' participation in governmental decision-making processes (Chang & Jacobson, 2010), in order to achieve greater efficiency, acceptance and legitimacy of political processes and in the delivery of public services (Hui & Hayllar, 2010).

However, there remain several research areas that have yet to be widely discussed, such as problems related to the different barriers and restrictions limiting citizens' access to these new interactive tools, making their participation incomplete, and how the different strategies implemented by governments can encourage this participation (Julnes & Johnson, 2011). Due to the relevance to disabled and older people, this is a research topic with high potential to be considered in the future, and it should be analyzed deeply by the academic community.

These investigations should identify whether the accessibility policies implemented by public administrations are really accomplishing with the access requirements and appropriated use of new technologies. Also, these investigations should research the motives and perceptions of disabled and older people on the advantages of new technologies and if they own capacity and learning skills needed to be involved and to participate in the social affairs. Research should highlight the problems to which citizens are faced, and whether these policies actually get to meet the needs of these citizens, even to make comparisons between governments in different countries with the aim of identifying synergies on good social policies and practices necessary to reduce this digital divide.

In addition, e-voting is another research topic that needs to receive greater attention, not only during elections but also in contributing to resolving other decisions (Kenski, 2005). In this regard, researchers should show whether or not these technological tools are being used by citizens in their daily lives, if they let citizens participate in decision-making process of possible adjustment measures implemented by a government, favoring a better democracy or, conversely, if these technologies are only used at specific times—general elections—where governments put all the means available to the citizens, without this being maintained over time.

Similarly, no studies have yet been made analyzing needs and difficulties and barriers that citizens face as actors in e-participation processes (Saebo et al., 2008). Empirical research has analyzed the policies implemented by the government, but very few of them are actually focused on knowing the opinion of citizens, and even analyzing their behavior in the use and access to a new tool, identifying if there is really a symbiosis that could enhance a two-way communication and participation between government and citizens.

Our analysis shows that the evolution of e-participation bears certain similarities with that of e-government (Rodríguez Bolivar et al., 2010). Both research areas combine different disciplines, fields and research areas, features specific theories and methodologies, and thus diverse methods and techniques are applied to the phenomenon in question, which does not favor the maturing of the scientific discipline (Saebo et al., 2008). Our study shows that these patterns in the evolution of research vary between Europe and the United States. Thus, while the subject matter examined is similar in both regions, the use of methodological tools is quite different.

The research carried out in Europe is characterized by the use of qualitative methods and, in particular, case studies, which usually offer a purely practical approach, lacking a theoretical base; this is characteristic of a young research area (Sandford & Rose, 2007). Such studies make use of surveys and content analysis, and conclude by presenting merely descriptive data and opinions, thus reflecting a relatively shallow research effort (Saebo et al., 2008).

However, in the United States, the methodologies used are mostly quantitative, which requires the investigation of causal relations, through a combination of statistical techniques such as regression analysis and structural equation models, which produces more reliable and robust results (Bailey, 1992). With this type of methodology, theoretical arguments can be created, enhancing understanding, on the basis of empirical data corroborating deductive hypotheses, thus giving rise to new theories and enriching existing ones. Both quantitative and qualitative studies are needed, but the latter tend to offer the current state of the art and they are usually very descriptive. Thus, the emphasis is on improving the quality of existing descriptive work, and on filling in knowledge gaps.

Overall, e-participation studies bring together researchers from various areas of knowledge, with different research traditions and methodologies, and encourage collaboration among diverse researchers, who seek to obtain mixed theories common to various areas. This diversity and heterogeneity could lead us to affirm that this is an emerging research field, in which each academic area has conducted researchers with its own methodologies and research topics, taking place in the existence of a variety of heterogeneous research topics, without achieving to the scope of a maturity stage of this field of knowledge in the immediate future, since there is no proper basis and common theories that favor it. In addition, our results indicate that far from obtaining synergies with the participation of researchers from different research areas, what often occurs is cooperation among researchers from the same university and area of expertise.

Results of our study also indicate there is a need to improve the existing descriptive work, using more sophisticated research methods to provide an adequate response to governmental and social demands. Such an improvement would require greater involvement by professionals, in collaboration with scholars. However, this collaboration does not exist (Rodríguez Bolivar et al., 2010). The participation of professionals would enable greater understanding of the roles of key stakeholders in e-participation: politicians, governmental institutions, businesses, and even software providers. In this regard, there is a lack of research on which all the parties involved are analyzed, especially on the opinions of public policy makers, analyzing if they really believe in the potential given to e-participation or, if by contrary, they are not convinced that the citizen participation, new technologies and efforts really enhance the flexibility of the public administrations promoting the democratic process by fostering debate and discussion on important issues of public interest.

In summary, e-participation is an immature field of research, requiring theoretical underpinning to its methodological approaches. The overview provided by the present study could be considered a starting point that would help researchers guide their future research projects, through alliances with other scholars and interested professionals, seeking to apply joint theories and methods, in response to social demands within a dynamic, globalized environment, and thus support the development of a theoretical framework for the application of e-participation tools in order to enhance democracy and the formal political process, by means of effective communication among citizens, politicians, public officials and other stakeholders who may be affected by collective decisions.

APPENDIX 10.1

Table 10.1   Definitions of E-Participation Research Topics

E-Democracy. Facilitate the participation of citizens in democratic processes, with the consequent change and/or improvement of democracy in society, increasing citizen participation in public affairs.

E-Governance. New governance model of democratic systems and public policy, which allows participation in the institutions, control of public resources and public activities.

E-Activism. Spontaneous participation of stakeholders (NGOs, associations, etc.) in public affairs and public policy, using new technologies -blogs, social networks, and so on-.

E-Campaigning. Use of new technologies -Internet, blogs, facebook, twitter, etc,- by candidates and political parties to conduct political campaigns.

E-Community. The use of ICTs by communities that interact using email, Internet, social networks, to share ideas with political agendas, such as local political discussion forums.

E-Consultation. The use of mechanisms -Web pages and/or Web 2.0 tools- for enhancing the disclosure of information –financial information, forms, procedures, charter services, etc.- by governments, encouraging interaction with stakeholders -citizens, enterprises, social groups, etc.-.

E-Decision making. The use and implementation of technological tools that facilitate participation in the processes of political decision-making.

E-Deliberation. The empowerment of citizen participation in debates and discussions on politics and public affairs, using online media.

E-Inclusion. Measures and public policies that favor the electronic participation of disadvantaged citizens, trying to reduce social differences (digital divide), promoting the availability and access to technology and resources needed to make this participation possible.

E-Petition. Citizens have the option to apply through the Internet, a specific topic being discussed at scrutiny by public agencies.

E-Politics. Participation in the processes of political parties.

E-Polling. Using vertical mechanisms for governments to obtain the opinion of citizens on public affairs, online surveys, without initiating dialogue among stakeholders.

E-Rulemaking. Facilitates participation in processes to issue and approve laws and legal regulations.

E-Voting. Promotion of citizen participation in elections by issuing the vote over the Internet or other electronic means, such as electronic machine voting.

Table 10.2   Dimensions of E-Participation

Dimension	Description
1. Level of participation	*what level of detail, or how far* to engage citizens
2. Stage in decision-making	*when to engage*
3. Actors	*who should be engaged and by whom*
4. Technologies used	*how and with what to engage citizens*
5.Rules of engagement	*what personal information will* be needed/collected
6. Duration & sustainability	for what period of time
7 Accessibility	*how many citizens participated* and from where
8. Resources and promotion	*how much did it cost and how wide was it advertised*
9. Evaluation and Outcomes	methodological approach and results;
10. Critical factors for success	political, legal, cultural, economic, technological factors

Source: Macintosh (2004).

Table 10.3   Articles on E-Participation Found in Each JCR Journal (2000–2010)

Abbreviated Journal Title	Total Articles	e-Participation Articles	Articles Excluded	USA Articles	Europe Articles
PUBLIC ADMINISTRATION JOURNALS					
PUBLIC ADMIN REV	743	10	2	8	0
ADMIN SOC	333	7	0	6	1
AM REV PUBLIC ADM	279	6	1	3	2
PUBLIC ADMIN	510	5	0	0	5
LOCAL GOV STUD	320	5	0	1	5
J PUBL ADM RES THEOR	332	3	1	1	1
GOVERNANCE	288	2	0	1	2
AUST J PUBLIC ADMIN	344	2	0	1	2
ENVIRON PLANN C	548	1	0	1	0
J SOC POLICY	308	1	0	0	1
POLICY SCI	169	1	0	0	1
INT REV ADM SCI	361	2	1	1	0
POLICY STUD J	308	1	0	1	0
PUBLIC MONEY MANAGE	432	1	0	0	1
PUBLIC MANAG REV	336	1	1	0	0
PUBLIC ADMIN DEVELOP	359	1	1	0	0
GEST POLIT PUBLIC	127	2	2	0	0
CAN PUBLIC ADMIN	216	1	1	0	0
TOTAL	6,313	52	10	24	21
INFORMATION SCIENCE AND LIBRARY SCIENCE JOURNALS					
SOC SCI COMPUT REV	376	15	3	5	8
ASLIB PROCEEDINGS	401	13	1	0	12
GOV INFORM Q	277	11	6	3	2
INFORM SOC	427	10	4	2	4
J COMPUT-MEDIAT COMM	573	7	2	5	0
J GLOB INF MANAG	120	2	1	1	0
J INFOR SCI	528	1	0	0	1
ONLINE INFORM REV	238	1	0	1	0
INFORM SYST J	421	1	0	0	1
INT J INFORM MANAGE	404	1	1	0	0
TOTAL	3,765	62	18	17	28
COMMUNICATION JOURNALS					
NEW MEDIA AND SOCIETY	518	26	9	11	6
JOURNAL OF COMMUNICATION	447	13	0	13	0
J COMPUT-MEDIAT COMM	573	7	2	5	0
EUROPEAN JOURN COMM	191	9	4	0	5
MEDIA CULTURE SOC	472	13	9	1	3
INT J PUB OPIN RESEARCH	181	4	0	4	0
CYBERPSYCH BEHAVIOUR	502	1	0	1	0
HARVARD INT J PRESS/POLITICS	285	1	0	0	1
TOTAL	3,169	73	24	35	15
TOTAL	**13,247**	**188**	**52**	**76**	**64**

Notes:
1. We have excluded items that, although they address e-participation, either constitute a general review of the literature or which analyse e-participation in countries outside Europe or the USA.
2. Four articles examined e-participation in the USA and Europe, providing data for both contexts.
3. The Journal of Computer-Mediated Communication is included in two categories: Information Sciences and Library Sciences and Communication.

Table 10.4 Chronological Distribution of Different Subjects Dealt with in E-Participation (USA Studies vs. Europe Studies)

Research Themes / Years	2000 %	2000 Num.	2001 %	2001 Num.	2002 %	2002 Num.	2003 %	2003 Num.	2004 %	2004 Num.	2005 %	2005 Num.	2006 %	2006 Num.	2007 %	2007 Num.	2008 %	2008 Num.	2009 %	2009 Num.	2010 %	2010 Num.	TOTAL
e-Democracy	(4.7)	1	(9.52)	2		0	20.00 (14.3)	6	6.67 (4.76)	2	20.00 (14.29)	6	13.33 (14.29)	5	13.33 (4.76)	3	6.67 (9.52)	3	(4.76)	1	20.00 (19.05)	7	36 (37.5%)
e-Governance		0		0		0		0	(16.67)	1	28.57 (16.67)	4	42.86 (33.33)	4		0	14.29	1	(16.67)	1	14.29 (16.67)	2	13 (13.5%)
e-Activism		0		0	100	1		0		0		0		0		0		0		0		0	1 (1.04%)
e-Campaigning	9.09	1	(7.14)	1	9.09 (7.14)	2		0	(7.14)	1	9.09 (14.29)	3	18.18 (14.29)	5	9.09 (21.4)	3	9.09 (14.29)	3	8.18 (14.29)	4	18.18	2	25 (26.1%)
e-Community	(20.0)	1		0	8.33	1	8.33	1	8.33	1	16.67	2	25.00	3	8.33 (10.0)	2	(40.00)	2	8.33	1	16.67 (20.00)	3	17 (17.7%)
e-Consultation		0	(20.0)	1		0	16.67 (20.0)	2	(20.00)	1		0	16.67	1	33.33 (20.0)	2	16.67 (20.00)	2	16.67	1	(20.00)	1	11 (11.5%)
e-Decision Making	(7.69)	1	7.14	1		0	21.43	3	14.29 (7.69)	3	(15.38)	2	14.29 (7.69)	3	14.29	2	7.14	1	(7.69)	1	21.43 (53.85)	10	27 (28.1%)
e-Deliberation	(6.67)	1	(6.67)	1	6.67	1	6.67 (6.67)	2	13.33 (13.33)	4	13.33 (6.67)	3		0	6.67 (20.0)	4	6.67	2	20.00 (6.67)	4	26.67 (26.67)	8	30 (31.3%)
e-Inclusion		1		0		0	25.00	1	25.00	1		0		0	(100)	1		0	25.00	1	25.00	1	5 (5.2%)

(continued)

Table 10.4   (continued)

Research Themes / Years	2000		2001		2002		2003		2004		2005		2006		2007		2008		2009		2010		TOTAL
	%	Num.	%	Num.	%	Num.	%	Num.	%	Num.	%	Num.	%	Num.	%	Num.	%	Num.	%	Num.	%	Num.	
e-Petition		0		0	(50.0)	0		1	(50.00)	0		1		0		0		0		0		0	2 (2.1%)
e-Politics		0		0		0	(100)	1	25.00	1		0	25.00	0		1		0	50.00	0		2	5 (5.2%)
e-Polling		0		0		0		0		0		0		0	100	0		1		0		0	1 (1.1%)
e-Rulemaking		0		0		0		0	50.00	1	50.00	1		0		0		0	(50.00)	1	(50.00)	1	4 (4.2%)
e-Voting		0		0		0	(33.3)	1		10	75.00	3		0		0	(66.67)	2	25.00	0	25.00	1	7 (7.3%)
TOTAL		5		6		5		18		16		25		21		18		17		15		38	184

*The first horizontal line of each research theme refers to research in the USA and the second to research in Europe, except for the research themes "e-Petition", which only refers to Europe and "e-Polling", which only refers to the USA.

Table 10.5 Chronological Distribution of the Use of Methodologies

Year	USA			Europe		
	%Non-Empirical	Qualitative Methodology	Quantitative Methodology	%Non-Empirical	Qualitative Methodology	Quantitative Methodology
2000	0.00%	100.00%	0.00%	0.00%	100.00%	0.00%
2001	0.00%	100.00%	0.00%	0.00%	100.00%	0.00%
2002	0.00%	33.33%	66.67%	0.00%	100.00%	0.00%
2003	11.11%	66.67%	22.22%	16.67%	83.33%	0.00%
2004	20.00%	40.00%	40.00%	0.00%	100.00%	0.00%
2005	16.67%	25.00%	58.33%	0.00%	57.14%	42.86%
2006	10.00%	0.00%	90.00%	25.00%	75.00%	0.00%
2007	16.67%	16.67%	66.67%	0.00%	80.00%	20.00%
2008	0.00%	50.00%	50.00%	0.00%	42.86%	57.14%
2009	0.00%	16.67%	83.33%	0.00%	60.00%	40.00%
2010	14.29%	50.00%	35.71%	7.14%	78.57%	14.29%
TOTAL	11.27%	35.21%	52.52%	6.25%	75.00%	18.75%

Table 10.6 Methodologies Used to Analyze Each of The Phenomena Related to E-Participation (Percentage)

Research Themes / Methodologies	Qualitative Methodologies													Quantitative Methodologies						
	Non-Em	Cs	Coman	Conan	Cit	Etb	Eval	Expl	Fea	Her	Heu	Lbm	Others*	Reg	Coman	Conan	Cs	Eval	Sem	Others**
e-Democracy	33.33 (19.05)	13.33 (42.86)	6.67 (4.76)	(4.76)		(9.52)	6.67	(4.76)			(4.76)	6.67	6.67	13.33 (4.76)		6.67	(4.76)			
e-Governance	28.57	(66.67)		14.29 (16.67)			14.29							14.29 (16.67)		14.29				14.29
e-Activism		100.00																		
e-Campaigning		16.67 (14.29)		16.67 (7.14)		8.33		(21.43)			(7.14)		(7.14)	41.67 (14.29)		8.33 (14.29)	(7.14)		8.33	(7.14)
e-Community		18.18 (40.00)		(20.00)		(20.00)							9.09	63.63 (20.00)		9.09				
e-Consultation		(20.00)	(20.00)	16.67 (40.00)		(20.00)						16.67 (20.00)	(20.00)	50.00						16.67
e-Decision Making	9.09	27.27 (69.23)	(7.69)	(7.69)					9.09	9.09			(7.69)	27.27 (7.69)				9.09		9.09
e-Deliberation	5.56	5.56 (66.67)	(6.67)	5.56 (6.67)		(6.67)	5.56			5.56	(6.67)		5.56	55.56			(6.67)		11.11	
e-Inclusion		25.00	25.00	25.00								25.00		25.00			(100.00)			
e-Petition		(100.00)																		
e-Politics		(100.00)											25.00	50.00						25.00
e-Polling																		100.00		
e-Rulemaking		(50.00)	(50.00)										(33.33)	25.00		50.00				50.00
e-Voting	25.00				(33.33)									25.00				25.00		25.00 (33.33)

*TREAD (2), SNW (2) USA; USAB (1), AR (1), EXP (1) EUROPE
**EXP (2), CIT (2), LONG (1), FAC (1) USA; LONG (1), CIT (1) EURO

Table 10.7 E-Participation Research Topics in the Main Journals

Research Topic / Main Journals	Public Administration			Information Science and Library Science			Communication	
	PAR	AS	ARPA	SSCORE	ASLIB	INFSOC	NEWME	JCOMM
e-Democracy	18.18%	20.00%	11.11%	36.36%	16.67%	33.33%	11.11%	5.56%
e-Governance	18.18%	10.00%	11.11%				5.56%	
e-Activism								
e-Campaigning					46.67%		22.22%	33.33%
e-Community	9.09%		22.22%	18.18%		16.67%	11.11%	5.56%
e-Consultation				9.09%	6.67%		11.11%	11.11%
e-Decision Making	27.27%	40.00%	22.22%			16.6/%	5.56$	11.11%
e-Deliberation		20.00%	22.22%	18.18%	6.67%	33.33%	16.67%	27.78%
e-Inclusion	9.09%			9.09%			5.56%	
e-Petition					6.67%			
e-Politics	9.09%	10.00%					11.11%	
e-Polling	9.09%							
e-Rulemaking			11.11%					
e-Voting				9.09%	6.67%			5.56%
TOTAL	100%	100%	100%	100%	100%	100%	100%	100%

LIST OF ABBREVIATIONS

METHODOLOGIES

CS	Case Studies	HER	Hermeneutic Exploration
CONAN	Content Analysis	HEU	Heuristic Approach
COMAN	Comparative Analysis	LHM	Life History Method
CIT	Critical Incident Technique	LONG	Longitudinal Design
ETH	Ethnographic Studies	NON-EM	Non-empirical
EVA	Evaluation Research	REG	Regression Analysis
EXPL	Exploratory Analysis	SNA	Social Network Analysis
EXP	Experimental Study	SEM	Structural Equation Model
FAC	Factorial Analysis	TREAD	Tread Analysis
FEA	Feasibility Studies	USAB	Usability Study

DEPARTMENTS

PA	Public Administration	CS	Computer Science and Information Systems
P&PS	Public and Political Science	PRAC	Practitioners
MS	Management Science		

	JOURNALS		
ARPA	American Review of Public Administration	**JCOMM**	Journal of Communication
AS	Administration and Society	**NEWME**	New Media and Society
ASLIB	Aslib Proceedings	**PAR**	Public Administration Review
INFSOC	The Information Society	**SSCORE**	Social Science Computer Review

REFERENCES

Bailey, M. T. (1992). Do physicists use case studies? Thoughts on public administration research. *Public Administration Review, 52*(1), 47–55.

Bingham, R. D., & Bowen, W. (1994). Mainstream public administration over time: A topical content analysis of public administration review. *Public Administration Review, 54*(2), 204–208.

Bowman, J. S., & Hajjar, S. G. (1978). The literature and American public administration: Its contents and contributions. *Public Administration Review, 38*(2), 156–165.

Braadbaart, O., & Benni, Y. (2008). Public sector benchmarking: A survey of scientific articles, 1990–2005. *International Review of Administrative Sciences, 74*(3), 421–433.

Chang, L., & Jacobson, T. (2010). Measuring participation as communicative action: A case study of citizen involvement in an assessment of a city's smoking cessation policy-making process. *Journal of Communication, 60,* 660–679.

Coursey, D., & Norris, D. F. (2008). Models of E-government: Are they correct?. An empirical assessment. *Public Administration Review, 68*(3), 523–536.

Forrester, J. P., & Watson, S. S. (1994). An assessment of public administration journals: The perspective of editors and editorial board members. *Public Administration Review, 54*(5): 474–482.

Hartley, J. (2005). Innovation in governance and public services: Past and present. *Public Money and Management, 25*(1), 27–34.

Hartley, J. & Kostoff, D. N. (2003). How useful are "key words" in scientific journals?. *Journal of Information Science, 29* (5), 433–438.

Heeks, R., & Bailur, S. (2007). Analyzing e-government research: Perspectives, philosophies, theories, methods, and practice. *Government Information Quarterly, 24*(1), 243–265.

Hui, G., & Hayllar, M. R. (2010). Creating public value in e-government: A public-private-citizen collaboration framework in Web 2.0. *Australian Journal of Public Administration, 69*(S1), S120–S131.

Jaeger, P. T. (2005). Deliberative democracy and the conceptual foundations of electronic government. *Government Information Quarterly, 22,* 702–719.

Jiang, M., & Xu, H. (2009). Exploring online structures on Chinese government portals: Citizen political participation and government legitimation. *Social Science Computer Review, 27*(2): 174–195.

Johnston, P., & Stewart-Weeks, M. (2007). The connected republic. New possibilities and new value for the public sector. Cisco Internet Business Solutions Groups. Retrieved from www.ictparliament.org. Accessed in July 2011.

Kenski, K. (2005). To i-vote or not to i-vote? Opinions about Internet voting from Arizona voters. *Social Science Computer Review, 23*(3), 293–303.

Klijn, E., Edelebons, J., & Steijn, B. (2010). Trust in governance networks: Its impact and outcomes. *Administration and Society, 42*(2), 193–221.

Lan, Z., & Anders, K. K. (2000). A paradigmatic view of contemporary public administration research: An empirical test. *Administration and Society, 32*(2), 138–165.

Lattimer, C. (2009). Understanding the complexity of the digital divide in relation to the quality of House campaign websites in the United States. *New Media and Society, 11*(6), 1023–1040.

Legge, J. S., Jr., & Devore, J. (1987). Measuring productivity in U.S. public administration and public affairs programs 1981–1985. *Administration and Society, 19*(2), 147–156.

Macintosh, A. (2004) Characterizing e-participation in policy-making. *Proceedings of the Thirty-Seventh Annual Hawaii International Conference on System Sciences (HICSS-37),* January 5–8, Big Island, Hawaii.

McCurdy, H. E., & Cleary, R. E. (1984). A call for appropriate methods. *Public Administration Review, 44*(6), 49–55.

McMillan, P., Medd. A., & Hughes. P. (2008). Change the world or the world will change you: The future of collaborative government and Web 2.0, Deloitte Touche Tohmatsu. Retrieved from www.deloitte.com

Nabatchi, T. (2010). Addressing the citizenship and democratic deficits: The potential of deliberative democracy for public administration. *American Review of Public Administration, 40*(4), 376–399.

Osimo, D. (2008). Web 2.0 in government: Why and how? European Commission. Joint Research Centre. Institute for Prospective Technological Studies. Retrieved from www.ec.europa.eu. Accessed in July 2011.

Pratchett, L. (2007). Comparing local e-democracy in Europe: A preliminary report. In United Nations, *E-participation and e-government: Understanding the present and creating the future.* New York: United Nations.

Quintelier, E., & Vissers S. (2009). The effect of Internet use on political participation. An analysis of survey results for 16-year-olds in Belgium. *Social Science Computer Review, 26*(4), 411–427.

Raadschelder, J. C. N., & Lee, K. H. (2010). Trends in the study of public administration: Empirical and qualitative observations from *Public Administration Review,* 2000–2009. *Public Administration Review, 71*(1), 19–33.

Robbins, M. D., Simonsen, B., & Feldman, B. (2008). Citizens and resource allocation: Improving decision making with Interactive Web-based citizen participation. *Public Administration Review, 68*(3), 564–575.

Rodríguez Bolívar, M. P., Alcaide Muñoz, L., & López Hernández, A. M. (2010). Trends of e-government research. Contextualization and research opportunities. *The International Journal of Digital Accounting Research, 10,* 87–111.

Rose, J., Grönlund, Å., & Andersen, K. V. (2008). Introduction. In A. Avdic, K. Hedström, J. Rose, & Å. Grönlund (Eds.), *Understanding eParticipation—Contemporary PhD eParticipation studies in Europe.* Sweden: Örebro University Library.

Saebo, O., Rose, J., & Flak, L. S. (2008). The shape of e-participation: Characterizing an emerging research area. *Government Information Quarterly, 25*(3), 400–428.

Sanford, C., & Rose, J. (2007). Characterizing e-participation. *International Journal of Information Management, 27*(4), 406–421.

Scholl, H. J. (2010). *E-government: Information, technology, and transformation.* Volume 17. Advances in Management Information Systems. Armonk, NY: M. E. Sharpe.

Wilkinson, S. (1997). Focus group research. In Silverman, D. (Ed.), *Qualitative research: Theory, method and practice,* London (UK): Sage Editorial(pp. 177–199).

Wright, B. E., Manigault, L. J., & Black, T. R. (2004). Quantitative research measurement in public administration: An assessment of journal publications. *Administration and Society, 35*(6), 747–764.

Yildiz, M. (2007). E-government research: Reviewing the literature, limitations, and ways forward. *Government Information Quarterly, 24*(3), 646–665.

11 Rational Choice Theory
Using the Fundamentals of Human Behavior to Tackle the Digital Divide

Porche Millington and Lemuria Carter

CHAPTER OVERVIEW

The introduction of the Internet and personal computers changed the way people gather and store information. People across the globe have been classified into two groups: the "haves" and the "have-nots." The growth and use of Internet-based technology has led to a disparity known as the digital divide. Recently, calls for more research on the digital divide and its subsequent subdivisions have been emphasized in several studies (Barzilai-Nahon, Gomez, & Ambikar, 2008; Dewan & Riggins, 2005; van Dijk, 2006). This chapter uses rational choice theory to offer a fresh perspective on the link between human behavior and the digital divide. It presents an overview of existing literature on rational choice theory and offers suggestions for future research on the digital divide.

1 INTRODUCTION

Most research on the digital divide highlights the variation in access to technology and the Internet by socioeconomic status (Robinson, Dimaggio, & Hargittai, 2003). The literature on the digital divide usually analyzes this gap in terms of individual demographic factors and ignores the impact of the social class those individuals belong to (Wattal, Hong, Mandviwalla, & Jain, 2011). Despite government intervention and large investment, the digital divide remains a prominent debate that encompasses social, economic and political issues (Helbig, Gil-Garcia, & Ferro, 2009). In 2009, roughly 63.5 percent of American households were connected to broadband, up from just 9.2 percent in 2001 (Anonymous, 2010). According to the Department of Commerce, only 4 out of every 10 households with an annual household income of $25,000 or less have Internet access at home (Anonymous, 2010; NTIA, 2011). In comparison to the 94 percent of households with higher incomes, low-income households' growth in access lags tremendously. The disparity in Internet access and use is not unique to the United States. About 30 percent of individuals in developing countries use the Internet and only 20 percent of households in developing countries have access to the Internet (Anonymous, 2011). According to Seybert (2011), Greece and Romania continue to lack growth in Internet access compared to neighboring countries.

Reports show that education plays a role in creating the digital divide as well. Approximately 84 percent of households with at least one college degree have broadband and just over 28 percent of households without even a high school diploma are connected (Anonymous, 2010). Other factors that seem to cause the disparity are geographic regions and ethnic groups. Statistics even show an inequality of Internet users in older age groups. In Europe, only 40 percent of individuals between the ages of 55 and 74 use the Internet at least once a week which is below the continent's average of 68 percent (Seybert, 2011). Some researchers even use the phrase "grey digital divide" when discussing the disparity of Internet users in older age groups (Livermore, 2011; Morris, 2007).

The gaps are beginning to close but researchers question if it is closing fast enough (Fontenay & Beltran, 2008; van Dijk & Hacker, 2000). The digital divide is both an economic and social phenomenon (Wattal et al., 2011). Numerous studies on the digital divide have taken one of two theoretical perspectives on technology diffusion: sociological or public policy (Dewan & Riggins, 2005). The purpose of this chapter is to offer a new perspective on how to bridge the digital divide. Some enthusiasts proclaim that the shrink in the digital divide will be the key to reducing inequality because of its potential to lower barriers to information which may lead people of all types of backgrounds "to improve their human capital" and in turn increase their opportunities (Hargittai, 2003). In order to improve human capital, researchers must find the relationship between a human's choice to enhance his opportunity and the tools provided to make the choice (Lehtinen & Kuorikoski, 2007).

Rational choice theory states that "the choices a person makes tend to maximize total utility or satisfaction" (Herrnstein, 1990). Rational choice theory is also known as optimal choice theory which serves as the fundamental principle of behavioral sciences (Simon, 1955). This chapter uses rational choice theory to understand the impact of information communication technologies (ICT) on human behavior. By discussing the fundamentals of human behavior, we posit that more research on the digital divide supplemented with theories from other referent disciplines may help shed light on this phenomenon. In particular, we present a list of potential researcher questions that integrate the elements of rational choice theory and the digital divide.

2 BACKGROUND LITERATURE

2.1 Digital Divide

The most common definition of the digital divide is "the gap between people with effective access to digital information and communications technology, and those with very limited to no access to ICT" (Wattal et al., 2011).

Hargittai (2003) labels those with effective access to ICT as the "haves" and those with limited to no access to ICT as the "have-nots."

Measurements of the digital divide often engage in simple or single factor measurements that do not illustrate the whole picture (Barzilai-Nahon et al., 2008; Korupp & Szydlik, 2005; van Dijk, 2006; van Dijk & Hacker, 2000). The concept in fact encompasses a range of information disparities including material access, use and skill (Barzilai-Nahon et al., 2008). For this reason, the simplistic approach continues to be criticized (Barzilai-Nahon, 2006). According to Barzailai-Nahon et al. (2008), researchers need to develop a multifaceted concept that thoroughly measures the divide inequality. Epstein, Nibset, and Gillespie (2011) use two "frames" to explore the digital divide—material access and skills access. Hsieh, Rai, and Keil (2008) cite van Dijk's model. Van Dijk (1999) outlines four kinds of access which surround the digital divide:

1. Psychological Access—low digital experience caused by lack of interest, computer fear, and unattractiveness of the new technology;
2. Material Access—little to no access to computers and network connections;
3. Skills Access—lack of digital skills caused by inadequate education;
4. Usage Access—little to no significant usage opportunities within the home or workplace.

Psychological access, the "mental barrier," is commonly thought to only affect old people (van Dijk & Hacker, 2000). However, the "mental barrier" affects other groups of people like housewives and illiterates (van Dijk & Hacker, 2000). Researchers hardly address this type of access divide (van Dijk, 2006). Van Dijk (1999) refers to material access as "hurdles" or "barriers" to the information and network society. Material access is seen to describe both access to computers and network infrastructure (Epstein et al., 2011). Van Dijk and Hacker (2000) argue that public policy is "engrossed" with material access and think the problem of information inequality is solved with just giving computer and Internet access to the population. The lack of digital skills is described as inadequate knowledge to operate the technology and manage hardware and software (van Dijk & Hacker, 2000). Van Dijk (1999) argues that the skills access is a temporary phenomenon and people overcome the lack of knowledge after using the technology over a period of time. According to van Dijk (2006), access problems gradually shift from psychological access and material access to skills access and usage access. The shift in access problems results in a larger usage gap where the population is split into those who gain significant benefits from technological advancements and those who only use the technology for basic applications (van Dijk & Hacker, 2000). About 16 percent of non-users live in households where an individual uses the Internet (Smith, 2010a). Those with low interactions with computers cite usability and availability as the key reasons they do not access the Internet (Smith,

2010a). According to Kettemann (2008), a Working Group on e-inclusion established within the eEurope Advisory Group approach the divide as "both a technical ('access') and a personal dimension ('inclusion', 'ability')."

One approach to understanding the full concept is to study the phenomenon in a continuum alongside other socioeconomic inequities (Barzilai-Nahon, 2006). The first step to identifying a problem concerning equality according to Sen (1992) is answering the question: what inequality does the digital divide concept refer to? Although social and economic literature have pointed out ten potential answers to that question, the most popular is still physical or material access (van Dijk, 2006). A problem with focusing on physical access is the never ending evolution of the technology on the market (Vehovar, Sicherl, Husing, & Dolnicar, 2006). Van Dijk (2006) suggests the digital divide phenomenon is always as new as the technology it is linked to at a particular time.

Dewan and Riggins (2005) link access to ICT to community interaction and e-commerce as well as improving social welfare. Belanger and Carter (2009) point out the concerns about the digital divide and its impact on the growth of e-services. Studies found that the digital divide hindered e-government services (Belanger & Carter, 2009; Fang, 2002). By analyzing the digital divide at three levels—individual level, organizational level, and global level—researchers found overlapping topics which include the impact on economies, social opportunities and human capital (Dewan & Riggins, 2005; Korupp & Szydlik, 2005; Wattal et al., 2011). One general finding across the digital divide is that the widening or closing of the gap is parallel to economic inequality and choice (Fontenay & Beltran, 2008).

2.2 Rational Choice Theory

Rational choice theory (RCT) is an approach used to understand human behavior. RCT is based on the assumption that people make choices that help them achieve their objective and maximize their utility (Simon, 1955). Rational choice theorists have become increasingly mathematical and formal (Scott, 2002). However, the trend towards more formal models of rational action has not discouraged researchers from adapting the models to explain diverse domains including political science (Johnson, 1997; Riker, 1990; Simon, 1985), criminology (Akers, 1990; Becker, 1968; Cornish & Clarke, 1987), and economic growth (North, 1994; Sidrauski, 1967). Sociologists and political scientists now adapt theories around the assumption that people are essentially rational in character (Masatilioglu & Ok, 2005). Scott (2002) states that rational choice theory denies the existence of any actions not directed by ration which distinguishes RCT from other forms of theory.

One popular study that focuses extensively on behavior and rational choice theory is Becker (1968). Becker (1968) uses rational choice theory to understand the impact of human behavior on public and private policies on illegal behavior (Becker, 1968). Becker (1978), Hogarth and Reder (1987), and Green and Shapiro (1996) discuss rational choice theory beyond conventional economic issues. The theory developed by Becker (1968) can be applied to any effort to impede or support human behavior (Li, Zhang, & Sarathy, 2010).

Various studies apply rational choice theory to explain a multitude of behavioral topics from security policy compliance to consumption (Chai, 2008; Li et al., 2010; Vale, 2010). Li et al. (2010) applied rational choice theory to examine employees' intentions to comply with their workplace Internet use policy. According to Li et al. (2010), employees' compliance intentions are based on competing perceived benefits and security risks. D'Arcy, Hovav, and Galletta (2009) also explores IS security using rational choice. Vale (2010) analyzes rational choice theory and the standard model of inter-temporal decision making to reduce the gap between the theory and clinical definition of addiction. The study also emphasizes one of the theory's assumptions—individuals are "forward-looking and their decisions rational" (Vale, 2010).

Previous predictive models of behavior have involved economic theory intertwined with a social dilemma by using rational choice theory as its framework. According to Chai (2008), further discussion and the call for more robust knowledge on applying RCT to other disciplines prompted researchers to use it in more social and economic issues. The subsequent development of rational choice theory took place in economics, political science and sociology (Chai, 2008). Chai (2008) argues that the predictive behavioral modeling could apply to social sciences as well as hard scientists like computer scientists approach to technology diffusion. RCT is believed to assist in the dialogue between social and hard science studying a social phenomenon (Chai, 2008). Chai (2008) states that "no other existing major theoretical approach equals conventional rational choice in meeting a combination of criteria" which justifies the dominance the theory has in social and economic studies. The ability to predict behavior around choosing to connect to a network or to gain the skills to enhance usage would be an advantage in closing the technology gap known as the digital divide.

3   RCT AND THE DIGITAL DIVIDE

We draw upon rational choice theory to understand the four types of access divides. Prior to physical access comes the desire to own a computer and to be connected to a network. In 2011, the two most commonly cited reasons for not having Internet access in the home are that the access is not needed and the access is too expensive (NTIA, 2011). Researchers can use RCT to develop techniques to engage the population with low motivation. Table 11.1 shows the four types of access divides and examples of each. Table 11.2 includes diverse research questions related to the interaction of the digital divide and RCT. Each access divide has factors that hinder the population from receiving the full benefits of technology innovation. We use RCT to formulate research questions that address how to tackle narrowing each type of access divide. Backed by the idea that people make decisions based on rationality, we recommend using research questions to understand the thought process to reach a rational decision. Tables 11.1 and 11.2 can be used to direct future research on the diverse types of access divides.

Table 11.1   Four Types of Access Divides

Psychological Access	Material Access
• Fear of the unknown • Lack of interest • Unattractive technology	• No network connection • No access to a computer • Lack of income to purchase computer or network connection
Skills Access	**Usage Access**
• Inability to navigate computer system • Low social support • No assistance to grasp digital skills	• Limited technology use in the workplace • Little opportunity to use the computer for personal tasks • Low interaction with computers

Table 11.2   Rational Choice Theory to Understand the Access Divide

Psychological Access	Material Access
1. How can training be used to minimize computer anxiety in the elderly population? 2. How can user awareness programs be used to increase the perceived benefits of adopting technological innovations? 3. What factors entice non-users to try technological innovations?	1. What impact will computer/technology subsidies from the government have on the diffusion of computer-based systems and services? 2. Should technology providers be held responsible for helping to close the digital divide? 3. What is the impact of community centers equipped with computers and network connection on the desire to own a personal computer?
Skills Access	**Usage Access**
1. What types of programs should be implemented to increase digital skills? 2. What impact does technology design and the user-interface have on the digital divide? How can the IS community make technology more user-friendly? 3. What types of training are most effective at reducing the skill divide?	1. Does access to computers in the workplace enhance usage at home? 2. Will the availability of e-services increase the use of technology? 3. What types of technological innovations promote more computer usage beyond basic tasks such as sending an email?

This chapter explores the growth and use of Internet-based technology as well as the disparity associated with it. The digital divide is a multifaceted issue and requires solutions to address all four of the access divides. For this reason, the identification of non-user and user groups is an essential step toward implementing proper policies and recommendations. The quadrant in the table below provides an initial framework of gaps associated with each access divide. According to Fuller, Vician, and Brown (2006), there is a correlation between computer self-efficacy and technology usage. Computer self-efficacy refers to an individual's judgment of his capabilities to use computers and complete goals (Venkatesh & Davis, 2000). Researchers suggest that socio-economic status is the most significant power in distinguishing non-users from users (Hsieh et al., 2008; Lenhart et al., 2003). Table 11.3 highlights the relationship between socio-economic status and computer self-efficacy with the four access divides.

We propose this quadrant as an effort to identify common barriers to access among certain groups of people. Individuals with high socio-economic status and low computer self-efficacy face barriers associated with psychological and skill access divides. The usage access divide is a potential barrier for individuals with high socio-economic status and high computer self-efficacy. Individuals with low socio-economic status and low computer self-efficacy face barriers associated with material access. Individuals with low socio-economic status and high computer self-efficacy also face barriers associated with material access but not in its traditional sense. Although income level and geographical location plays a role in their material access, they still have access to the Internet through alternative devices. African

Table 11.3   Gaps Associated with the Four Access Divides

Socio Economic Status		Low	1. Age groups ("Grey Digital Divide") 2. Computer anxiety or computer fear	1. Lack of interest 2. Lack of perceived benefits
			Psychological and Skills Access Divides	Usage Access Divide
			1. Education level 2. ICT knowledge 3. Income level	1. Income level 2. Geographical location
		High	Material Access Divide	Material Access Divide
			Low High	
			Computer Self-Efficacy	

Americans and Latinos continue to outpace Caucasians in their use of handheld devices. According to Smith (2010b), minority Americans lead the way in mobile access using handheld devices. Additionally, minorities tend to take advantage of their phones' data functions compared to Caucasian cell phone owners (Smith, 2010b). This would explain why minorities with low socio-economic status often have high computer self-efficacy.

As previously stated, rational choice theory assumes that people are essentially rational in character (Masatilioglu & Ok, 2005). Rational choice theory defines rationality different from the philosophical use—behaving sane or in clear-minded manner. Rationality is defined as an individual's ability to balance costs against benefits to arrive at a rational decision (Herrnstein, 1990). Using rational choice theory to understand individuals who are affected by access barriers, garners understanding of their motivations. Individuals with high socio-economic status but low computer self-efficacy would use rational choice to weigh the perceived benefits against the costs of overcoming their fear or anxiety. Individuals with high socio-economic status and computer self-efficacy would be most susceptible to intervention because the benefits would most likely outweigh the costs. Individuals with low socio-economic status as well as low computer self-efficacy might not buy into government initiatives or social policies to increase their access to ICTs. This group might be hesitant because the benefits might not balance the costs of participating. Individuals with low socio-economic status but high computer self-efficacy would buy into community and pricing initiatives. The perceived benefits of participating could outweigh costs—if the costs of ICTs were within their budget or access was free within the community.

Discussion & Limitations

This chapter represents an initial response to Chai's (2008) call for more research on the relationship between rational choice theory and social science issues. Chai (2008) also calls for more vigorous dialogue between social scientists and hard scientist studying a social phenomenon. Few studies have linked rational choice to the digital divide. This occurrence could be largely due to the misunderstanding of the theory (Hechter & Kanazawa, 1997). One of the most common arguments against using rational choice theory outside of economics is association with unrealistic assumptions about individual behavior (Lehtinen & Kuorikoski, 2007). Recent criticism of rational choice theory states that people tend to deviate from systematic decision making (Rooderkerk, Heerde, & Bijmolt, 2011). However within the last 5 years, rational choice theory has been closely related to philosophy and law research (Bar-Gill, 2008; Higgins, 2007; Seipel & Eifler, 2010). The theory can also be used to understand other social and economic behavior. Gul and Pesendorfer (2005) state "our main point is that the separation of economics and other social sciences are a consequence of specialization around different questions and different data." RCT enables researchers to take a more comprehensive approach to studying the digital divide. This chapter is an initial attempt toward highlighting the potential benefits of using RCT to explore the digital divide; future research should conduct a qualitative or quantitative empirical study that explores the impact of rational choice theory on the digital divide. Future studies should identify theory from other referent disciplines that may help shed light on this phenomenon.

This chapter does not address alternative devices such as mobile phones and tablets that may impact an individual's rational choice to use the Internet. Future research should explore the impact of alternative devices on closing the gap. Future empirical research may allow researchers to find patterns in individuals affected by access barriers. Statistics show that physical disabilities also impact Internet use. In America, one in four adults live with a disability that interferes with their day-to-day activities (Fox, 2011). About 81 percent of adults in the survey stated they use the Internet while only 54 percent of adults with a disability use the Internet (Fox, 2011). Future research should address users and non-users with disability and how this group of individuals fall within the four access divides.

4   CONCLUSION

The digital divide is a challenge with immense social, economic and technological implications. Wattal et al. (2011) posit the diffusion of technology is highly correlated to the existing social class lines; with an arrival of new technologies comes the perpetuation of the divide. International organizations continue to call for research dealing with global and regional digital divide and digital environment (Anonymous, 2012). This chapter is an initial step toward an enhanced understanding of the multiple elements of the digital divide and their impact on society. It shows possible connections from the digital divide to theories from referent disciplines. According to Wei et al. (2011), there is a lack of research that uses a "theoretical account for the effects of the digital divide." The chapter highlights the need for more research on the various components of the digital divide.

REFERENCES

Akers, R. L. (1990). Rational choice, deterrence, and social learning theory in criminology: The Path not taken. *The Journal of Criminal Law & Criminology, 81*(3), 653–676.
Anonymous. (2010). U.S. Census Bureau, Current Population Survey: Computer and Internet Use. Washington, DC: U.S. Department of Commerce.
Anonymous (Producer). (2011). ICT Facts and Figures. Retrieved from http://www.itu.int/ITU-D/ict/facts/2011/material/ICTFactsFigures2011.pdf on January 25, 2012
Anonymous (Producer). (2012). Digital Divide Working Group Call for Papers. Retrieved from http://iamcr.org/s-wg/mcpl/digital-divide-mainmenu-146/825-iamcr2012ddicfp on January 25, 2012.

Bar-Gill, O. (2008). *The law, economics and psychology of subprime mortgage contracts.* The Berkeley Electronic Press. Retrieved from http://law.bepress.com/alea on September 18, 2011.

Barzilai-Nahon, K. (2006). Gaps and bits: Conceptualizing measurement for digital divides. *The Information Society, 22*(5), 269–278.

Barzilai-Nahon, K., Gomez, R., & Ambikar, R. (2008). Conceptualizing a contextual measurement for digital divides: Using an intergrated narrative. In E. Ferro, Y. K. Dwivedi, & R. G. Williams (Eds.), *Overcoming digital divides: Constructing an equitable and competitive information society.* Seattle, Washington:University of Washington, Center of Information & Society.

Becker, G. S. (1968). Crime and punishment: An economic approach. *Journal of Political Economy, 76*(2), 169–217.

Becker, G. S. (1978). *The economic approach to human behavior.* Chicago: University of Chicago Press.

Belanger, F., & Carter, L. (2009). The impact on the digital divide on E-government use. *Communications of the ACM, 52*(4), 132–135.

Chai, S.-K. (2008). *Rational choice theory: A forum for exchange of ideas between the hard and social sciences in predictive behavioral modeling.* Paper presented at the Social Computing, Behavioral Modeling, and Prediction, Phoenix, Arizona.

Cornish, D. B., & Clarke, R. V. (1987). Understanding crime displacement: An application of rational choice theory. *Criminology, 25*(4), 933–948.

D'Arcy, J., Hovav, A., & Galletta, D. (2009). User awareness of security countermeasures and its impact on information systems misuse: A detterence approach. *Information Systems Research, 20*(1), 1–20.

Dewan, S., & Riggins, F. J. (2005). The digital divide: Current and future research directions. *Journal of Association for Information Systems, 6*(12), 298–337.

Epstein, D., Nibset, E. C., & Gillespie, T. (2011). Who's responsible for the digital divide? Public perceptions and policy implications. *The Information Society, 27*, 92–104.

Fang, Z. (2002). E-government in digital era: Concept, practice, and development. *international Journal of The Computer, The Internet and Management, 10*(2), 1–22.

Fontenay, A. B. d., & Beltran, F. (May 20, 2008). *Inequality and economic growth: Should we be concerned by the digital divide?* Paper presented at the Information Technology Systems, Montreal.

Fox, S. (Producer). (2011, January 25, 2012). Americans living with disability and their technology profile. Retrieved from http://pewinternet.org/Reports/2011/Disability.aspx on January 26, 2012.

Fuller, R. M., Vician, C., & Brown, S. A. (2006). E-learning and individual characteristics: The role of computer anxiety and communication apprehension. *Journal of Computer Information Systems, 46*(4), 103–115.

Green, D. P., & Shapiro, I. (1996). *Pathologies of rational choice theory: A critique of applications in political science.* New Haven, CT: Yale University Press.

Gul, F., & Pesendorfer, W. (2005). *The Case for Mindless Economics.* Princeton: Princeton University.

Hargittai, E. (2003). The digital divide and what to do about it. *New economy handbook* (pp. 821–839). San Diego, California: Elsevier Science.

Hechter, M., & Kanazawa, S. (1997). Sociological rational choice theory. *Annual Review of Sociology, 23*, 191–214.

Helbig, N., Gil-Garcia, J. R., & Ferro, E. (2009). Understanding the complexity of electronic government: Implications from the digital divide literature. *Government Information Quarterly, 26*(1), 89–97.

Herrnstein, R. J. (1990). Rational choice theory: Necessary but not sufficient. *American Psychologist, 45*(3), 356–367.

Higgins, G. E. (2007). Digital piracy, self-control theory, and rational choice: An examination of the role of value. *International Journal of Cyber Criminology*, 1(1), 33–55.

Hogarth, R. M., & Reder, M. W. (1987). *Rational choice: The contrast between economics and psychology*. Chicago: University of Chicago Press.

Hsieh, J. J. P.-A., Rai, A., & Keil, M. (2008). Understanding digital inequality: Comparing continued use behavioral models of the soci-economically advantaged and disadvantaged. *MIS Quarterly*, 32(1), 97–126.

Johnson, C. (1997). Preconception vs. observation, or the contributions of rational choice theory and area studies to contemporary political science. *Political Science and Politics*, 30(2), 170–174.

Kettemann, M. C. (2008). E-inclusion as a means to bridge the digital divides: Conceptual issues and international approaches. In W. Benedek, V. Bauer & M. C. Kettemann (Eds.), *Internet governance and the information society: Global perspectives and European dimensions*. The Netherlands: Eleven International Publishing.

Korupp, S. E., & Szydlik, M. (2005). Causes and trends of the digital divide. *European Sociological Review*, 21(4), 409–422.

Lehtinen, A., & Kuorikoski, J. (2007). Unrealistic assumptions in rational choice theory. *Philosophy of the Social Sciences*, 37(2), 115–138.

Lenhart, A., Horrigan, J., Rainie, L., Allen, K., Boyce, A., & Madden, M. (2003). The ever-shifting Internet population: A new look at Internet access and the digital divide. Pew Internet and American Life Project. Retrieved from http://www.pewinternet.org/~/media//Files/Reports/2003/PIP_Shifting_Net_Pop_Report.pdf.pdf on October 13, 2011.

Li, H., Zhang, J., & Sarathy, R. (2010). Understanding compliance with Internet use policy from the perspective of rational choice theory. *Decision Support System*, 48(4), 635–645.

Livermore, C. R. (2011). Intelligent technologies for bridging the grey digital divide. *Australasian Journal on Ageing*, 30(33), 170–171.

Masatilioglu, Y., & Ok, E. A. (2005). Rational choice with status quo bias. *Journal of Economic Theory*, 121(1), 1–29.

Morris, A. (2007). E-literacy and the grey digital divide: A review with recommendations. *Journal of Information Literacy*, 1(3), 13–28.

North, D. C. (1994). Economic performance through time. *The American Economic Review*, 84(3), 359–368.

NTIA. (2011). *New commerce department report shows broadband adoption rises but digital divide persists*. Retrieved from http://www.ntia.doc.gov/press-release/2011/new-commerce-department-report-shows-broadband-adoption-rises-digital-divide-pers on January 22, 2012.

Riker, W. H. (1990). Political science and raional choice *Perspectives on positive political economy*. Cambridge: Cambridge University Press.

Robinson, J. P., Dimaggio, P., & Hargittai, E. (2003). New social survey perspectives on the digital divide. *IT & Society*, 1(5), 1–22.

Rooderkerk, R. P., Heerde, H. J. V., & Bijmolt, T. H. A. (2011). Incorporating context effects into a choice model. *Journal of Marketing Research*, 48(4), 767–780.

Scott, J. (2002). Rational choice theory. In G. Browning, A. Halcli & F. Webster (Eds.), *Understanding contemporary society: Theories of the present*. Thousand Oaks, California: Sage Publications.

Seipel, C., & Eifler, S. (2010). Opportunities, rational choice, and self-control. *Crime & Delinquency*, 56(2), 167–197.

Sen, A. (1992). *Inequality reexamined*. Oxford: Oxford University Press.

Seybert, H. (Producer). (2011). Internet use in households and by individuals in 2011. *Statistics in Focus*. Retrieved from http://epp.eurostat.ec.europa.eu/

cache/ITY_OFFPUB/KS-SF-11–066/EN/KS-SF-11–066-EN.PDF on January 25, 2012

Sidrauski, M. (1967). Rational choice and patterns of growth in a monetary economy. *The American Economic Review, 57*(2), 534–544.

Simon, H. A. (1955). A behavioral model of rational choice. *The Quarterly Journal of Economics, 69*(1), 99–118.

Simon, H. A. (1985). Human nature in politics: The dialogue of psychology with political science. *The American Political Science Review, 79*(2), 293–304.

Smith, A. (Producer). (2010a). Home Broadband 2012. Retrieved from http://pewinternet.org/Reports/2010/Home-Broadband-2010/Part-1/Most-non-internet-users-have-limited-exposure-to-online-life.aspx on January 29, 2012.

Smith, A. (2010b). Mobile Access 2010: Pew Internet &American Life Project. Retrieved from http://www.pewinternet.org/~/media//Files/Reports/2010/PIP_Mobile_Access_2010.pdf on October 24, 2011

Vale, P. H. (2010). Addiction—and Rational Choice Theory. *International Journal of Consumer Studies, 34*(1), 38–45.

van Dijk, J. (1999). *The Network Society, Social Aspects of New Media*. London, Thousand Oaks, New Delhi: Sage.

van Dijk, J. (2006). Digital divide research, achievements and shortcomings. *Poetics, 34*, 221–235.

van Dijk, J., & Hacker, K. (2000). *The digital divide as a complex and dynamic phenomenon*. Paper presented at the International Communication Association, Acapulco.

Vehovar, V., Sicherl, P., Husing, T., & Dolnicar, V. (2006). Methodological challenges of digital divide measurements. *The Information Society, 22*, 279–290.

Venkatesh, V., & Davis, F. D. (2000). A theoretical extension of the technology acceptance model: four longitudinal field studies. *Management Science, 46*, 186–204.

Wattal, S., Hong, Y., Mandviwalla, M., & Jain, A. (2011). *Technology diffusion in the society: analyzing digital divide in the context of social class*. Paper presented at the Hawaii International Conference on System Sciences.

Wei, K.-K., Teo, H.-H., Chan, H. C., & Tan, B. C. Y. (2011). Conceptualizing and testing a social cognitive model of the digital divide. *Information Systems Research, 22*(1), 170–187.

12 E-Government for All

From Improving Access to Improving the Lives of the Disadvantaged

Jeremy Millard

CHAPTER OVERVIEW

Applying ICT to public services has attracted huge investment in Europe over the past 10 to 15 years. The impact of this, though generally positive, has been mixed, with two main areas of concern: the disappointing take-up of e-government services and the general failure of e-government to improve the lives of the socially and digitally disadvantaged. Various strategies have and are being applied to address these challenges, including e-accessibility and e-skills, multi-channel service delivery, the role of intermediaries, citizen-centric services, better integration of services, and collaborative service production and delivery. This has lead policy-makers and practitioners to realise that seeing the 'digital divide' as purely about ICT access is far from adequate. The real success or otherwise of inclusive e-government (or e-government for all) is instead the impact it has on the lives of users, particularly those who are disadvantaged in some way, whether or not they themselves have access. This conclusion has important policy implications for how e-government services are designed and deployed.

This chapter is a meta-study of selected previous studies, largely undertaken for the European Commission. It examines a relatively unexplored but increasingly important area of e-government (i.e., how ICT used by the public sector can improve the lives of disadvantaged people whether or not they themselves are using ICT). It identifies common trends and conclusions relevant for both practitioners and policy-makers, whilst researchers are also invited to undertake follow-up empirical studies to test them.

1 INTRODUCTION

1.1 Context and Rationale of Chapter

In developing Europe's Information Society, the emphasis has always been that it should be an "inclusive" society. Not only is this necessary to avoid new technologies leading to further exclusion of the groups in society that are already on the margins (the unemployed, less well educated, elderly people, etc.), but the aim is also to use these technologies to offer new opportunities for "inclusion."

Since the early 2000s, much evidence has emerged that e-government can provide more inclusive services in an effective, appropriate and accessible manner for specific groups at risk of exclusion, such as younger people in situations of disadvantage, low-income groups, the unemployed, retired people, older citizens, ethnic groups and the disabled. However, it has also since become clear that for, the foreseeable future, no matter what is done to extend and improve access, there will remain large numbers of citizens who continue to use traditional channels only. Up to one-third of the EU population are unlikely themselves to be using e-government services for the foreseeable future, and these are often those who are most in need of social services because they are disadvantaged in some way. They are thus doubly disadvantaged.[1]

This chapter examines a relatively unexplored but increasingly important area of e-government (i.e., how ICT used by the public sector can improve the lives of disadvantaged people, for example by supporting their literacy, employability and social integration. As this chapter will show, this can happen successfully in two ways. First, by improving ICT access, skills, and use by these groups and, second, by the use of ICT somewhere in the service delivery value chain to improve service targeting and quality. In both cases, disadvantaged people improve their lives, whether or not they themselves have access to or use ICT.

1.2 European Policy Development 2000–2020

E-Inclusion and e-government have been central ICT policy priorities since the EU's 2010 Lisbon objectives agreed in 2000 (European Commission, 2000). Halfway through the decade, their importance was strongly reinforced by the i2010 initiative launched in 2005 (European Commission 2005b). First, this led to the 2006 Ministerial "Riga Declaration" on *ICT for an inclusive information society* in which EU Member States agreed a set of six targets and themes: enhancing e-accessibility, addressing the needs of older workers and elderly people, improving digital literacy and competences, reducing the geographical digital divide, promoting cultural diversity, and promoting inclusive e-government. Participating in the information society is seen as an absolute must for getting a job, enjoying social and healthcare, aging well, accessing education, being creative, and nurturing entrepreneurship and participation.

Second, building on the Ministerial e-Government Declaration from November 2005, the i2010 e-Government Action Plan (European Commission, 2006) recognised that no citizen should be left behind. It stated that e-government should advance inclusion by fighting the digital divide through inclusive e-government to ensure that *"all citizens benefit from trusted, innovative services"* in which *"users will continue to want channels other than the Internet to access public services, such as digital TV, mobile and fixed phone and/or person-to-person."*

In November 2009, a new e-Government Ministerial Declaration laid the basis for the next 2015 Action Plan covering the period 2011–2015 to build on both the achievements and shortcomings of the 2010 Action Plan. (European Commission, 2010c). Amongst four political priorities, the empowering citizens and businesses theme focuses on *"services designed around users' needs and Inclusive services through providing flexible and personalised ways of interacting and performing transactions with public administrations. In addition, the usability of and access to e-government services should be improved by delivering them via multiple channels (including Internet, TV, telephone, mobile devices, or where appropriate through intermediaries)"*.

The 2015 e-Government Action Plan is also firmly embedded in the flagship initiative a *Digital Agenda for Europe* (DAE) agreed in August 2010 to speed up the roll-out of high-speed Internet and reap the benefits of a digital single market for households and firms (European Commission, 2010b). A main plank of the DAE is the action on Public Digital Services which will embed innovation and cost effectiveness into e-government through the systematic promotion of open standards and interoperable systems. Inclusion also remains a priority in one of the eight Action Areas of the DAE *Enhancing digital literacy, skills and inclusion*. The DAE is itself an important plank of the broader *EU2020—A strategy for smart, sustainable and inclusive growth*, agreed in March 2010, with a focus on getting the European economy back on track after the economic and financial crisis. (European Commission, 2010a).

2   PATTERNS OF EUROPEAN E-GOVERNMENT SERVICE USE

2.1   E-Government Service Take-up

It is only in the past 5 years that comprehensive measurements of e-government service use has taken place across all twenty-seven EU Member States. However, in this timeframe there was an increase from 23 percent take-up by individual adults in 2005 to only 32 percent in 2010, the latest available data.[2] This is disappointing given the huge investments in e-government service roll-out over the last decade. For example, full online availability of the basket of twenty e-government services increased from 40 percent in 2005 to 81 percent in 2010 for EU27 (Capgemini 2005; 2010).

2.2   Channels Used to Access Government Services

There have been even fewer data on the usage of government services by channel, across different countries and by different types of users.[3] The main comprehensive survey comes from a 2006 study (Millard, 2006) based on telephone interviews with 10,000 adults across ten EU Member States,[4] focusing on the use of both government and e-government services. This showed that, although almost 70 percent of adults had contact with the public administration in the previous 12 months, only 20 percent of adults used ICT in some form, compared to 80 percent by the more traditional channel of face-to-face, 42 percent by telephone, and 40 percent by post.[5] However, the data also show that there are very large differences between countries, so that in 2006 Denmark was the leading country in the sample with over 40 percent of government service users using ICT, compared to 9 percent in the Czech Republic. Furthermore, in the United Kingdom and Ireland the use of the postal services and the telephone had overtaken face-to-face, probably because of the large investment by these countries into public service call centers.

2.3 Socio-economic Characteristics of E-Government Users

When different socio-economic groups are examined, the 2006 data show that e-government users compared to individuals not using e-government services are significantly more likely to:

- Be in employment,
- Be well educated,
- Have medium to high income,
- Be aged 25 to 34,
- Be male.

Furthermore, e-government users tend to live in countries with high Internet and e-government roll-out, and have well developed e-skills and e-attitudes, which may explain some of the differences between Denmark and the Czech Republic mentioned above. Thus, users who may be disadvantaged in some way, due to their own situation or where they live, are much less likely to use e-government services than more mainstream users.[6]

2.4 Usage Patterns of Different Types of Government Service User

The 2006 data also show that the usage patterns of three different types of government service user are quite distinct. Figure 12.1 shows these types as e-government users, plus two types of non e-government user, i.e. those using the Internet and those not.

Figure 12.1 shows that e-government users used government services on average 3.1 times a year (i.e., 311 percent) compared with non-eGovernment users who only tended to use government services 1.5 times. Further, when examining the range of channels used, e-government users can be

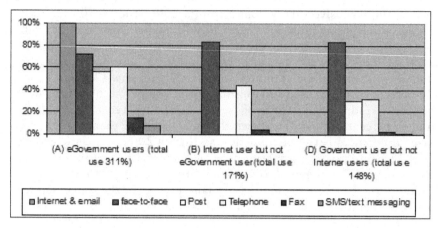

Figure 12.1 Usage patterns of three types of government service user (Source: Millard 2007).

described as "flexi-channellers" and "channel balancers," in that up to 70 percent of them also use other channels and clearly make channel choices suited to their preference, to the specific service and to the specific task in hand. This is in some contrast to non-e-government users who tend to be "single channellers," relying mainly on the traditional face-to-face channel to access government services.

Overall, these and other data in the survey show that e-government service users use government services more often than other service users, but also use a wider range of government services, as well as many more channels, not only ICT. Their use is thus more varied as well as intensive. In turn, this means that disadvantaged users are much less likely to enjoy these more varied and intensive government service experiences, despite the fact that they also tend to be those who need government services most. They are thus doubly disadvantaged.

The following two sections show how new strategies aim to counter this double disadvantage.

3   STRATEGIES TO CHANGE THE DESIGN AND FOCUS OF E-GOVERNMENT SERVICES

3.1   Strategies to Move from Access to Training to Impact

A number of studies have examined how the double disadvantage illustrated by the data above is being tackled (European Commission, 2007a; 2007b). Figure 12.2 provides an overview of documented leading edge practices in inclusive e-government in 2005 and 2007. In 2005, almost 70

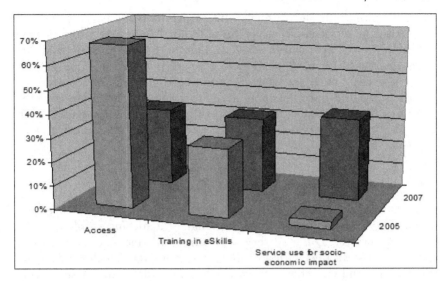

Figure 12.2 The focus of leading edge inclusive e-government practices, 2005–2007 (Source: European Commission, 2007b).

(2005: n = 124 from 72 cases; 2007: n = 178 from 90 cases)

percent of leading edge cases focused primarily on providing ICT access to disadvantaged users, with only about 25% focused on providing such users with e-skills. By 2007, however, the balance had completely changed with access now at 33% of the total, training at 32% and a focus on the use of services for positive impacts on the lives of disadvantaged users at 35%. Although access remains essential and is typically a necessary precursor or first stage, the need for training in e-skills, and then attempting to promote positive service use, had become more important as stages 2 and 3 in the progression to fully inclusive e-government.

Evidence from the same survey shows that the large majority (about 75 percent) of inclusive e-government practices in 2007 were designed and delivered at the local or regional level, and only then (if successful and cost-effective) rolled out more widely. This also reflects an analysis made in 2005 that the success of strategies for social and digital inclusion is largely dependent on a context-based approach, whereby targeted groups were considered within their specific geographical, social and cultural environment (European Commission, 2005a).

3.2 Channel and Targetization Strategies

Figure 12.3 shows how strategies for tackling disadvantage have also shifted from a one-size-fits-all, single (online) channel approach to ones which employ multiple channels and target individuals. Personalized e-government services targeting the individual increased from 27 percent in 2005 to 73 percent in 2007, and multi-channel personalized targeting increased from 19 percent to 62 percent over the same period. There is a clear move away from assuming that all users are more or less the same and have the same needs to group segmentation (such as older or disabled people) and even to fully personalized services. Both segmentation and personalization are examples of "citizen centricity" (cc:eGov, 2007).

3.3 Strategies to Tackle Multiple Disadvantage

One of the main challenges to both the policy and practice of e-government for disadvantaged groups is that of achieving combined and joined-up services. Different services traditionally tackle different problems, but most disadvantaged people suffer from multiple deprivation so their unique individual situations need to be addressed. These include poverty, poor or no housing, low education and skills, poor health, old age, disability, difficulties in obtaining steady work, perhaps also crime and anti-social behavior, in addition to technical difficulties with information and communication technology (ICT). Addressing these disadvantages in a systematic and joined-up manner is essential for a fully

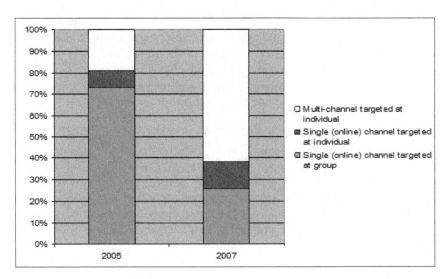

Figure 12.3 Channel and targeting strategies of leading edge inclusive e-government practices, 2005–2007 (Source: European Commission, 2007b).

(2005: n = 124 from 72 cases; 2007: n = 178 from 90 cases)

inclusive society. The different service providers need to ensure that their efforts do not overlap or counteract each other and that signals picked up by one service can act as early warnings for another. In most cases, disadvantaged users are confronted with overlapping rules, different agencies, an enormous amount of paperwork, and complicated forms to complete, all of which increase still further the difficulties they have in trying to arrange their lives.

An interesting strategy to tackle these challenges, followed in some parts of the UK over the last five years, is to understand an individual's holistic needs using Maslow's needs hierarchy[7], as shown in Figure 12.4. Disadvantaged users tend to have unmet needs at the bottom and in the middle of the pyramid compared to mainstream users whose service needs from government are more likely to be near the top. Thus, focusing on whether and how the unmet needs of disadvantaged users can be at least partially met by ICT has been a useful U.K. strategy, more recently also taken up in Denmark and elsewhere. Government ICT policy has typically not addressed these needs, but rather focused on ICT access and use to meet the mainstream needs of the mainstream population. The focus has been on existing services, often irrelevant to the disadvantaged groups. To the right of the pyramid, some examples are given of how each type of need could and is being met by government.

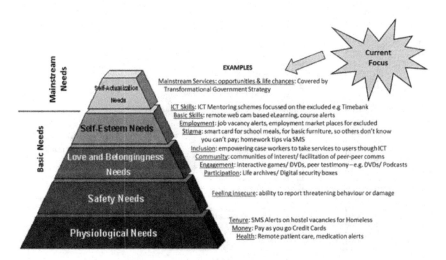

Figure 12.4 Maslow's needs hierarchy adapted to individual needs (Source: Internal papers, Digital Inclusion Team, UK Cabinet Office, 2006).

4 STRATEGIES TO CHANGE THE CONFIGURATION OF THE VALUE CHAIN

4.1 Strategies for Intelligent Use of ICT by Front- and Back-Office Staff

Figure 12.5 also shows another important development over the last 5 years in which the public sector uses ICT to better target services to dis-advantaged people who are not themselves expected to use ICT directly. Two strategies are being used. First, front-line staff (e.g., home helpers or care workers visiting persons in need in their own homes or commu-nities) use ICT to provide a more intelligent and quicker service. They can link directly to databases in the back-office, fill out and send forms, and obtain relevant information in real time in the field whilst physically with the disadvantage person. Second, ICT is being increasingly used in government back-offices to join-up and simplify services as well as reduced duplication of effort by back-office staff. This enables such staff to use ICT and data to more intelligently target disadvantaged commu-nities, families or individuals, for example unemployment black spots or families most likely to need social help. Although this trend even in leading edge initiatives in 2007 was small, the European Commission as well Blakemore and Wilson (both in 2009) showed that it was becoming increasingly prominent.

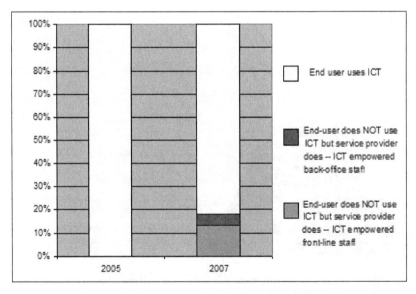

Figure 12.5 Changing where ICT is used in the inclusive e-government service delivery value chain, 2005–2007 (Source: European Commission, 2007b).

(2005: n = 124 from 72 cases; 2007: n = 178 from 90 cases)

4.2 Strategies to Involve Other Actors in the Value Chain

Millard (2006) documented for the first time the importance of intermediaries in e-government (i.e., actors who mediate between a public service and the intended end user). Importantly, intermediaries can be both government staff (as exemplified by the front-office staff using ICT mentioned above) or non-government actors and can be particularly important for disadvantaged individuals who tend to have less ability than mainstream users to know what services are available and how to access and use them. Data from the 2006 study show that 53 percent of users of e-government do so for their own purpose, 51 percent as part of their job, and 42 percent on behalf of family or friends,[8] the latter thus being termed "social intermediaries." Moreover, each social intermediary on average assists 2.6 other individuals who are not themselves direct e-government users, thereby dramatically extending the actual impact of e-government. Interesting, the profile of social intermediaries also differs from that of e-government users generally, in that they tend to be older and perhaps retired, often unemployed and living in a country with undeveloped e-government services and roll-out. The profile of individuals receiving assistance from social intermediaries also strongly mirrors that of non-e-government users generally (i.e., having low e-skills and e-attitudes, unemployed or in unskilled occupations, lower income and educational levels, in higher age groups including retired, and living in countries with undeveloped e-government services). Overall, it is clear that social intermediaries considerably extend the benefits of e-government to individuals who otherwise are not being reached.

One conclusion from these data is that, in contrast to the relatively modest 32 percent direct usage of e-government services in 2010 by individuals cited in Section 2, and although comparing data over time needs to be treated with some caution, this figure should probably be multiplied by between 2 and 3 to get an idea of how many are actually benefitting from e-government services.

4.3 New Business Model Strategies for Delivering E-Government Services

The intelligent and innovative use of ICT can make partnerships between government and actors from the third and private sectors more efficient and effective. It can support multi-channel organizational interactions, including human contact, in providing sustainable user-centric services for socially excluded people, often taking place through an intermediary person or organisation as described above. This is an example of so-called collaborative service production and delivery. Figure 12.6 exemplifies this type of new business model in comparison to a more traditional "before" approach. It also shows that e-government does not always require disadvantaged people to use ICT themselves, as noted above, but does involve using ICT somewhere in the vale chain to improve service quality, delivery. and impact.

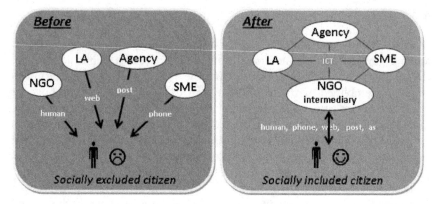

Figure 12.6   New types of business model for delivering services to disadvantaged people (Source: Prepared for the European Commission E-Government Ministerial Conference in Malmö, Sweden, in November 2009 by J. Millard, based on European Commission, 2009, and Blakemore & Wilson, 2009)

The problems of socially excluded people are almost invariably highly personal and complex. They often require an intermediary person or organisation (whether governmental or non-governmental) to enable them to benefit from a combination of information and transactions, put together to meet their highly specific and complex needs. Intermediation and partnership take place mostly at local level, vital because many interactions are likely to remain human to human through direct engagement with end users in service creation and governance.

Typically, this "partnership" approach is not a loose coalition of interested parties, but a formalized network where the objectives and tasks are shared through agreements or contracts. All actors need to be trained and supported, and should be responsible for achieving the outcomes, rather than on delivering particular services. The combined knowledge and resources ensure that the partnership works in a sustainable way and is acceptable to the user. The links in the delivery network are crucially enabled by ICT, in a mix of systems, technologies and media, including human interactions.

It is through this multi-channel approach and flexible availability of services, personalized and configured around users' needs and preferences, that sustainable service delivery can be achieved. Multi-channel thus comes to mean the organisational interactions which make up the network, rather than only a collection of access routes for delivering services. Therefore, the operational, sustainable inclusive e-government model is in reality much more like a flexible and dynamic network that joins up services from government and other organisations from the third sector (civil societies, NGOs, etc.) as well as the private sector in some cases, around the needs of the socially excluded, in a way that is not possible only at the government end, due to relative government remoteness and the considerable variety of end-user needs.

Although still rare, these approaches are beginning to have an impact, for example, the *Day Activity* initiative in Amsterdam, the Netherlands, sketched in Figure 12.7. This recognizes that many socially excluded people suffer from multiple problems, covering employment, skills, accommodation and crime, the Local Authority, charitable groups and employers have formed partnerships to find solutions. They themselves provide the core funding, but extra resources also come from a local insurance company and a charitable lottery fund. By sharing their resources, knowledge and databases, they use a flexible mix of channels (Internet, email, phone and face-to-face) to deliver personalised services. This results in triple win benefits: greater efficiency, increased tax revenue, fewer social costs in the longer term for the Local Authority; additional labor and more flexibility for employers; and work, dignity, societal worth, plus greater independence for the socially excluded.

5 CONCLUSIONS AND RECOMMENDATIONS

This chapter is a meta-study of selected previous studies, largely undertaken for the European Commission. It examines a relatively unexplored but increasingly important area of e-government (i.e., how ICT used by the

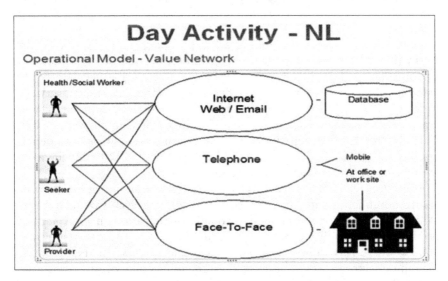

Figure 12.7 Day Activity project, the Netherlands (Source: Blakemore & Wilson, 2009).

public sector can improve the lives of disadvantaged people whether or not they themselves are using ICT). It identifies common trends and conclusions relevant for both practitioners and policy makers, whereas researchers are also invited to undertake follow-up empirical studies to test them.

Many, but not all, policy-makers and practitioners have realised that seeing the 'digital divide' as purely about ICT access is far from adequate. The real success or otherwise of inclusive e-government is instead the impact it has on the lives of users, particularly those who are disadvantaged in some way, whether or not they themselves have access. Clear benefits for disadvantaged groups have been documented by a number of studies (Millard, 2006; European Commission, 2007a; 2007b; Blakemore & Wilson, 2009), whether through the direct or indirect use of e-government services:

- Better service access through complementary channels;
- Easing daily life burdens, including engagement with the public administration;
- Improvements to government-citizen relations;
- Better access to education, training, healthcare, work, and jobs;
- Improvements to personal capacity and skills, life chances, social networks, and quality of life.

Previous studies have shown this to be possible, even though impacts are still on a small scale. (Blakemore & Wilson, 2009; Millard, 2007). According to an analysis of EU Member State questionnaires (European Commission, 2009), this shift in thinking has been a difficult and ongoing learning curve. This conclusion has important policy implications for how e-government services are designed and deployed. There are two main issues.

First, given that we know that upwards of 30 percent of European citizens will not be online in the foreseeable future, the question becomes "do we forget about these 30% for the time being, or can ICT somewhere in the value chain be used to target, reach and deliver better government services to them, even though they may not themselves be directly using or accessing services through such technology?" (European Commission, 2009). This also means that deploying multiple channels should be considered, not just ICT, each of which is likely to have specific suitability for the user, the type of service used and the usage context.

Second, ICT dramatically increases the ability of public service providers from public, private, and civil sectors, targeting disadvantaged users, to develop new business models through collaboration in joint service production and delivery, as well as to deploy social and other intermediaries where this improves service reach and quality. In this context, the public sector in some countries is establishing collaborative platforms where this can take place, for example the United Kingdom's "opening up government" platform,[9] which offers both online and offline spaces for joint working, using shared resources, accessing open government and other data, debating, accessing good practices, etc. Many of these resources and activities are increasingly cloud based and also offer mobile government services highly suitable for disadvantaged users, given that their use of standard or smart phones is often much greater than their access to the Internet.

NOTES

1. Presentation by David Broster, Head of Unit eGovernment and CIP Operations, June 19, 2007, at the Inclusive eGovernment Stakeholders Workshop, Brussels. See also European Commission (2007a).
2. From Eurostat: http://appsso.eurostat.ec.europa.eu/nui/show.do?dataset=isoc_si_igov&lang=en (accessed January 2012).
3. Raw Eurobarometer data could, however, be used to undertake the necessary research.
4. The Czech Republic, Denmark, France, Germany, Hungary, Ireland, Italy, Poland, Slovenia and the United Kingdom.
5. Note the percentages total more than 100 percent because most individuals used more than one channel.
6. These data are very similar to other sources examining the digital divide in the context of European e-government, for example EPAN (2005), Foley and Alfonso (2005), European Commission (2008; 2010d).
7. Abraham Maslow (1954) viewed human needs as occurring in a hierarchy, such that the lower needs had to be met before the higher ones become salient for the individual. His original scheme included, in order, physiological needs, safety needs, belongingness and love needs, esteem needs, and the need for self-actualization. The bottom four examples presented in Figure 12.4 correspond to the first two of Maslow's needs. The next three have to do with belongingness. Participation and democracy, as well as inclusion, are measures of esteem, and empowerment is part of self-actualization. This is, of course, just one example of one articulation of needs.
8. Note the percentages total more than 100 percent because most e-government users act in more than one capacity.
9. http://www.data.gov.uk

REFERENCES

Blakemore, M., & Wilson, F. (2009) .MC-eGov: Study on multi-channel delivery strategies and sustainable business models for public services addressing socially disadvantaged groups, published by the ICT for Government and Public Services, DG INFSO, European Commission.

Capgemini (2005, March). Online availability of public services: How is Europe progressing? Web based survey on electronic public services. Brussels: European Commission, Directorate General for Information Society and Media.

Capgemini, IDC, Rand Europe, Sogeti and DTI (2010, December). Digitizing public services in Europe: Putting ambition into action—9th Benchmark Measurement. Brussels: European Commission, Directorate General for Information Society and Media.

cc:eGov. (2007). Organisational change for citizen-centric eGovernment project: Retrieved from http://www.ccegov.eu/downloads/Handbook_Final_031207. pdf April 2010.

EPAN (European Public Administrations Network). (2005). eAccessibility of public sector services in the European Union: executive briefing. Published in cooperation with the U.K. Presidency of the EU. November 2005. Retrieved from http://www.dgaep.gov.pt/media/0601010000/uk/eAccessibility.pdf. April 2012.

European Commission. (2000). eEurope—an information society for all, 23–24 March 2000, Lisbon, published by in Brussels 14 June 2000.

European Commission. (2005a). e-Inclusion revisited: The local dimension of the information society, DG Employment, SEC(2005)206. Retrieved from http://europa.eu.int/comm/employment_social/news/2005/feb/einclusion_en.html

European Commission. (2005b). i2010—A European Information Society for growth and employment. Brussels. 1.6.2005, {SEC(2005) 717}, COM(2005) 229 final.

European Commission (2006) i2010 eGovernment Action Plan: Accelerating eGovernment in Europe for the Benefit of All, COM(2006) 173 final, Brussels, 25 April 2006.

European Commission. (2007a). European e-government 2005–2007: Taking stock of good practice and progress towards implementation of the i2010 e-Government action plan, J. Millard (Ed.) on behalf of DG Information Society and Media, September 2007.

European Commission. (2007b). Inclusive e-government: survey of status and baseline activities, J. Millard (Ed.) on behalf of DG Information Society and Media, December 2007.

European Commission. (2008). EQUAL opportunities for all: Delivering the Lisbon Strategy through social innovation and transnational cooperation. DG EMPLOY, October 2008.

European Commission. (2009). i2010 eGovernment Action Plan Progress Study. DG Information Society and Media, November 2009.

European Commission. (2010a). EUROPE 2020—A strategy for smart, sustainable and inclusive growth. Brussels. 3.3.2010, COM(2010) 2020.

European Commission. (2010b). A Digital Agenda for Europe. Brussels. 26.8.2010, COM(2010) 245.

European Commission. (2010c). "The European eGovernment Action Plan 2011–2015—Harnessing ICT to promote smart, sustainable & innovative government. Brussels. December 15, 2010, COM(2010) 743.

European Commission. (2010d). Independent panel report Interim Evaluation of the Ambient Assisted Living Joint Programme: Unlocking innovation in ageing well. DG INFSO, December 2010.

Foley, P., & Alfonso, X. (2005). An international study of technology initiatives to enhance social inclusion: Extending the reach of what works. A report prepared by IECRC for the Social Exclusion Unit of the Office of the Deputy Prime Minister, U.K. Government, August 2005.

Maslow, A. H. (1943). A theory of human motivation. *Psychological Review, 50*, 370–396.

Millard, J. (2006). eGovernment services. In: Deliverable D5.2, Current Demand/Supply Match. eUSER project: Evidence-Based Support for the Design and Delivery of User-Centred Online Public Services, European Commission IST 6th Framework IST Program.

Millard, J. (2007.) E-government for an inclusive society: How different citizen groups use e-government services in Europe. In D. Norris (Ed.), *E-government research: Policy and management*. Hershey, PA: IGI Global.

Part III

T-Government and Public Service Delivery

13 Collaborative Government

E-Enabled Interagency Collaboration as a Means for Government Process Redesign

Ari-Veikko Anttiroiko

CHAPTER OVERVIEW

Global and national changes pose various challenges to service quality and integration, productivity, innovativeness, and change management in the public sector. Such challenges have increased politicians' and public managers' interest in finding ways of improving public organizations' performance. Discussions about administrative simplification and more radical government process redesign have a vital role in such an agenda. This chapter discusses approaches to government process redesign, which may be incremental, radical, or revolutionary, focusing respectively on the simplification of administrative procedures, the redesign of service and governance processes, and the reassessment of the role and scope of government in society. Redesign is approached from a supply-side perspective with a focus on four aspects of interagency collaboration: framing, harmonizing, sharing, and acting. In terms of methods and tools, attention is paid to the utilization of information and communication technologies. In the empirical part of this chapter, selected cases of simplification and redesign are presented to illustrate real-life developments and to demonstrate their transformational potential. The conventional approach to redesign is action-oriented interagency collaboration. Yet, this chapter also points to a more radical redesign, which opens up visions for collaborative government or joined-up government with streamlined and integrated service systems. Such a change emphasizes the systemic nature of the service redesign and innovation processes, which requires that special attention is paid to the governance of the "systemization" process as a prerequisite of translating public policies smoothly into cost-effective, integrated, and high value-adding public services.

1 INTRODUCTION

The roles and working methods of governments have been changing considerably since the 1980s in practically all developed countries. Many such changes can be derived from increased competition in both public and private sector and demand from customers for better services (Hammer & Champy, 1993, p. 17), which implies that public organizations must pay special attention to service quality and integration, productivity and innovativeness, and also change management. There seems to be a universal tendency in the provision of public services toward streamlining administrative machinery and increasing partnerships and contracting out. Public organizations are becoming coordinators in the multi-sectoral governance field (see, e.g., Felbinger & Holzer, 1999; Mälkiä et al., 2004; Argyriades, 2002).

Intense pressure for efficiency and responsiveness has increased politicians' and public managers' interest in finding ways of improving public organizations' performance. Discussions about administrative simplification and more radical government process redesign have a vital role in such an agenda (OECD, 2009).

This chapter discusses approaches to incremental and radical government process redesign. The aim is to systematize this conceptual field and to map out strategic options and key tools for managing planned change. Special emphasis is placed on the use of information and communication technologies (ICTs) in supply-side-oriented redesign, in which the success depends to a large extent on exchange of data and collaboration between public service providers. In the empirical part of this chapter selected cases of redesign are presented to illustrate real-life developments and to demonstrate their transformational potential.

2   MANAGERIAL APPROACHES TO REDESIGN

There are various management concepts that reflect the need to simplify administrative processes and to redesign governance and service processes. Some of these concepts can be grouped under the label "incremental government redesign," which means that their primary focus is on making incremental changes to existing administrative and service structures and processes. Examples of such approaches are administrative simplification, Organization Development and Total Quality Management.

Administrative simplification is a primary managerial approach to cut red tape originating from excessive unnecessary regulations and procedures that may be redundant, and thus may have a negative overall impact on society (OECD, 2009). *Organization Development* (OD) is a planned, organization-wide educational effort to improve an organization's effectiveness and viability and to better adapt to new technologies and challenges. It has a close connection to human resource management (HRM) (McLean, 2006). In the context of government process redesign *Total Quality Management* (TQM) is usually seen as a paradigmatic form of incremental redesign. Its roots are in quality management in manufacturing with an emphasis on reducing the errors that may occur during the manufacturing processes.

Previous approaches have been essentially incremental in changing the ways of working of public organizations. Besides these, there is a family of concepts that depict more radical rethinking of the role of public sector organizations and the scope and mode of their actions. A generic concept that refers to radical redesign is *business process reengineering* (Hammer & Champy, 1993; Hammer, 1996; Motwani et al., 1998; Malhotra, 1998). In the public sector it is occasionally referred to as government process reengineering (Hughes, Scott, & Golden, 2007; da Cunha & Costa, 2004, p. 14; Chaba, n/a; Linden, 1994). Another well-known conceptualization of radical change in the public sector is *reinventing government*, which is essentially about the introduction of entrepreneurial government which is high-performing, business-like and enabling (Osborne & Gaebler, 1992, p. 35; Osborne & Plastrik, 1997; Anttiroiko, Bailey, & Valkama, 2011, p. 7). Another slightly similar yet more abstract concept is *transformational government*, which is used as a generic term to refer to a fundamental change in the role of government in society. (On e-transformation in government see Mälkiä et al., 2004, and on transformational politics see Woolpert, Slaton, & Schwerin, 1998).

The concepts that depict both incremental and radical redesign reflect various degrees of change in government, as illustrated in Figure 13.1.

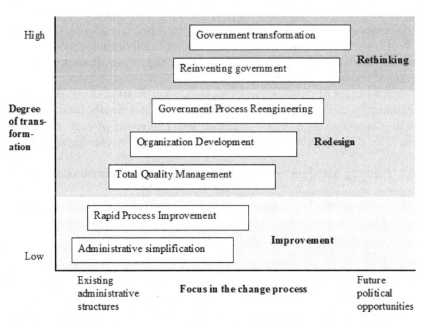

Figure 13.1   Approaches to government process redesign.

The idea illustrated in Figure 13.1 can be summarized as a three-layered model, indicating incremental, radical, and revolutionary changes: *simplifying* administrative procedures and practices, *redesigning* service and governance processes, and *rethinking* the role and scope of government in society (cf. Venkatraman, 1994).

3   COLLABORATION AS AN ENABLER OF CHANGE

The public sector has a long history of expanding their responsibilities, personnel, and organizations relying on a supply-oriented "silo" approach, which has created rather fragmentary service systems. It has been generally recognized that collaboration is one answer to the problem of improving efficiency in the public sector, reducing service fragmentation, improving public service quality, and changing organizational culture (Kaiser, 2011; cf. NSW Government, 2010).

Different change processes create new relations between public agencies, ranging from voluntary *ad hoc* collaboration to system-based redesign and finally to mergers as a part of large-scale reforms. Theoretically, we may distinguish three levels of collaboration associated with the level of government process redesign: operational collaboration (improvement), strategic collaboration (redesign), and structural or transformative collaboration (rethinking).

Collaboration has different modes or forms, such as cooperation among peers, coordination, mergers, integration, networks, and partnerships (Kaiser, 2011). Such forms mainly reflect the organizational continuum of collaboration, which is not particularly useful when considering the utilization of e-enabled tools in a wide set of cases of collaboration of independent public organizations. For the analysis of this chapter, an alternative classification of the forms of collaboration is constructed on the basis of a review of various cases of public service redesign, identification of the discernibly collaborative nature of activities in these cases and finally their grouping under a manageable number of categories. The result of such an applied heuristics is the typology of four distinguished aspects of collaboration:

1. *Framing* based on "principles" that guide collaborative reforms (policy, regulation, and institutional framework);
2. *Harmonizing* based on "standards" that serve to provide isomorphic objects or processes affecting the relationships of public authorities and service providers (service integration, standardization, back-office rationalization);
3. *Sharing* based on joint use and dissemination of value objects among public authorities or service providers (joint resources, databases, and information); and
4. *Acting* based on coordinated "action" within a given group of actors (collaboration, coordinated actions, and brokerage).

These categories match loosely with the radical nature of change depicted in Figure 13.1, for *framing* is generally associated with a transformative change; *harmonizing* is a tool for strategic redesign operating at the systemic level, *sharing* is paradigmatically associated with interagency sharing and exchange relationships, and *acting* is generally an action-oriented arrangement in incremental service design. However, such connections are only indicative. One of the key points is the extent to which the decision-making on services goes beyond organizational competence and thus requires either formal arrangements between organizations or, as in some cases, conditioning sector-wise or inter-sectoral regulation. This is in line with the hypothesis that the more radical service innovation or service redesign scheme in question, the more systemic nature it tends to have (cf. Consoli, 2007).

4 E-GOVERNMENT AS A TOOL OF REDESIGN

What has changed in public sector reform agenda in recent decades is the increased role given to *information and communication technologies* (ICTs) in cutting red tape and in transforming public organizations (Fountain, 2001; Norris, 2003; Scholl, 2005; Andersen, 2006; Hinnant & Sawyer, 2007; Wauters & Lörincz, 2008). We may envision the future e-government services being inter-linked within a joined-up government framework to provide multi-channel access to seamless public services. To reach such an ideal situation through government process redesign projects or reform programs is hardly possible without the critical role given to ICTs.

ICTs offer new opportunities for the reduction of administrative burdens as they improve communication, information processes, interaction and transactions. First, the capacity to deal with enormous amounts of data can improve government's capacity to utilize and share information. Second, the capacity for information dissemination is multiplied exponentially with the use of electronic means. Third, the electronic exchange of data is a powerful tool to increase efficiency in case handling and in performing government functions. Finally, time and space limits can be effectively eliminated through 24x7 access to online services. Nonetheless, *the use of ICT should be accompanied by a parallel review and reengineering of existing traditional administrative processes* to avoid waste and inefficiencies resulting from the automation of already non-performing processes. (OECD, 2009). This symbiotic relationship brings about the need to investigate how ICTs may support redesign processes, and as its flip side, how should government process redesign be integrated with information systems development (Weerakkody & Currie, 2003).

The most common tools used in the e-government area for simplification and redesign are: (1) digitalization of administrative forms; (2) simplification through reengineering and automation of back-office processes; (3) systems for data reporting from business to government; (4) portals for information and services; and (5) electronic data storage and exchange. (OECD, 2009). In the next section we discuss the application of such tools as an integral part of collaborative government process redesign initiatives.

5   CASES OF E-ENABLED INTERAGENCY COLLABORATION

This section presents system and producer-centered cases of public service simplification and redesign measures adopted in European countries. The cases were selected to represent different aspects of the Framing-Harmonizing-Sharing-Acting aspects of collaborative redesign, starting from policy framework and ending with hands-on collaboration: (a) the case of the Dutch regulatory reform program, (b) the case of eInvoice in Denmark, (c) shared databases as used by Crossroads Bank of Belgium and by pre-completed tax return in Finland, and lastly (d) the cases of the Virtual Customs Office of Sweden and the TYVI Model of Finland.

5.1   Regulatory Reform Program of the Netherlands

Practically all developed countries started to consider administrative simplification decades ago. However, the most recent wave emerged in the 2000s (OECD, 2003; 2007; Ziller, 2008). An excellent example of a national approach to better regulation and administrative simplification is the Dutch regulatory reform program. Its origin is in the mid-1990s, when the Dutch government as a part of a broad deregulation agenda set a goal to reduce administrative burdens on enterprises by 10 percent. In 1998 it set up a temporary advisory committee known as the Slechte Committee, which proposed several projects intended to promote simplification. The committee based its work on re-use of information already provided by enterprises to public authorities and the use of IT. A major step forward was the establishment of the Dutch Advisory Board on Administrative Burden (abbreviated to ACTAL) in 2001 as an independent watchdog of the reform. (OECD, 2003; Djankov & Ladegaard, n/a). This case indicates that successful framing requires strong political support, clear organizational solutions with sufficient mandates, clear—most preferably measurable—objectives, and the identification of benefits that are tangible and can be achieved within a reasonable timespan. Such a frame encourages and sometimes imposes interagency collaboration and helps to achieve efficiency gains through systemic innovations.

5.2   E-Invoice in Denmark

One of the applications in back-office rationalization is e-invoice. A good example of the introduction of e-invoice is the case of Denmark. In 2005 all public institutions in the country were required to accept invoices from suppliers in electronic format only, which can be read directly by the public sector's accounting systems. This means that all public sector entities have been required to convert all systems and administrative processes from physical to digital processing of invoices, credit notes and other transactions. This reform affects approximately 15 million invoices a year and applies to the entire public sector. It is expected to save the public some 120 million Euros annually, in addition to savings in internal administrative processes. (Trias telematica, 2007a). As this case illustrates, the harmonization of transaction processing systems has a potential to bring tangible benefits to collaborating agencies, customers, and the society as a whole. The idea is to replace agency-based solutions by a standardized system, which contributes to the transition of the entire government structure towards collaborative government or joined-up government.

5.3   Crossroads Bank of Belgium

An interesting simplification case from Belgium is Crossroads Bank, which facilitates the sharing of information between government agencies to rationalize information exchanges. A major business process reengineering and computerization was carried out during the past 15 years by about 2,000 Belgian public and private actors in the social sector from local to national levels, under the coordination of the *Crossroads Bank for Social Security* (CBSS). This collaboration led to the implementation of a network for joint electronic service delivery. All actors connected to the network can consult their databases and exchange up to 180 different types of electronic standard messages within the system framework in a secure way. In 2004, 380 million messages were exchanged, which reduced the printing of documents by roughly the same number. The reciprocal data exchange guarantees unique collection of data from the citizens and their employers by the social sector as a whole, and enables the automatic granting of social benefits. (Trias telematica, 2008; Cabinet Office 2009, p. 41). This case reveals how important agenda data-sharing is in government process redesign. This kind of change has similar kind of systemic dimension as in harmonizing transaction processing systems.

5.4   Pre-completed Tax Return in Finland

A classic example of redesign is the pre-completed tax return. In the Finnish system every individual with taxable income needs to submit a tax return. Taxpayers receive pre-completed tax return forms in an envelope in spring. They include a set of data on income, such as wages, pensions, and receipts of dividends, which are collected by the tax authority from employers. Such a procedure is possible due to a comprehensive system of basic registers. If a taxpayer finds that the facts are correct, he/she need not take any further action. If there are errors or omissions, the individual is expected to complete the form for corrections and return the documents to the tax office for reprocessing. (Nordisk eTax, n/a). In the latter case, a user may sign in to a secure online tax return site. The pre-completed tax returns is also a case for how IT can be incorporated in the radical process reengineering. Instead of just providing e-forms which can be used to fill in a tax return, the idea is to dispense with unnecessary forms, reduce unnecessary work, coordinate information processes and streamline the whole process with a special view to reducing the administrative burden of citizens and businesses. In this case the efficient collection of information and back-office data sharing serve as a building block of an entire society, as it guarantees transparency, coherence, and efficiency in taxation. It also provides benefits to ordinary citizens, as their obligations in taxation are reduced to a minimum.

5.5   Virtual Customs Office of Sweden

Simplification of protection and control functions performed by government have a lot of potential due to the volume and importance of these functions in society. One example of the rethinking and redesigning of such services is the customs in Sweden, which, through the application of process management, has come to the conclusion that the customs process does not start or even end with the customs itself. This has increased discussion with other public stakeholders in the foreign trade process. The result was the creation of a *Virtual Customs Office*, through which Swedish Customs on behalf of other public entities performs a number of integrated, interdepartmental e-services adding value to the overall foreign trade process for the Swedish business community. Besides the traditional Single Window solutions, the virtual customs collect value added taxes on imports on behalf of the taxation authorities, trade statistics on behalf of Statistics Sweden, and facilitate foreign trade regarding licenses through innovative e-services in partnership with the Board of Trade and the Board of Agriculture. This means that a customer can apply for, monitor and compute given license quantities and/or values by using My Customs Office through the Virtual Customs Office, hence creating an integrated front-office solution. The long-term objective for the Virtual Customs Office is to enable seamless electronic processes covering the full value chain through the use of sophisticated e-services. (Trias telematica, 2007b). The previous cases were 'systemic' in the truest sense of the word, whereas this Virtual Customs Office represents the case of action-oriented interagency service collaboration.

5.6   TYVI Model of Finland

Another actor-based case to be discussed here is the *TYVI Model* (the Finnish name of the system is *Tietovirrat Yritysten ja Viranomaisten välillä*, literally Information Flows between Companies and Public Authorities) set up by the

Ministry of Finance in 1997. It is a standardized data collection and exchange system used by several authorities, which aims at improving data reporting from companies to public authorities. TYVI started as a small pilot project with the option of scaling up. From the beginning it was planned to become financially self-supporting and to rely on private providers as brokers. (Valtioneuvoston kanslia, 2005). The TYVI Model has been expanding steadily since its inception. For example, in 1998 monthly and quarterly reporting from companies included some 2000 companies, the number tripled in the following year and has increased yearly since then. Yet in Finland a large part of taxation related information is still transmitted from companies to the tax authority conventionally on paper. This last case, the TYVI Model, is another example of basically voluntary interagency collaboration and also of brokerage, which brings an action-oriented dimension into the picture of government process redesign. This, just like the previously discussed Swedish case, is essentially a case in which some agency acts on behalf of others, which brings efficiency gains through coordinated actions.

Key aspects of government process redesign together with abovementioned examples are presented in Figure 13.2.

The most critical aspect of interagency collaboration in various types of redesign processes seems to be the governance of the service redesign with regard to its systemic nature. Yet, we may also hypothesize that there are nuances and differences which reflect the varying aspects of collaboration: framing requires more than anything strong political leadership and

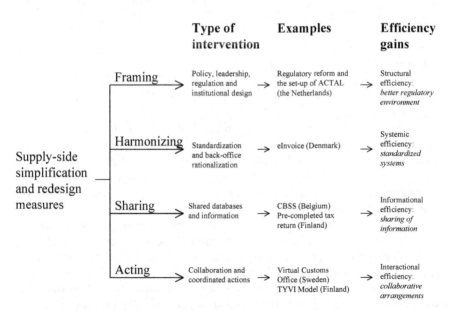

Figure 13.2 Benefiting from e-enabled administrative simplification and redesign.

firm organization of coordinated policy measures, harmonizing requires power over agencies operating within the system, sharing requires trust and tangible benefits in order to look persuasive to potential collaborators, and acting requires clear benefits and arrangements in order to guarantee smooth operations. As systemic nature is a kind of determining factor at the threshold of strategic or radical change, we may assume that "systemization" is a critical strategy-level design activity. Such "systemization" is needed to attune the components of services—such as service provider, value-adding core and support services, service setting, service process and delivery channel, and service user—within the public sector context so that jurisdictional and sectoral boundaries do not impede the creation of integrated value-adding services. This implies that such an approach is not only an application of some ready-made model but a learning process, marked by tensions and contradictions (cf. Warmington et al., 2004). Such a policy paves the way to radically new collaborative arrangements and to joined-up or seamless production models (see, e.g., Drüke & Klinger, 2011).

6   FUTURE TRENDS

The future of e-enabled interagency collaboration as a means for government process redesign is a political issue that is shaped according to the key characteristics and challenges of each national context. However, it is obvious that administrative simplification and redesign will continue to be important elements in the public sector reform throughout the developed world.

Impetus from research and the private sector is directing public sector reforms from supply-side approaches toward a user-centered approach, even though at the practical level this development is gaining ground only slowly. Anyhow, when customers are involved in the process not only in the design phase but also in implementation, we will enter a truly new phase in the development of public service provision, which can be called the co-creation model of public service (cf. Bailey, 2011). To simplify, the current trend of e-enabled interagency collaboration within systemic context may transform into e-enabled co-creation taking place on platforms that enable open innovation and seamless composition of tailored service packages.

It goes without saying that emerging technological trends will affect the future of public administration, including interagency collaboration. The current approach emphasizes interoperability and standardized solutions, but it is highly likely that new opportunities will arise from the utilization of ubiquitous technologies, augmented reality and social media by revolutionizing the user-centered redesign of public services. All this will strengthen the transition from supply-side oriented e-government toward collaborative, joined-up, ubiquitous, or seamless government, depending on what features are emphasized or will dominate the future development.

7 CONCLUSION

Administrative simplification and redesign form an important part of the reshaping of the way public organizations operate and interact with each other and with their stakeholders. Cutting red tape is usually an incremental change but may also be a part of a radical reform with the aim of reengineering government processes and reconsidering the scope of government activities.

In this chapter we have systematized the potential of e-enabled interagency collaboration as a means of government process redesign by categorizing both degrees of the radical nature of change and the modes of collaboration, which are combined in framing–harmonizing–sharing–acting framework. The conventional approach to redesign is action-oriented interagency collaboration, which through the changing roles and division of labor paves the way for rationalization, simplification, and incremental redesign. Yet this chapter points out to a more radical redesign as well, which opens a vision for truly collaborative government.

Simplification and redesign are challenging processes, as they relate to collective actions that are associated with structural change, which naturally increases ambiguity, inertia, and tensions. In addition, they are embedded in cultural, political, and administrative contexts, which condition the agenda-setting and implementation of related processes. Such observations boil down to a systemic nature of most of the service redesign and innovation processes, especially the radical ones, which in turn entails paying special attention to the governance of "systemization" process, which is needed in translating public policies into practices of integrated service systems.

Our perspective on simplification and redesign may need to be much more radical in the future than it is today, for after major simplification measures have been accomplished within existing political-administrative systems and their underlying rationalities, there will be—under the pressure of global competitiveness, financial distress, and a legitimation crisis—an urgent need to rethink the entire role of government in society.

REFERENCES

Andersen, K.V. (2006). Reengineering public sector organisations using information technology. *Research in Public Policy Analysis and Management, 15,* 615–634.

Anttiroiko, A.-V., Bailey, S., & Valkama, P. (Eds.). (2011). *Innovations in public governance.* Amsterdam: IOS Press.

Argyriades, D. (2002). Governance and public administration in the 21st century: New trends and new techniques. In *General Report. Twenty-fifth International Congress of Administrative Sciences: Governance and Public Administration in the 21st Century: New Trends and New Techniques, Athens, July 2001.* Proceedings (pp. 31–64). Brussels: IIAS.

Bailey, S. J. (2011). The evolving governance of public services in England: Extending competition, choice, co-design and co-production. In A.-V. Anttiroiko, S. J. Bailey, & P. Valkama (Eds.), *Innovations in public governance* (pp. 140–157). Amsterdam: IOS Press.

Cabinet Office. (2009). *Power in people's hands: Learning from the world's best public services.* London: Cabinet Office.

Chaba, A. (n/a). *Government process reengineering in context of e-governance.* Ppt presentation. National Informatics Centre, New Delhi. Retrieved September 20, 2011, from http://elearning.nic.in/training-section/government-trainings/workshop-on-e-governance/presentation/l5-government-processes-re-engineering-doc.ppt/

Consoli, D. (2007). Services and systemic innovation: A cross-sectoral analysis. *Journal of Institutional Economics, 3,* 71–89.

da Cunha, A. M., & Costa, P. M. (2004). Towards key business process for e-government. In W. Lamersdort, V. Tschammer, & S. Amarger (Eds.), *Building the e-service society. E-commerce, e-business, and e-government* (pp. 3–21). Boston: Kluwer Academic Publishers.

Djankov, S., & Ladegaard, P. (n/a). *Review of the Dutch administrative simplification programme.* The World Bank Group. Retrieved March 31, 2010, from http://www.ifc.org/ifcext/fias.nsf/AttachmentsByTitle/Review_Dutch_AdminSimplProgram/$FILE/World+Bank+Group+Follow-Up+Review+of+Reg Ref+in+The+Netherlands.pdf

Drüke, H., & Klinger, P. (2011). Networked public administration for better service: New production model for local service delivery in Germany. In A.-V. Anttiroiko, S. J. Bailey, & P. Valkama (Eds.), *Innovations in public governance* (pp. 140–157). Amsterdam: IOS Press.

Felbinger, C. L., & Holzer, M. (1999). Public Administration in transformation: Three global challenges. *International Review of Public Administration, 4*(2), 3–11.

Fountain, J. E. (2001). *Building the virtual state: Information technology and institutional change.* Washington DC: Brookings Institution Press.

Hammer, M. (1996). *Beyond reengineering. How the process-centered organization is changing our work and our lives.* New York: HarperBusiness.

Hammer, M., & Champy, J. (1993). *Reengineering the Corporation. A Manifesto for Business Revolution.* London: Nicholas Brealey Publishing.

Hinnant, C. C., & Sawyer, S. B. (2007). Technological innovation in public organizations through digital government. In A.-V. Anttiroiko & M. Mälkiä (Eds.), *Encyclopedia of digital government* (vol. 3, pp. 1511–1518). Hershey, PA: Idea Group Reference.

Hughes, M., Scott, M., & Golden, W. (2007). Business process redesign in implementing e-government in Ireland. In A.-V. Anttiroiko & M. Mälkiä (Eds.), *Encyclopedia of digital government* (vol. 1, pp. 151–157). Hershey, PA: Idea Group Reference.

Kaiser, F. M. (2011). *Interagency collaborative arrangements and activities: Types, rationales, considerations.* Congressional Research Service, CRS Report for Congress, 7-5700, May 31, 2011. Retrieved January 25, 2012, from http://www.fas.org/sgp/crs/misc/R41803.pdf

Linden, R. M. (1994). *Seamless government: A practical guide to re-engineering in the public sector.* San Francisco: Jossey-Bass.

Malhotra, Y. (1998). Business process redesign: An overview. *IEEE Engineering Management Review, 26*(3), 27–31.

McLean, G. N. (2006). *Organization development. Principles, processes, performance.* San Francisco: Berrett-Koehler Publishers.

Motwani, J., Kumar, A., Jiang, J., & Youssef, M. (1998). Business process reengineering: A theoretical framework and an integrated model. *International Journal of Operations & Production Management, 18*(9/10), 964–977.

Mälkiä, M., Anttiroiko, A.-V., & Savolainen, R. (Eds.). (2004). *eTransformation in governance.* Hershey, PA: Idea Group Publishing.

Nordisk eTax. (n/a). Web site of Nordisk eTax. Retrieved April 24, 2010, from http://nordisketax.net/?l=eng

Norris, D. F. (2003). Leading-edge information technologies and American local governments. In G. D. Garson (Ed.), *Public Information Technology: Policy and Management Issues* (pp. 139–169). Hershey, PA: Idea Group Publishing.

NSW Government. (2010). Interagency collaboration: Making it work. NSW Government, Human Services, Community Services. Research to Practice Note, March 2010. Retrieved January 25, 2012, from http://www.community.nsw.gov.au/docswr/_assets/main/documents/researchnotes_interagency_collaboration.pdf

OECD. (2003). *From red tape to smart tape. Administrative simplification in OECD countries.* Paris: OECD. Retrieved April 2, 2010, from http://unpan1.un.org/intradoc/groups/public/documents/APCITY/UNPAN022212.pdf

OECD. (2007). *Cutting red tape: National strategies.* Policy Brief, January 2007. Paris: OECD. Retrieved April 2, 2010, from http://www.oecd.org/dataoecd/12/9/38016320.pdf

OECD. (2009). *Overcoming barriers to administrative simplification strategies: Guidance for policy makers.* Regulatory Policy Division—Directorate for Public Governance and Territorial Development. Paris: OECD. Retrieved March 20, 2010, from http://www.oecd.org/dataoecd/13/40/42306414.pdf

Osborne, D., & Gaebler, T. (1992). *Reinventing government: How the entrepreneurial spirit is transforming the public sector.* New York: Penguin.

Osborne, D., & Plastrik, P. (1997). *Banishing bureaucracy: The five strategies for reinventing government.* Reading, MA: Addison-Wesley.

Scholl, H. J. (2005). E-government-induced business process change (BPC): An empirical study of current practices. *International Journal of Electronic Government Research, 1*(2), 25–47.

Trias telematica. (2007a). *Case: EInvoicing in Denmark.* Web site modified June 12, 2007. Retrieved March 24, 2010, from http://wiki.triastelematica.org/index.php/Case:EInvoicing_in_Denmark

Trias telematica. (2007b). *Case: Virtual customs office.* Web site modified July 16, 2007. Retrieved March 24, 2010, from http://wiki.triastelematica.org/index.php/Case:Virtual_Customs_Office

Trias telematica. (2008). *Case: Cross road bank Belgium.* Web site modified March 13, 2008. Retrieved March 24, 2010, from http://wiki.triastelematica.org/index.php/Case:Cross_road_bank_Belgium

Valtioneuvoston kanslia. (2005). *Tieto- ja viestintätekniikalla aikaansaadut tehostamishyödyt julkisessa hallinnossa* [Efficiency gains through information and communication technologies in public administration]. Valtioneuvoston kanslian julkaisusarja 9/2005. Helsinki: Valtioneuvoston kanslia.

Venkatraman, V. (1994). IT-enabled business transformation: From automation to business scope redefinition. *Sloan Management Review, 35*(2), 73–87.

Warmington, P., Daniels, H., Edwards, A., Brown, S., Leadbetter, J., Martin, D., & Middleton, D. (2004). *Interagency Collaboration: a review of the literature.*

TLRPIII: Learning in and for interagency working. The Learning in and for Interagency Working Project, 2004. University of Birmingham & University of Bath. Retrieved January 25, 2012, from http://www.bath.ac.uk/research/liw/resources/Microsoft%20Word%20-%20Interagency_collaboration_a_review_of_the_literature_initial.pdf

Wauters, P., & Lörincz, B. (2008). User satisfaction and administrative simplification within the perspective of eGovernment impact: Two faces of the same coin? *European Journal of ePractice*, 1(4), August 2008. Retrieved March 20, 2010, from http://www.epractice.eu/files/4.5.pdf

Weerakkody, V., & Currie, W. (2003). Integrating business process reengineering with information systems development: Issues & implications. In W. M. P. van der Aalst, A. T. Hofstede, & M. Weske (Eds.), *Business Process Management*. International Conference, BPM 2003. Proceedings (pp. 302–320). Berlin: Springer.

Woolpert, S., Slaton, C.D., & Schwerin, E.W. (Eds.). (1998). *Transformational Politics: Theory, Study, and Practice*. Albany: State University of New York Press.

Ziller, J. (2008). *Developing administrative simplification: Selected experiences from recent administrative reforms in EU institutions and member states*. Seminar on Administrative Simplification, Ankara, 8–9 May 2008. SPO Headquarters. Retrieved April 1, 2010, from http://www.oecd.org/dataoecd/40/50/41327209.pdf

14 Diffusion of Personalized Services among Dutch Municipalities

Evolving Channels of Persuasion

Vincent Homburg and Andres Dijkshoorn

CHAPTER OVERVIEW

In the Netherlands, municipalities are autonomous with respect to issues of design and management of electronic government services. One of the horizons for development is the implementation of personalized electronic services. In this chapter, we investigate how and why various municipalities adopt personalized electronic services by analyzing the channels of persuasion that are being used in the diffusion process. In order to do this, we analyze (1) a time series of personalization prevalence in more than 400 municipalities in the years 2006 through 2010 with a quantitative "rate of diffusion" model and (2) qualitative data that were gathered during interviews with key stakeholders in ten selected municipalities. We present an explanatory model of diffusion of personalized electronic service delivery that includes notions of institutional pressure, organizational search activities, and "framing" of innovations.

1 INTRODUCTION

Within the e-government literature, increasing attention has been given to explanatory models of e-government diffusion (see Table 14.1 for a literature review).

What can be noticed in these explanatory studies is that there is an emphasis on *structural-functionalist* characteristics. Although useful in itself, these explanations do not provide insights in questions like *how* public sector organizations actually adopt e-government innovations. Theoretical insights like Orlikowski's (2000) practice lens and Cziarniawska and Sevon's (2005) travelling of ideas point toward human agency and environmental pressures as explanations for the varieties of observed outcomes (i.e., prevalence of e-government services) in public organizations. By focusing on "agency" next to "structure" (Orlikowski & Barley, 2001), it is hoped to shed light on the process of technological and organizational change, so that eventually diffusion can be more effectively stimulated.

Table 14.1   Review of Explanatory E-Government Studies

Author(s)	Dependent variable	Determinant(s)
Moon (2002)	E-government adoption (following Hiller & Belanger, 2001)	City size (economies of scale), council-manager forms of government
Holden, Norris & Fletcher (2003)	E-Government adoption (following Layne & Lee, 2001)	Citizen demand, form and type of government, geographical characteristics of city
Gilbert, Balestrini & Littleboy (2004)	Citizens' willingness to use E-Government	Perceived time savings, financial security, trust, information quality, cost savings
Reddick (2004)	E-Government adoption (following Layne & Lee (2001) and Hiller and Belanger (2001)	City size (economies of scale), council-manager forms of government, geographical location tangible benefits, separate IT department
Moon & Norris (2005)	E-Government effectiveness through e-government adoption	Managerial innovation orientation, financial resources, technical capabilities, city size
Norris & Moon (2005)	E-Government adoption (websites & online services)	City size (economies of scale), council-manager forms of government, geographic location
Horst, Kuttschreuter & Gutteling (2007)	Citizens' willingness to use E-Government	Perceived usefulness of services (determined by trust in government, risk perception)
Reddick (2009)	Managers' perception of e-government effectiveness	Management capacity, collaboration
Homburg & Dijkshoorn (2011)	Adoption of personalized service delivery	City size

In this chapter we examine the diffusion of a specific, more or less mature form of e-government, personalized e-government, in a specific setting (municipalities in the Netherlands).

2   PERSONALIZATION AND PERSONAL SERVICE DELIVERY IN DUTCH MUNICIPALITIES

Various authors have suggested that various "stages" or "levels of maturity" can be discerned in electronic service delivery (Anderson & Henriksen,

2006), with delivery of static information being one extreme of a continuum and integrated services being the other extreme. Characteristic for the latter is that there is supposed to be a seamless integration of information services across administrative boundaries.

Recently, the idea of integration has been pushed a bit further by the discussion of personalized integrated services (Pieterson, Ebbers, & Van Dijk, 2007; Homburg & Dijkshoorn, 2011). These kinds of services take into account previous interactions of citizens with government, and through authorization, profiling, and customization, one-to-one relationships between service providers and users are established (examples at national or federal levels include the Belgian MyMinFin e-tax initiative, the Danish borger.dk portal, the Estonian eesti.ee initiative, the French mon.service-public.fr website, the Norwegian Norway.no portal, the British direct.gov.uk site, and the Dutch mijnoverheid.nl site). This kind of service delivery can be viewed as an attempt to realize the ambitions of customer orientation and delivery of high-quality, more individualistic services that have been brought forward by advocates of New Public Management wave of reforms (Homburg, 2008).

In this chapter, we do not argue that personalized e-government service delivery is or should be a necessary next step; rather, we analyze personalized e-government services as a "case" of diffusion of a specific innovation and analyze *how* the diffusion of personalized e-government service delivery takes place. In order to be able to actually explain the diffusion, we analyze the diffusion in a population of more than 400[1] municipalities in a single national jurisdiction, the Netherlands. The Netherlands can be categorized as a decentralized unity state (Esping Andersen, 1990; Pollitt & Bouckaert, 2004), implying that municipal governments are relatively autonomous vis-à-vis central government with respect to issues of management, including the design and management of electronic services (Van Os, 2011). At the central level, e-government initiatives are coordinated by the Ministry of the Interior and Kingdom Relations (services for citizens) and the Ministry of Economic Affairs, Agriculture and Innovation (services for businesses). A chief information officer (CIO) coordinates e-government initiatives that involve various ministries. Development and implementation of initiatives that involve various layers of government (provinces, municipalities) takes place under the heading of the ICTU Foundation (which implements the National Implementation Program i-NUP and is jointly governed by central and local governments) and the Logius agency (who owns and maintains infrastructural components like authentication facilities and is part of the Ministry of the Interior and Kingdom Relations). Municipalities may jointly purchase services under the heading of the GovUnited initiative. Furthermore, there are various forms of cooperation between municipalities and ministries in specific sectors like social security, policing, spatial planning, etc. These initiatives and organizations are mentioned here to illustrate that explanations that explicitly include contexts might be very relevant.

3   THEORETICAL ANTECEDENTS OF DIFFUSION

Diffusion of a new idea, product or service is defined as the spread of its use in a population of potential adopters (Rogers, 1995). The process of diffusion has been linked to characteristics of the innovation itself, the social system (community of potential adopters), channels of communication, and time (Mahajan & Peterson, 1985).

Advancements in the disciplines of sociology and organization studies such as the emergence of the new institutionalism (DiMaggio & Powell, 1983; Tolbert & Zucker, 1996) have highlighted cognitive structures, norms, and prevailing values in which innovation takes place. Institutionalism holds that adoption of innovations does not take place because individuals or (private as well as public organizations) organizations make rational, calculated decisions regarding costs and benefits but are under the influence of social context criteria that together form the concept of *institutions*. Hence, institutionalism emphasizes the persuasive control over practices of individuals or organizations under the institution's sway (King et al., 1994). Persuasion can be achieved not only through directives, but also through more gentle means like deployment of specific knowledge, subsidies of activities deemed 'appropriate', standard-setting and raising awareness (King et al., 1994).

Various authors have explicitly or implicitly analyzed vertical channels of communication (emphasizing activities undertaken by actors outside the set of potential adopters) through which persuasive control over adoption of innovations is exerted. Adoption at any time is supposed to be dependent on the number of potential adopters that has yet to adopt the innovation and prior adopters do not influence potential adopters. Thus, adoption begins rapidly and slows down as the number of adopters increases. The formal description of this model is presented in Table 14.2.

As opposed to vertical channels of communication and persuasion, Rogers (1995) has identified horizontal channels of communication and persuasion between potential adopters through which innovations are promoted through processes of mimicking. Innovation by means of mimicking is likely to occur under the conditions that the innovations are socially visible (Mahajan & Peterson, 1985); causes, conditions and consequences are known (absence of causal ambiguity); and the success of the innovation is unlikely to be determined by path dependencies (Loh & Venkatraman, 1992). Adoption at any time in this line of reasoning is related to the number of adopters, as well as the number of potential adopters (see Table 14.2).

Bass (1969) has also identified a mixed-influence model as a rival model to both the internal as well as the external model and in which adoption is both determined by vertical as well as horizontal channels of communication and persuasion. The formal description (Table 14.2) yields an asymmetrical S-shaped adoption function in which external influence results in more rapid early adoption than with imitation alone.

Table 14.2   Summary and Formal Descriptions of Three Rival Diffusion Models

Labels	Formal Description of Model
External influence (Mahajan & Peterson, 1985; Mahajan, Muller & Bass, 1990)	$dN_t/d_t = p[m - N_t]$ which (after integration) equals to the adoption function: $N_t = m[1 - e^{-pt}]$ N_t: cumulative number of adoption at time period t p: coefficient of external influence (p>0) m: number of potential adopters (m>0)
Mixed influence (Bass, 1969)	$dN_t/d_t = [p + q.N_t][m - N_t]$ which (after integration) equals to the adoption function: $N_t = m[p(m - m_0)/(p + q. m_0)].e^{-[(p + qm).t]}.$ $[1 + [q(m - m0)]/(p + qm_0)]. e^{-[(p + qm).t]}]^{-1}$ N_t: cumulative number of adoption at time period t p: coefficient of external influence (p>0) q: coefficient of internal influence (q>0) m: number of potential adoptersm 0: number of adopters at t=0
Internal influence (Mahajan & Peterson, 1985), 'word of mouth' diffusion (Wang & Doong), imitation (Loh & Venkatraman, 1992), institutional isomorphism (DiMaggio & Powell, 1983)	$dN_t/d_t = q.N_t [m - N_t]$ which (after integration) equals to the adoption function: $N_t = m / (1 + ([m - m_0]/m_0). e^{-qmt})$ N(t): cumulative number of adoption at time period t q: coefficient of internal influence (q>0) m: number of potential adoptersm 0: number of adopters at t=0

Additionally, according to the so-called Scandinavian Institutionalism, innovations can be viewed as "ideas" as much as they can be viewed as artifacts. In order for ideas (such as "personalization") to spread (either through internal or external influence), they must be translated into a success story or tale. During the travel, the idea itself is likely to change (Czarniawska & Sevon, 2005). As such, the idea of translation is a much more complex change than the notions of "mimicking" and "direction" suggest, and it adds to the diffusion literature the notion that diffusion is an intricate social process that involves translation activities of experts, boundary spanning agents and knowledge brokers. In the analysis of his paper, we attempt to provide a diffusion model that takes the above notions of change into account.

4　METHODS AND DATA

In order to explain the diffusion of personalized e-government services among relatively autonomous Dutch municipalities, we employ two methods.

First, we fit three quantitative diffusion-of-innovation models (see Table 14.2) for the purpose of comparing and specifying relevant communication and persuasion channels in the adoption of personalized e-government services (phase 1 of the study). The data that are used in the analysis have been extracted from a larger data set that was commissioned by the Dutch Ministry of the Interior and composed by the "Government has an answer" program committee. The data set covers e-government characteristics in the time frame 2006–2010.[2] The fitting procedure requires time series of a minimum of five consecutive observations (Mahajan & Peterson, 1985), a condition to which our data satisfy and were performed using basic statistics software.[3] The analytical procedure is as follows: (1) parameters of alternative models are estimated; (2) all models are tested against the null hypothesis that diffusion is a random event (White Noise), and (3) remaining models are contrasted to determine the best diffusion model (Wang & Doong, 2010).

Second, in line with our objective to further extend the e-government body of knowledge, we added a phase 2 of the study and analyzed adoption processes in more detail in ten selected municipalities, five early adopters and five laggards, selected from the data set described above. As the e-government literature consistently reports city size as being a major determinant of e-government adoption in general (see Table 14.1), we selected both the adopters as well as the laggard from substrata of the population, based on city size. In each of the selected municipalities, qualitative interviews were held with key stakeholders using a topic list. Responses were recorded, transcribed, and analyzed[4] using back-and-forth coding techniques (Miles & Huberman, 1994).[5] The categories resulting from the coding techniques in the selected municipalities allowed us to compare characteristics of both adopters with non-adopters in various, and through induction to explain diffusion of personalized e-government services.

5　ANALYSIS: EXPLAINING THE DIFFUSION OF PERSONALIZED E-GOVERNMENT

5.1　Description of Personalized E-Government Services in Dutch Municipalities

Table 14.3 lists the prevalence of attributes of personalized electronic service delivery by Dutch municipalities in the years 2006, 2007, 2008, 2009 and 2010.

Table 14.3   Prevalence of Personalization Attributes in Dutch Municipal
E-Government Services

	2006 (n=458)	2007 (n=443)	2008 (n=443)	2009 (n=441)	2010 (n=418)
DigiD authentication	20.7%	56.7%	76.3%	88.2%	94.6%
Personalized newsletter	16.4%	21.2%	21.2%	N/A	27.9%
Tracking & tracing	10.0%	16.0%	28.2%	26.5%	41.3%
Payment	15.9%	42.4%	61.4%	80.0%	91.6%
Pre-completed forms	N/A	N/A	17.8%	19.1%	33.9%
Personalized counters (MyGov.nl)	5.2%	14.2%	23.7%	28.8%	40.9%
Personalized policy consequences	N/A	N/A	19.4%	18.7%	22.2%

5.1.1   Phase 1: Models of Diffusion

To determine which influence model best explains adoption, we fit each of the three models described in Table 14.2 using an iterative non-linear sum of squared residuals regression analysis[6] and apply it to the time series of prevalence of personalized counters (see Table 14.4).

As all R^2 indicate a reasonable fit, and p and q estimates are all positive, additional procedures must be taken into account as to compare alternative diffusion models. In a pairwise comparative test, if one or more of the alternative models fail to reject the White Noise model, there is no need to proceed further (Mahajan & Peterson, 1985). From Table 14.5 it can be concluded that all three rival models can reject the null hypothesis (which states that diffusion is a random event).

Table 14.4   Parameters for Best Fit for E-Government Personalization Adoption in Municipalities in the Netherlands 2006–2010

	Influence Model		
	External	Internal	Mixed
p	0.11	-	0.079
q	-	0.04	0,000
Adjusted R^2	0.96	0.94	0.50

Table 14.5   Model Comparisons against White Noise Model

	Alternative Models		
	Internal Influence	Mixed Influence	External Influence
H_0: White noise	t = 3.116 (p<0,05)	t = 2.830 (p<0,05)	t = 2.879 (p<0,05)

Table 14.6 Model Comparisons among Alternative Diffusion Models

	Alternative Models		
	Internal Influence	Mixed Influence	External Influence
H_0: Internal influence	-	t = .89 (p=.438)	t = 1.10 (p=.349)
H_0: Mixed influence	t = -0,05 (p=.962)	-	t = .394 (p=.72)
H_0: External influence	t =-.439 (p=.69)	t = 0,113 (p=.917)	-

This leaves us the task of determining which of the three alternatives, if any, is the model that best explains diffusion. In order to determine the best explanation, the P-test is used, which determines the truth of H_0 in the presence of an alternative model H_1. In any one of the paired confrontations, if α is statistically no different from zero, then H_0 is the true model.

From the results of the P-test reported in Table 14.6 and given the quite small sample, we cannot decide on a "winning" fitting model. Based on the values in Table 14.4, we infer that horizontal *and* vertical channels of communication and persuasion can be identified in the diffusion of personalized e-government in the time frame 2006–2010 in the Netherlands.

5.1.2 Phase 2: Qualitative Field Work

To further analyze the process of communication, persuasion, and adoption beyond the issue of relevant channels, we compared experiences and consideration of five "adopters" (municipalities offering personalized electronic services as of 2008) with experiences and considerations of five "non-adopters."

5.2 Pressure on Adoption Decisions

Respondents in municipal organizations reported perceived expectations of citizens as the most important source of influence on adoption decisions regarding personalized e-government services. As one alderman phrased it:

> *a clamor for service provision, less bureaucracy, transparency: that is external pressure, as I perceive it. (. . .) Just because society does not tolerate other kinds of organizational behavior.* (Alderman)

Another kind of influence that was mentioned quite frequently was the existence of benchmarks with which the presence of municipalities is exposed. As a manager of service provision explained:

> *To score is felt to be important among municipalities. How often is your municipality being mentioned in professional journals, are you*

Table 14.7   Sources of Pressure

Source of Pressure	Frequency
Citizen demand	121
Benchmarks	88
Legislation	81
National initiatives	80
Peer rivalry	5

in the Top 3. . . . that is considered to be very important. (Manager of service provision)

The fact that municipalities keep a sharp eye on benchmarks and rankings sometimes results in somewhat perverse incentives to adopt personalized services, as one respondent reported.

Our decision to implement personalized service delivery was due to our low ranking . . . Our alderman wanted to improve our ranking, and we found out that we could improve our ranking quite easily by implementing a Personalized Internet Page . . . and so we did. (Project manager)

Table 14.7 lists reported sources of pressure, including legislation (not as a direct source of influence, but for instance national environmental legislation that instigates municipalities to issue one permit covering a variety of conditions stemming from various acts) and national outreach activities. Together, these sources indicate that (institutional) pressure affects adoption in line with existing literatures on isomorphic pressure on adoption of innovations.

5.3   Organizational Search

One consequence of institutional pressure as reported by respondents is that municipalities, once confronted with pressure, start scanning their environments for relevant knowledge and experiences (see also Levinthal & March, 1981). As one respondent indicated:

One member of our support staff made an inventory of associations staff members are participating in, and she managed to compile a list of three or four pages. (Manager of service provision)

Respondents reported that pressure did not directly result in new connections with other organizations, but rather that organizational pressure resulted in more intensive contact with forums and associations (for instance, the Public Service Provision Managers' Association, the Association of Dutch Municipalities, but also outreach programs like GovUnited) one was already participating in.

Table 14.8   Organizational Search

Organizational search	Frequency
Forums & outreach programs	65
Companies	62
Alliances of municipalities	23

Table 14.8 lists the type of associations, programs, and alliances that are reported by respondents as sources of ideas, knowledge, and solutions. Forums in general relate to outreach organizations or—programs; companies refer in most cases to banks and publishing houses, but also to consultancy firms. Alliances refer to pre-existing forms of cooperation between municipalities.

5.4   Activation: Moderation between Pressure and Organizational Search

Although respondents indicated that organizational search activities follow up on institutional pressure, from the case study so-called activation triggers (Zahra & George, 2002) can be identified that result in episodic changes (Tyre & Orlikowksi, 1994). Activation triggers in municipal e-government development include disasters affecting municipal organizations (in the Dutch situation, the explosion of a fireworks factory in the city of Enschede triggered a political crisis and in the subsequent reorganization, personalized e-government services were seen as a opportunity to help shape the new organization) but also the merger of municipalities and the appointment of new senior managers or politicians. These occasions do not by themselves induce organizational change but rather amplify the pre-existing impact of pressure on organizational search activities.

5.5   Framing

In line with the Swedish Institutionalism mentioned in the section on Theoretical Antecedents of Diffusion, knowledge and ideas cannot simply be transfused from one organization to the other; rather, ideas, concepts, and knowledge is repacked and re-embedded (Isabella, 1990). In the field study, we observed that various adopters framed ideas and chunks of knowledge completely differently. Personalization was sometimes framed as a precursor of an organization being a service champion (actually enabling citizen-centric service delivery), a means for achieving efficiency (*"If the processes are well-organized, I am convinced that in the long run we can do without large number of members of staff,"* Alderman), reputation (*"We think that we, being part of a high technology region, are obliged to modernize our service delivery"*, Head of Customer Relations Department), and control

Table 14.9 Frames of Personalization

'Framing' of Innovations	Frequency
Service champion	102
Efficiency	48
Reputation	54
Control	27

("*Now the focus is on the front office . . . but in the near future we intend to reengineer processes in the back office as well, as to simplify and speed up processes,*" Project Manager Service Delivery).

5.6 Social Integration

From the observations in the field work, and informed by our theoretical discussion of the Swedish Institutionalism, we could observe that translation, transfusion and repackaging of knowledge and ideas are social integration processes in which specific actors play a role (Czarniawska & Sevon, 2005). The actual transformation and transfusion of knowledge and ideas regarding personalization takes place through exchange of staff among municipalities, but also by the activities of (internal) innovation champions that actively 'pitch' innovations, as well as by activities of external knowledge brokers.

> *John Doe, of Consulting Inc[7], that is a remarkable character. He has access to senior management levels, where normally no one understands the potential of modern ICTs. But he is able to come up with brilliant applications, stories and examples.* (Program manager)

5.7 Synthesis: Persuasion and Communication Underlying Adoption Decisions

The theory building reported above can be summarized in five conjectures:

- Conjecture 0: municipalities experience both internal as well as external influence to adopt personalized e-government services;
- Conjecture 1: institutional influence on municipalities to adopt personalized e-government services results in increased organizational search activities;
- Conjecture 2: activation triggers moderate the impact of institutional influence on organizational search activities;
- Conjecture 3: in order to inform adoption decisions, knowledge and ideas resulting from search activities are framed in such a way as to appeal to local priorities and ambitions;

- Conjecture 4: only knowledge and ideas that are framed as to appeal to local priorities and ambitions inform decisions to adopt personalized e-government services.

With these conjectures, a model of *how* municipalities (being public sector organizations) actually adopt e-government innovations, *how* these municipalities actually learn to innovate, and *how* institutional influence shapes e-government adoption, can be presented (see Figure 14.1 for a graphic representation). With this model, the channels of persuasion underlying the adoption of, in our case, personalized e-government services have been decomposed, thereby revealing both the structure as well as agency of adoption decisions in the public sector.

6   DISCUSSION AND CONCLUSION

This chapter has explored the process by which public organizations—more specifically, Dutch municipalities—adopt personalized e-government services. In doing so, it builds upon an institutional tradition of technology diffusion, in which technology diffusion and adoption is associated not primarily with individually rational cost/benefit considerations, but rather

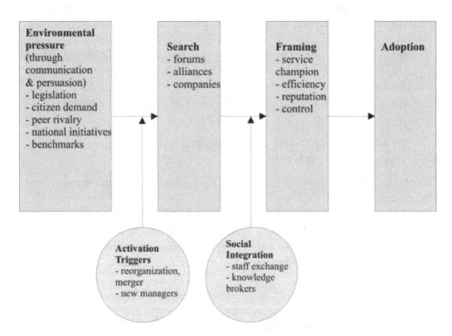

Figure 14.1   Model of institutional influence on adoption of personalized e-government.

with organizations' attempts to cope with a variety of prevailing norms, values, belief systems and rules that are imposed upon them. Furthermore, it has been our objective to highlight the role of human agency in the *process* of innovation, rather than focus on explaining the outcome as such.

Our analysis has concentrated on environmental pressure and ways in which knowledge and ideas regarding innovations are dealt with in municipal organizations.

One important finding of our research is that municipalities are confronted with horizontal and vertical channels of persuasion, by which pressure is put on municipalities to adopt innovations. Here, we add the element of "persuasion" to the existing notion of communication channels in the innovation literature, as communication to (potential) adopters was perceived as being compelling "evidence" to behave in a particular way.

A second finding was that environmental pressure imposed on municipalities was followed up by organizational search activities resulting in knowledge that was actively framed in terms of either (1) essential for service delivery, (2) efficiency, (3) reputation and/or (4) organizational control. Here we can infer how human agency plays a role in the eventual decision whether or not to adopt personalized e-government services.

These findings raise a number of questions for further research. First, direction and source of institutional pressure (horizontal, vertical, or mixed) may depend on differences in centralized, decentralized, or decentralized unity state regimes. Comparative research is needed to reveal differences and similarities in this respect. Second, we have analyzed the *antecedents* of personalization; it may be of interest to examine the *effects* of personalization, including possible unintended consequences of inequality in service provision and weakening of popular sovereignty (Fountain, 2001). Third and finally, we realize that the model depicted in Figure 14.1 is overly stylized and simplified, and additional research activities may be needed to include feedback loops and interactions between identified constructs.

NOTES

1. Note that population size has dropped from 458 (2006) to 418 (2010) throughout the time frame covered due to ongoing reorganizations and mergers, particularly of smaller municipalities.
2. Local elections were held in 2006 and 2010, implying that no major political changes have occurred in the time frame covered.
3. SPSS 16.0 and Marketing Engineering extensions of Microsoft Excel.
4. Note that interviews were held in Dutch; the authors present the quotations in the Analysis section in English.
5. Using the MaxQDA qualitative analysis tool.
6. We used SPSS 16.0 in combination with the Marketing Engineering utility for Excel.
7. Name of respondent and the consultancy firm were changed to maintain anonymity.

REFERENCES

Andersen, K. V. , & Henriksen, H. Z. (2006). E-government maturity models: Extension of the Layne and Lee model. *Government Information Quarterly, 23*(2), 236–248.

Bass, M. (1969). A new product growth model for consumer durables. *Management Science, 15*, 215–227.

Czarniawska, B., & Sevon, B. (2005). *Global ideas: How ideas, objects and practices travel in the global economy.* Copenhagen: Copenhagen Business School Press.

DiMaggio, P. J., & Powell, W. W. (1983). The iron cage revisited: Institutional isomorphism and collective rationality in organizational fields. *American Sociological Review, 48*(2), 147–160.

Esping-Andersen, G. (1990). *The three worlds of welfare capitalism.* Cambridge: Polity Press & Princeton: Princeton University Press.

Fountain, J. (2001). Paradoxes of public sector customer service. *Governance. 14*(1), 55–73.

Homburg, V. M. F. (2008). *Understanding e-government: Information systems in public administration.* London: Routledge.

Homburg, V. M. F., & Dijkshoorn, A.D. (2011). Diffusion of personalized e-government services among Dutch municipalities (an empirical investigation and explanation). *International Journal of E-Government Research, 7*(3), 21–37.

Isabella, L. (1990). Evolving interpretations as a change unfolds—How managers construe key organizational events. *Academy of Management Journal, 33*(1), 7–41.

King, J., Gurbaxani, V., Kraemer, K., McFarlan, F., Raman, K., & Yap, C. (1994). Institutional factors in information technology innovation. *Information Systems Research, 5*(2), 139–169.

Levinthal, D. A., & March, J. G., A Model of Adaptive Organizational Search. *Journal of Economic Behavior and Organization, 2* (1981) 307–333.

Loh, L., & Venkatraman, N. (1992). Diffusion of information technology outsourcing influence sources and the Kodak effect. *Information Systems Research, 3*(4), 334–358.

Mahajan, V., & Peterson, R. A. (1985). *Models for innovation diffusion.* Beverley-Hills CA: Sage.

Miles, M. B., & Huberman, A. M. (1994). *Qualitative data analysis (*2nd ed.). Thousand Oaks, CA: Sage.

Norris, D. F., & Moon, M. J. (2005). Advancing e-government at the grassroots: Tortoise or hare? *Public Administration Review, 65*(1), 64–75.

Orlikowski, W. J. (2000). Using technology and constituting structures: A practice lens for studying technology in organizations. *Organization Science, 11*(4), 404–428.

Orlikowski, W. J., & Barley, S. (2001). Technology and institutions: What can research on information technology and research on organizations learn from each other? *MIS Quarterly, 25*(2), 145–165.

Os, G. S. van (2011). The challenge of coordination: Coordinating integrated electronic service delivery in Denmark and the Netherlands. *Information Polity, 16*(1), 51–61.

Pieterson, W., Ebbers, W., & van Dijk, J. (2007). Personalization in the public sector: An inventory of organizational and user obstacles towards personalization of electronic services in the public sector. *Government Information Quarterly, 24*(1), 148–164.

Pollitt, C., & Bouckaert, G. (2004). *Public management reform: A comparative analysis.* Oxford: Oxford University Press.

Reddick, C. G. (2009). Factors that explain the perceived effectiveness of e-government: A survey of United States city government information technology directors. *International Journal of E-Government Research*, 5(2), 1–15.

Rogers, E. (1995). *Diffusion of innovations* (4th ed.). New York: Free Press.

Tolbert, P. S., & Zucker, L. G. (1996). The institutionalization of institutional theory. In S. R. Clegg, C. Hardy, & W. R. Nord (Eds.), *Handbook of organization studies* (pp. 175–190). Thousand Oaks, CA: Sage.

Tyre, M. J., & Orlikowski, W. J. (1994). Windows of opportunity—Temporal patterns of technological adaptation in organizations. *Organization Science, 5*(1), 98–118.

Wang, H., & Doong, H. (2010). Does government effort or citizen word-of-mouth determine e-government service diffusion? *Behaviour & Information Technology, 29*(4), 1–15.

Zahra, S. A., & George, G. (2002). Absorptive capacity: A review, reconceptualization, and extension. *The Academy of Management Review. 27*(2), 185–203.

15 E-Government Adoption of XBRL

A U.K./U.S. Comparison

Rania Mousa and Yu-Che Chen

CHAPTER OVERVIEW

This chapter examines the adoption of an e-government innovation utilizing the Extensible Business Reporting Language (XBRL). XBRL brings standardization to business and financial information for meaningful comparison. XBRL is viewed as the barcode of business and financial information. Moreover, XBRL enables efficient gathering, validation, and dissemination of business and financial data for regulators and investors alike. For e-government, XBRL plays a critical role in transforming the electronic regulatory reporting process.

This chapter investigates two prominent cases of e-government XBRL adoption: the Securities and Exchange Commission (U.S.) and Companies House (U.K.). Both are the main regulators of business and financial information for their respective countries. The emphasis is on identifying and analyzing the Critical Success Factors (CSFs) that contribute to the adoption of XBRL at both agencies.

The main findings of this research suggest that similarities in e-government adoption in United States and United Kingdom span a number of CSFs. These factors include the emphasis on making XBRL business case for government agencies, availability of in-house technical expertise, secure access to technical and non-technical stakeholders' support, and the agencies' capabilities in overcoming the technical difficulties encountered in adopting XBRL. These findings are relevant to the theory and practice of adopting innovative e-government in general and transforming regulatory reporting in particular.

1 INTRODUCTION

Throughout the world, there has been a significant paradigm shift where government agencies have recognized the importance of adopting technological initiatives that would serve as a transformative tool for innovative governments. Many government agencies have relied—and few still do—on conventional paper-based reporting methods, which have undermined the agencies' ability to provide efficient reporting services and streamline government operations. However, the landscape of government has changed, and new reporting technologies have become key components in governments' legacy reporting systems (Reddick, 2009; Pavlichev & Garson, 2004; Norris, 1999). One of these remarkable reporting technologies is the Extensible Business Reporting Language. Ushering in standardization, XBRL has revolutionized the electronic reporting systems by bringing additional cost savings, providing timely financial and business reports, and most importantly enhancing the quality of data dissemination and disclosure. All these important features of XBRL have commended XBRL as an imperative reporting technology that has transformed the e-government process in regulatory authorities.

In this chapter, two leading government agencies exemplify this technological paradigm shift by adopting XBRL to be an integral part of their existing electronic filing systems. These are the United Kingdom's Companies House (CH) and the United States' Securities and Exchange Commission (SEC). XBRL has been recognized as a strategic component of these agencies' e-filing agenda. Facilitated by the growth of the Internet, XBRL has had a prominent impact on the global regulatory adopters' community, which thrives on the processing of voluminous data and the efficient delivery of information services.

The XBRL adoption processes at CH and the SEC have been impacted by certain Critical Success Factors (CSFs). These factors have been examined in this chapter through conducting a comparative assessment of XBRL adoption process at CH and the SEC. Through this assessment, the CSFs are identified to determine the potential similarities and differences in each agency's approach toward adopting XBRL, and the impact such factors would have on XBRL adoption process. This comparative analysis will demonstrate the transformative role of XBRL as a notable interactive data reporting tool that has revitalized the e-government process in two leading government agencies in the United Kingdom and the United States.

The rest of the chapter is organized as follows: Section 2 provides a review of the literature on e-government reporting and technologies with focus on XBRL and the main CSFs that affect XBRL adoption; Section 3 provides a comparative analysis of each government agency's CSFs based on the empirical evidence. Section 4 provides the research findings. The practical significance and conclusions of the research are provided in the final section.

2 LITERATURE REVIEW

Electronic government initiatives have been considered one of the powerful mechanisms to improve the performance of the administrative and data processing tasks of government agencies (Kraemer & King, 2003). E-government provides the best example of utilizing the Internet and information and communication technologies (ICTs) such as databases, networking, multimedia, and reporting technologies. In the specific context of online services delivery, Brown and Brudney (2001, p.1) define e-government as the "use of technology, especially web-based applications to enhance access to and to efficiently deliver government information and services." Many innovative reporting technologies are instrumental to their regulatory adopters as such technologies help in improving existing reporting processes and systems. The adoption of those reporting technologies requires the collaboration of different individuals and stakeholder groups and the participation of different players in an organizational context. In a regulatory context, the adoption of e-government initiatives requires the inclusion of people, technology, organizational resources as well as government's stakeholders in the adoption process (Dawes and Pardo, 2002). One of these e-government initiatives that has played a crucial role in redefining the landscape of regulatory electronic reporting is the Extensible Business Reporting Language, or XBRL.

The adoption of e-government initiatives in general and XBRL in particular, has unique characteristics, particularly with references to many CSFs that impact the e-government adoption process. In the literature of technology adoption, Tornatzky and Fleischer (1990) provide a comprehensive framework for understanding technology adoption in an organizational context. This framework has been recognized by Cahill, Stevens, and Laplante (1990, p. 74) who indicate that the "configuration of hardware, software applications, individuals and procedures which together comprise information system technology in any organization is a "complex package," which is highly unique and differentiated among and between public sector organizations with varying purposes, charters, resource levels and access to technology." Cahill et al. (1990) emphasize that Tornatzky and Fleischer's Critical Success Factors provide great explanatory power for understating technology adoption process in various government settings. These CSFs have been closely re-examined in the context of XBRL regulatory adoption to determine their applicability and transformative role in developing e-government process (Mousa, 2010).

These CSFs include recognizing the importance of making the XBRL business case for the adopting government agency. This entails the realization of the benefits pertinent to the adoption of XBRL with regard to disseminating business and financial information and minimizing regulatory inefficiencies (Hampton, 2005). XBRL is perceived as an important reporting tool that would enhance data processing (Boyd, 2004) and facilitate the disclosure of publicly traded companies' data (Rezaee & Turner, 2002; Willis, 2007). XBRL literature also emphasizes the espoused benefits delivered by XBRL including data comparability, reliability and timeliness (ICAEW, 2004; Kull et al., 2007; Kull & Abraham, 2008; Rogers, 2010).

XBRL business case for stakeholders has been also identified as another Critical Success Factor. Identifying and meeting potential stakeholders' needs—especially end users-—during the process of adopting technologies has been reported in e-government literature (Barret & Green, 2001; West & Berman, 2001; Dawes & Pardo, 2002; GAO, 2001). In addition, Schwester argues that building a strong public support for adopted technologies helps to reduce public resistance towards using government information services (Schwester, 2009). The literature also indicates that government agencies should provide technology demonstration and prototypes to make the business case for potential users (Caffrey, 1998; Dawes & Pardo, 2002).

E-government literature indicates that the process of adopting e-government initiatives is not only a function of the adopted technology or the processed data but also a function of the availability of technical expertise needed to support such technology (Brudney & Selden, 1995; Heeks, 1999; Lee et al., 2003). Technical expertise has been recognized as another Critical Success Factor that emphasizes the importance of hiring and retaining qualified technical professionals and experts who have the education background and/or professional experiences that will enhance the adoption of e-government initiatives (Melitski, 2003).

The literature also recognizes the ability of government agencies to overcome the inherent technical difficulties associated with technology adoption as one of the Critical Success Factors. Ambite et al. (2002) and Dawes (1996) identify potential difficulties associated with data structure that cannot be easily processed by regulatory processing systems. Rogers (1983) considers technological complexity as an inhibitory to the adoption and DeLone and McLean (2003) make the argument by lining ease-of-use to more adoption. The sophisticated structure and the continuous proliferation of XBRL taxonomy versions are among the barriers that have been noted in XBRL literature that could decelerate XBRL adoption process (Rezaee & Turner, 2002; Cushing, 2003; Vun Kannon & Hannon, 2004; Dunne et al., 2009).

Heeks (1999), Norris (1999), and Lee et al. (2003) argue that external support—represented by business partnerships—could also be provided through software testing, product demonstration, and IT-tailored training to enhance the existing organizational skills of the adopting organization's staff members. The access to external technical and non-technical support and information from stakeholders has been recognized as a Critical Success Factor (Tornatzky & Fleischer, 1990). In addition, Irani (2002) and Dembla et al. (2003) suggest that a supportive regulatory role by top government officials could facilitate the adoption of technologies by government agencies.

The adoption of XBRL has been driven by regulatory authorities which utilize the functionality of data standardization and processing tools in their legacy reporting systems (Mousa, 2010). Mousa's research has assessed the impact of the previously discussed CSFs on the adoption of XBRL in a British government agency, Companies House (Mousa, 2010). This chapter builds on Mousa's findings and provides a comparative analysis of XBRL adoption processes at the United Kingdom's CH and the United States' SEC. The SEC has been selected as an instructive example of a government agency that recognized the significance of XBRL as a remarkable "interactive data" reporting technology that has facilitated the reporting and processing of financial and business information filed by publicly traded companies in the United States. CH has been selected as a pioneer executive government agency that recognized the capabilities of XBRL in processing the audit-exempt annual statutory information filed by small companies in the United Kingdom. The comparative analysis in the following section is based on examining XBRL adoption processes at CH and the SEC. A detailed description can be made available upon request.

3   COMPARATIVE ANALYSIS OF CRITICAL SUCCESS FACTORS

3.1   Making XBRL Business Case for the Adopting Government Agency

The Securities and Exchange Commission and Companies House realized the benefits of XBRL with regard to disseminating business and financial information and minimizing regulatory inefficiencies (Hampton, 2005). The SEC sought the adoption of XBRL to facilitate the disclosure of publicly traded companies' data. The use of XBRL by the SEC was also driven by XBRL's capability to provide meaningful and timely comparison of corporate data. XBRL was perceived as a machine-readable reporting medium that would enhance data capturing and manipulation in the audit-exempt companies' accounts at CH. This finding supports the importance of XBRL in facilitating the processing of information received from companies filing their statutory information. CH was also driven by the financial outcome of selling XBRL data to Internet users and data aggregators. Table 15.1 illustrates the profits (losses) generated by providing registration versus dissemination services during the period 2002–2010.

Both government agencies' decisions to adopt XBRL were aligned with their strategic vision to digitize the processing of regulatory filings and provide timely and reliable financial and business information to various XBRL user groups, including investors and public users. CH's and the SEC's recognition of XBRL's benefits was an important catalyst and a Critical Success Factor in the process of making XBRL business case for the agencies, which paved the way for integrating XBRL into their existing electronic reporting systems.

Table 15.1 Financial Results of CH's Registration and Dissemination Services (2002–2010)

Services	Profit (Loss) (£ million)							
	2002/ 03	2003/ 04	2004/ 05	2005/ 06	2006/ 07	2007/ 08	2008/ 09	2009/ 10
Registration Services— include incorporation, annual registration, dissolutions and late filing penalties.	3.0	3.4	(6.2)	2.0	0.1	2.0	(2.0)	(2.2)
Dissemination Services —include searches delivered on paper, electronically and to bulk users (data aggregators)	2.1	0.7	6.5	0.7	0.9	1.6	1.8	1.1

Source: CH Annual Reports

3.2 Making XBRL Business Case for Stakeholders

Addressing potential users' concerns varied between the Securities and Exchange Commission and Companies House. During the course of implementing the voluntary filing program, the SEC was keen to identify potential concerns of the impact of adopting XBRL on reporting businesses by taking a phase-in schedule starting with large companies to minimize the compliance cost for smaller companies. In the published final rule on XBRL reporting (Interactive Data to Improve Financial Reporting: Final Rule, Feb.10, 2009), the SEC made XBRL business case for investors by emphasizing the potential advantages of filing corporate data in XBRL. The SEC's efforts have been supported by e-government literature in terms of the need to build a strong public support for the adopted technology to reduce potential public resistance toward using government information services. The published final rule on XBRL was followed by the SEC's move to mandate the use of XBRL in June 2009. CH adopted a different approach in making XBRL business case for the small companies by offering reduced XBRL filing fees and by raising users' awareness through the showcase and testing sessions, which supports the ICAEW report (2009) on the importance of testing XBRL capabilities in coping with processing large volumes of data. While the SEC took a voluntary then mandatory phase-in approach, CH opted for introducing XBRL on a voluntary basis to small companies. However, in its future plans to expand the use of

XBRL for the filing of audited accounts presented by large companies, CH would follow the UK government mandate to receive XBRL-based audited accounts.

3.3   Availability of Technical Expertise

As an organization, CH did not have adequate in-house technical expertise to build XBRL taxonomy structure that would support the filing of the audit-exempt accounts. CH did not have a full-fledged IT department. When CH's XBRL team was formed, two members acquired practical IT knowledge, specifically in computer programming and XML languages. Upon implementing XBRL, CH struggled with recruiting and retaining additional IT professionals as they opted for better employment opportunities at private sector organizations. However, the SEC had a strong IT department of approximately 120 full-time employees who were responsible for the IT function of the agency direction and administrative support (U.S. Securities and Exchange Commission, 2009). The SEC's significant IT expertise was a Critical Success Factor in adopting XBRL, as the IT department successfully collaborated with different stakeholders during the implementation of the voluntary filing program, which eventually provided a stronger foundation for building XBRL taxonomy for the companies' data.

3.4   Overcoming XBRL Complexity

The sophisticated structure and the continuous proliferation of XBRL taxonomy versions were among the barriers faced by CH and the SEC. However, CH and the SEC managed to maneuver the data complexities associated with XBRL taxonomy. Due to CH's lack of technical expertise, especially in the area of XBRL implementation, the task of building XBRL taxonomy was outsourced to Adobe Systems. XBRL project team members at CH worked closely with Adobe Systems to create Adobe Intelligent Forms (AIFs) to support the filing of the audit-exempt accounts. However, the strength of the SEC's IT department to overcome the difficulty of tagging thousands of data elements in the corporate filings was evident during the experimentation and implementation of the voluntary filing program. In addition, the phase-in implementation approach allowed the SEC to focus on a small number of resourceful corporate filers and subsequently to take on a larger number of small filers.

3.5   Access to External Technical and Non-technical Support and Information from Stakeholders and Top Government

The strong interest and support of XBRL adoption among XBRL International Inc.'s members has contributed to building a "mass" of XBRL stakeholders (XBRL Progress Report, 2008). XBRL International has supported the global adoption of XBRL by building a network of regulators, consulting and accounting firms, providers of information services, professional bodies and business organizations. This type of networking has been one of the Critical Success Factors that fostered XBRL adoption at CH and the SEC. This network was represented by a diversified group of stakeholders, composed of software vendors, professional bodies (ICAEW, ICAS, and AICPA), XBRL U.S. and XBRL U.K. For example, CH's XBRL project manager is an active member of the Steering Committee of XBRL U.K. In addition, XBRL U.K. provided significant technical assistance on the presentation and format of XBRL-based Adobe forms. This type of strategic partnership was evident with the SEC which partnered with XBRL U.S. to provide technical assistance with building XBRL taxonomy structure. In addition, XBRL International provided a critical informational venue for CH and the SEC to meet with different regulatory adopters to share their XBRL adoption experience during the conferences organized by XBRL International.

The support extended by top government bodies was a common Success Factor at both agencies. At CH, legislative approval and advisory support was acquired from CH's overseeing top government agency: the Business, Innovation and Skills (BIS) Department, which played a strategic role in the decision making process of adopting XBRL. In addition, the BIS provided CH with the specialized accountancy expertise during the process of designing and building proper data structure and format of XBRL-based Adobe forms. The former SEC's Chairman, William Donaldson, saw the potential of XBRL as early as in 2004, while Chris Cox, a succeeding chairman, advocated and championed the XBRL adoption process. The E-Government Act of 2002 provided the institutional framework that served as the road map for adopting XBRL at the SEC. The U.S. government, represented by the Congress, was supportive of disclosing interactive financial data via the SEC's Interactive Data Initiative using XBRL. In addition, a generous financial budget of over $55 million was approved by the U.S. government to modernize the SEC's electronic filing systems in 2006, which was leveraged to adopt XBRL. Out of this budget ($55 million), $5.5 million was granted to XBRL U.S. to assist the SEC with building XBRL taxonomy structure for corporate companies.[1]

4   RESEARCH FINDINGS

In this chapter, we have provided a comparative overview of XBRL adoption process at two prominent government agencies in the United Kingdom and the United States with emphasis on the Critical Success Factors that have impacted this process. Based on the empirical evidence, five main CSFs were examined. The research findings show that CH and the SEC have followed different routes towards adopting XBRL. CH has opted for the voluntary filing of XBRL-based accounts (Adobe forms), while offering reduced electronic filing fees to encourage presenters to file in XBRL. The SEC followed a voluntary and then mandatory phase-in approach that allowed for the incremental adoption of XBRL over the course of 3 years. The differences in the adoption approaches reflect each agency's policy in adopting new technologies as part of its existing legacy reporting system. At CH, XBRL was viewed as a technical solution rather than a novel technology that was compatible with CH's existing web and electronic filing facilities. By law, small companies have to present annually their audit-exempt accounts to CH, and CH successfully made the business case for small companies' presenters to file these accounts electronically. CH did not see the need to mandate XBRL filing, as it was introduced inherently in the Adobe forms, in which XBRL data were embedded. Small companies' presenters were already accustomed to the utilization of CH's electronic filing facilities, so CH did not need to push any further for mandating XBRL. At the SEC, the phase-in approach allowed the SEC to focus on the corporate users' needs, widen the scale of XBRL implementation and eventually alleviate corporate users' concerns about their readability to file in XBRL. As corporate filers were ready to configure their filing systems to be XBRL-compatible, the SEC gradually moved to the next stage and applied XBRL mandate to provide the required legal authorization of XBRL usage.

XBRL business case was made for CH and the SEC as XBRL was perceived as a critical component of their regulatory filing systems which would improve data quality, dissemination and disclosure. This supports the regulatory provision for pushing the global efforts toward further development of XBRL capabilities to streamline government operations. The SEC was mainly driven by improving the quality of the data dissemination and disclosure, while CH viewed XBRL as a reporting medium that facilitates capturing and manipulating XBRL data, which could be sold to different Internet users and data aggregators. This difference reflects the varying nature and mission of each government agency's data management policy. SEC strictly uses data for filing and disclosure, while CH discloses basic business data to the general public, while selling other bulk data to potential data aggregators. It was also found that XBRL compatibility to CH and the SEC's electronic filing systems was an integral part of XBRL business case for both agencies, which facilitated the XBRL adoption processes at both agencies.

A significant finding in the comparative assessment highlights each agency's technical capabilities. While CH struggled with acquiring and retaining technical experts, the SEC was strongly equipped with a full-fledged IT and service support departments. Given the lack of CH's technical expertise, the task of building XBRL taxonomy structure was outsourced, while the SEC relied on its in-house experts to develop XBRL taxonomy, in collaboration with members from XBRL U.S. Despite CH's ability to overcome the shortage in technical skills, it is important to note that CH's reliance on outsourcing could potentially undermine the agency's ability to strengthen its own IT department. Such a weakness could have its own future ramifications, as CH plans to expand the use of XBRL for the filing of large companies' audited accounts, which contain thousands of data elements that need to be tagged.

Stakeholders' participation was found to be a key Success factor. The literature highlights the significance of having top government support, which facilitates the allocation of needed resources to drive e-government initiatives. Top government support was represented by the strategic assistance extended by the BIS and the U.S. government officials who provided appropriate technical and financial support to CH and the SEC, respectively. Several IT experts at government agencies, represented by the IT professionals at the SEC, and those at the private-sector software industry, represented by Adobe Systems, were among the most important providers of external technical support during the XBRL adoption process. Through formulating strategic partnerships with several members at XBRL U.S. and XBRL U.K., CH and the SEC managed to acquire and complement specialized technical expertise, which expedited the process of implementing XBRL.

5   CONCLUSIONS AND PRACTICAL SIGNIFICANCE

It can be concluded that the assessment of the Critical Success Factors across CH and the SEC provides an insightful comparative overview of the XBRL adoption process. The findings of this research support the importance of overcoming technical complexities, mobilizing organizational and technical resources, making the technology business case for the adopting agencies and potential stakeholders and seeking external support through building strategic partnerships with public and private-sector organizations. Understanding the Critical Success Factors encountered in adopting electronic government initiatives is a high priority for policy makers. This was evident at CH and the SEC which recognized the functionalities of XBRL as a remarkable data reporting and processing tool that transformed the electronic filing process and enhanced their e-government efforts. The process of adopting XBRL and identifying the Critical Success Factors affecting it highlight the importance of electronic reporting technologies to government agencies, and the applicability of the CSFs in devising strategic action plans for developing potential large-scale government projects in different national contexts.

This research has generated several practical management recommendations. We suggest that a broader critical mass of existing XBRL regulatory adopters and stakeholders is essential for fostering the XBRL adoption process for any future XBRL adopter. Evidence also suggests that strengthening the in-house technical capabilities of government agencies is an important driving force in e-government adoption. If technical capacities continue to be lacking, the process of adopting e-government initiatives could be severely undermined. Heightened awareness campaigns featuring success stories of XBRL adoption and building successful business partnerships are important catalysts in the adoption and development of sustainable e-government.

NOTES

1. http://www.cpa2biz.com/Content/media/PRODUCER_CONTENT/Newsletters/Articles_2007/CorpFin/Serious_About_XBRL.jsp

REFERENCES

Ambite, J.L., Y. Arens, L. Gravano, V. Hatzivassiloglou, E.H. Hovy, J.L. Klavans, A.Philpot, U. Ramachandran, K. Ross, J. Sandhaus, D. Sarioz, A. Singla, and B. Whitman.2002. Data Integration and Access: The Digital Government Research Center's EnergyData Collection (EDC) Project, In W. McIver and A.K. Elmagarmid (Eds.), *Advances inDigital Government: Technology, Human Factors and Policy* (pp. 85–106). Norwell, MA: Kluwer Academic Publishers.

Barret, K. and Green, R. (2001). *Powering up: How public managers can take control of information technology.* Washington, DC: CQ Press.

Boyd, G. (2004). XBRL in New Zealand—Past, present and future. *Chartered Accountants Journal of New Zealand, 83*(3), 9–11.

Brown, M., & Brudney, J. (2001, October). *Achieving advanced electronic government services: An examination of obstacles and implications from an international perspective.* Paper presented at the National Public Management Research Conference, Bloomington, Indiana.

Brudney, J., & Selden, S. (1995). The adoption of innovation by smaller local governments. *American Review of Public Administration, 25*(1), 71–80.

Caffrey, L. (1998). *Information sharing between and within governments: A research group report.* London: Commonwealth Secretariat.

Cahill, A., Stevens, J., & Laplante, J. (1990). The utilization of information-systems technology and impact on organizational decision-making. *Knowledge-Creation Diffusion Utilization, 12*(1), 53–79.

Cushing, K. (2003, May 20). XBRL is too complex for adoption. Retrieved from http://www.computerweekly.com/Articles/2003/05/20/194575/XBRL-is-too-complex-for-adoption.htm

Dawes, S. (1996). Inter-agency information sharing: Expected benefits, manageable risks. *Journal of Policy Analysis and Management, 15*(3), 377–394.

Dawes, S., & Pardo, T. (2002). Building collaborative digital government systems, In W. McIver & A. Elmagarmid (Eds.), *Advances in digital government, Technology, human factors, and policy* (pp. 259–274). Norwell, MA: Kluwer Academic Publishers.

DeLone, W. & McLean, E. (2003). The DeLone and McLean Model of information system success: A ten-year Update. *Journal of Management Information Systems, 19*(4), 9–30.

Dembla, P., Palvia, P., Brooks, L., & Krishnan, B. (2003). *Adoption of web-based services for transaction processing by organizations: A multilevel contextual analysis*. Paper presented at the 9th Americas Conference on Information Systems, Tampa, Florida.

Dunne, T., Helliar, C., Lymer, A., & Mousa, R. (2009). XBRL: The views of stakeholders. ACCA Research Report No. 111. Retrieved from http://www2. accaglobal.com/pubs/general/activities/library/technology/rr-111–002.pdf. Accessed January 27, 2012.

GAO (General Accounting Office) (2001). Electronic government: Challenges must be addressed with effective leadership and management. Retrieved from http:// www.gao.gov/new.items/d01959t.pdf. Accessed January 27, 2012.

Hampton, P. (2005). *Reducing administrative burdens: Effective inspections and enforcement*. London: HM Treasury.

Heeks, R. (1999). Management information systems in the public sector. In G. Garson (Ed.), *Information technology and computer applications in public administration* (pp.157–173). Hershey, PA: Idea Group Publishing.

ICAEW (Institute of Chartered Accountants in England and Wales). (2004). *Information for better markets, digital reporting: A progress report*. London. Retrieved from http://www.icaew.com/~/media/Files/Technical/Financial-reporting/Information%20for%20better%20markets/IFBM/Digital%20reporting%20a%20progress%20report.ashx. Accessed January 27, 2012.

ICAEW (Institute of Chartered Accountants in England and Wales). (2009, February 10). *Report by tax faculty on the compulsory online filing of company tax returns and electronic payment of corporation tax: Draft Legislation. Interactive Data to Improve Financial Reporting: Final Rule* (p. 6777).

Irani, Z. (2002). Information systems evaluation: Navigating through the problem domain. *Information and Management, 40*(1), 11–24.

Kraemer, K., & King, J. (2003). *Information technology and administrative reform: Will the time after e-government be different?* Center for Research on Information Technology and Organizations, University of California at Irvine.

Kull, J., & Abraham, C. (2008). XBRL & public sector financial reporting. *The Journal of Government Financial Management, 57*(2), 28–32.

Kull, J., Miller, L., St Clair, J., & Savage, M. (2007). Interactive Data—XBRL: A revolutionary idea. *The Journal of Government Financial Management, 56*(2), 10–14.

Lee, J.-N., Huynh, M., Kwok, R., & Pi, S.-M. (2003). IT sourcing evolution practices in human resources. *Communications of the ACM, 46*(5), 84–89.

Melitski, J. (2003). Capacity and e-government performance: An analysis based on early adopters of Internet technologies in New Jersey. *Public Performance & Management Review, 26*(4), 376–390.

Mousa, R. (2010). E-government adoption process: XBRL adoption in HM Revenue and Customs and companies house. Ph.D. dissertation. Birmingham Business School, University of Birmingham.

Norris, D. (1999). Leading edge information technologies and their adoption: Lessons from U.S. cities. In G. Garson (Ed.), *Information technology and computer applications in public administration: Issues and trends* (pp.137–156). Hershey, PA: Idea Group.

Pavlichev, A., & Garson, D. (2004). *Digital government: Principles and best practices*. London: Idea Group Publishing.

Reddick, R. (2009). The adoption of centralized customer service systems: A survey of local governments. *Government Information Quarterly, 26*(1), 219–226.

Rezaee, Z., & Turner, J. (2002). XBRL-based financial reporting: Challenges and opportunities for government accountants. *The Journal of Government Financial Management, 51*(2), 16–22.

Rogers, E. (1983). *Diffusion of innovations*. (3rd ed.). New York: The Free Press.

Rogers, R. (2010). Mandatory XBRL filing is coming soon to statutory agencies near you. *Accountancy Ireland, 42*(2), p.26

Schwester, R. (2009). Examining the barriers to e-government adoption. *Electronic Journal of e-Government, 7*(1), 113–122.

Tornatzky, L., & Fleischer, M. (1990). *The processes of technological innovation.* Lexington, MA: Lexington Books.

U.S. Securities and Exchange Commission. (2009, February 10). *Interactive data to improve financial reporting: final rule.* Retrieved from http://www.edgar-online.com/Portals/0/pdf/SEC/XBRLrule.pdf. Accessed January 27, 2012.

U.S. Securities and Exchange Commission. (2009, May). *In brief FY 2010 congressional justification.* Retrieved from http://www.sec.gov/about/secfy10congbudgjust.pdf

Vun Kannon, D., & Hannon, N. (2004). Why is XBRL so hard? *Strategic Finance, 86*(2), 49–51.

West, J., & Berman, E. (2001). The impact of revitalized management practices on the adoption of information technology: A national survey of local governments. *Public Performance and Management Review, 24*(3), 233–253.

Willis, M. (2007). Improving investor communications and analysis via standardization. *The International Journal of Digital Accounting Research, 7*(13), 153–165.

XBRL Progress Report. (2008). XBRL International Inc. Retrieved from http://www.xbrl.org/ProgressReports/2008_11_XBRL_Progress_Report.pdf. Accessed January 27, 2012.

16 E-Government Implementation in Times of Change
The Role of Shared Services in Transforming Government

Anton Joha and Marijn Janssen

CHAPTER OVERVIEW

Governments are looking for ways to reduce costs without eroding service provision. This vision is founded in the Whole-of-Government Approach (WGA) in which an integral perspective on government is taken and in which activities are bundled which were previously fragmented. Shared services have been embraced for realizing this as the basic premise is that decentralized services can be bundled into a semi autonomous business unit and provided to many users. Using shared services requires extensive transformations, yet there is little known about these transformations. In this chapter, we examine an in-depth case study of the largest shared service center (SSC) for human resource management (HRM) within the Dutch central government, a project that initially failed and only became successful after redefining the scope, governance, and implementation strategy. We describe the initial plan to implement the HRM SSC and the reasons why this transformation initially failed by identifying the lessons learned from a strategic, organizational, political, economic, and technical perspective. We then describe the change and transformation management process that was required to re-design and re-initiate the SSC in a different form. Finally, we discuss the role and effects the SSC had on the WGA.

1 INTRODUCTION

Especially in the current economic climate, governments are continuously looking for ways to work more efficiently and effectively by reducing costs, while at the same time maintaining or even improving customer service levels. Shared services have been embraced for realizing organizational transformations by bundling decentralized services into a semi-autonomous business unit that can be reused by many agencies, therefore avoiding the need to develop and maintain similar services many times. *Transformational government* encompasses a broad perspective of public administration, in which structures are radically changed (Irani, Love, & Jones, 2008; Weerakkody & Dhillon, 2008; Weerakkody, Janssen, & Dwivedi, 2011) and an essential element of this is the reengineering of back office processes and IT systems (Weerakkody et al., 2011).

The aim of the research presented in this chapter is to show the necessary changes that are required when introducing and implementing a shared service center (SSC). To this end, we examine an in-depth case study of the largest shared service center for human resource management (HRM) within the Dutch central government (P-Direkt), a project that initially failed and only became successful after redefining the scope, governance, and implementation strategy. The lessons learned from the implementation are identified and the role of shared services for transforming government will be discussed. The research conducted in this chapter has an explorative-descriptive nature. We investigated a case study involving the introduction of an SSC and studied documentation, in this way creating a retrospective view on the decision process that should contribute to the understanding of such processes.

The structure of the chapter is as follows. In the following section we discuss the background of transformational government and how the concept of shared services fits into this. Section 3 presents the research approach, whereas in Section 4 our case study is introduced. In Section 5 the case study is further analyzed and discussed, and finally, in Section 6, conclusions are drawn.

2　BACKGROUND

2.1　Transforming Government in the Netherlands

In the Netherlands there have been many changes in the organization of the central government over the past decades. All of these changes can be characterized by participative approaches in which coalition of usually two or three political parties were in charge. In situations in which coalitions of different parties are in control, only incremental changes can be made. This change strategy is found in the very nature of the Dutch political and cultural landscape in which creating consensus is an important aspect. Driven by the financial crisis, the ambition of government is to lower government spending and to reduce the administrative burden for businesses and citizens. Therefore, the next challenge is to transform government. This vision was founded in the Whole-of-Government Approach in which an integral perspective on government was taken as a response to the fragmentation (Christensen & Lægreid, 2007). Three spearheads for this policy were defined to transform government (Donner, 2011):

1. Creating a government-wide infrastructure enabled by shared services;
2. Bundling supporting services driven by process harmonization and standardization;
3. Avoiding task duplication among execution and enforcement agencies.

2.2 Shared Services for Transforming Government

Shared services are an important strategy for creating WGA and in many countries the promising benefits of sharing services resulted in the establishment of SSCs. By unbundling services and then concentrating them in a semi-autonomous business unit, the basic premise for shared services is that services provided by one department can be provided to others with relatively few efforts (Bergeron, 2003). This could result in service quality improvements as well as cost reduction (Janssen & Joha, 2006). Public sector organizations act as service requesters, users, and share their role as service provider by joint development, operation, and control of a shared service center.

The choice for sharing services is a major decision having a long-term and strategic impact, which often competes with outsourcing arrangements (Janssen & Joha, 2006). Just as in outsourcing arrangements (Baldwin, Irani, & Love, 2001; Fowler & Jeffs, 1998; Hirschheim & Lacity, 2000), the intended benefits are not always met, and there are many factors affecting the decision making, as the different stakeholders have different resources, capabilities, needs, interests, and goals (Janssen et al., 2007).

3   RESEARCH APPROACH

Given the need to understand the development of SSC arrangements, a qualitative approach based on in-depth case study research was adopted for this research (Yin, 2003). Case study research is one of the most common qualitative methods used in information systems (IS) (Orlikowski & Baroudi, 1991) and particularly well-suited for IS as the focus is on understanding a system in an organizational context (Benbasat, Goldstein, & Mead, 1987). This research was primarily based on document collection and evaluation in a qualitative setting. There are many theories underpinning sourcing theory (Baldwin et al., 2001; Hirschheim & Lacity, 2000; Lee et al., 2003) and given that SSCs can be considered as a sourcing arrangement, we opted to use Baldwin et al.'s (2001) model to examine documents about P-Direkt and acquire a good understanding of the strategic, organizational, political, technical, and economic aspects as well as issues and problems faced during the SSC initiation and implementation process. This approach is consistent with guidelines for qualitative research suggested by researchers such as Miles and Huberman (1994) and Baskerville (1999). They propose the study of official publications, organizational records, documents, and reports to identify detailed descriptions of people's activities, behaviors, actions, and interactions within and around the organization. The analysis of documents regarding P-Direkt allowed the creation of a retrospective view of the decision and implementation process that contributed to the understanding of SSC arrangements.

4   CASE STUDY

Mid 2003, the Dutch government decided to combine the personnel registration and salary administration of different ministries and to automate procedures such that staff members could independently request leave or retrieve salary information (P-Direkt, 2002; 2003). By centralizing human resource management and giving staff a self-service function, the government hoped to save approximately 400 million euro by 2015. Figure 16.1 provides a simplified model of the HRM SSC that is called "P-Direkt."

The design and development of the ICT infrastructure of the SSC was contracted out to a third party, and in September 2004 a contract was signed with a consortium of two IT service providers for the development and maintenance of the IT infrastructure underlying the HRM solution. After not meeting different milestones and many discussions regarding the progress of the project, this contract was terminated in October 2005. At that moment, the project was stopped and the Minister was ordered to do an investigation into the failure of P-Direkt. He also expressed that the government wanted to continue with the project to achieve the initially estimated cost savings. After a year of investigations and redefining the project plans, P-Direkt was re-initiated in the beginning of 2007. Compared to the first implementation plans in 2004, changes were made regarding the scope, governance, and implementation strategy. Using an incremental growth model, P-Direkt was

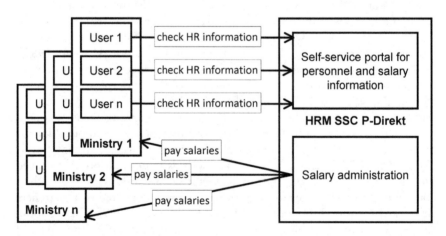

Figure 16.1   Simplified model of the HRM SSC P-Direkt with its customers.

able to become a mature SSC organization that is providing HRM services to almost the whole of the Dutch central government nowadays. Table 16.1 provides a chronological overview of the different stages of the SSC. We can differentiate two main phases of the P-Direkt case study:

1. Phase I—Initiation of P-Direkt and its initial failure.
2. Phase II—Re-design and re-initiation of P-Direkt.

These two phases will be used to further analyze and discuss the lessons learned in the next section.

Table 16.1   Chronological Timeline of the HRM SSC P-Direkt

Phase	Timeline	
I	2001 and 2002	Political discussions took place and reports have been written about changing the HRM system of the central government, by making it more efficient and effective in different ways, including the use of a SSC.
	January 2003	Political approval for renewing the HRM system of the central government, where the initial plans are mentioned for an HRM SSC.
	July 2003	Final green light for the realization of the HRM SSC that should be operational on the January 1, 2006.
	March 2004	The design, implementation, and maintenance of the ICT infrastructure will be outsourced to a third party and only two consortiums are bidding on this project. One of them decides to retreat as they consider the financial risks too high.
	September 2004	The only consortium left signs an outsourcing contract regarding the ICT infrastructure for the HRM SSC, which has now been renamed as P-Direkt.
	December 2004	The architectural design of the ICT infrastructure for P-Direkt is politically not approved, and it is decided that the implementation date of the SSC will have to be postponed to January 1, 2007.
	October 2005	When he architectural redesign that was completed by July 2005 was also not approved by the government, the consortium decides to retract itself from this process as no agreement could be made about the next steps.
	November 2005	The minister responsible for this project confirms that he wants to go forward with the SSC and demands an investigation into why the project failed.

(continued)

Table 16.1 (continued)

Phase	Timeline	
	2006	During this year, different investigations took place about the reasons for the failure of the SSC, the lessons learned and a redefinition of the project in terms of the scope, the services and the implementation strategy for the re-initiation of P-Direkt in 2007.
II	2007 and 2008	HR processes have been standardized and defined across most of the ministries. Also the governmental personal systems (payroll, portal) have been developed and implemented.
	2009	The contact center is built up, and the services for different ministries are implemented.
	2010 and 2011	The HR service level quality is maintained, and the services for the other ministries are implemented, providing the total HR service delivery to the majority of ministries.

Source: Lievense, 2005; P-Direkt, 2002; 2003; 2004a; 2004b; 2005a; 2005b; 2007; 2008; 2011.

5 ANALYSIS AND DISCUSSION

5.1 Phase I: Initiation of P-Direkt and Its Initial Failure

A key aspect of defining a new HRM system was to increase the efficiency and quality of the HR function of the different individual ministries by bundling these activities into one central entity that could provide HR services to the central government. The government therefore decided to implement an SSC to both benefit from economies of scale as well as increase the service quality, as scarce HR expertise could then be shared among the ministries. When the decision would have to be made, certain actions needed to have been completed. This was however not the case. The division of responsibilities was still insufficiently defined and moreover, no arrangements were made regarding the way P-Direkt would have to be managed during the period it would be operational. The business case was unclear and not convincing in terms of realizing the expected efficiency gains, reduction of personnel costs and of bureaucracy (P-Direkt, 2005b). Still, because of political pressure to quickly get results, the government decided to go ahead with the implementation.

In July 2003, there is final green light for the realization of the HRM SSC that should be operational on January 1, 2006. The scope of the HRM SSC would initially consist of the following activities: salary administration; personnel contract administration, annual and sick leave registration; other financial staff compensation, e.g. expenses and data about the department and internal organization (P-Direkt, 2003; 2004a; 2004b). It is decided that the design, implementation, and maintenance of the ICT infrastructure for the SSC will be outsourced to a third party and the most important reason to do so, was that the government wanted to use the market's best practices and common uniform standards. Moreover, the government wanted to have the third party pay for the design costs in exchange for a multi-year contract to maintain the system. It can be questioned whether this was a good strategy, as it created a significant dependency on an external party. After a European tender process, a consortium of two IT providers was selected and an outsourcing contract was signed. During the negotiations, it was decided that there was not enough time to define the product specifications and acceptance criteria and this would therefore all be done in a next phase, which was not a proper basis to start the realization phase (P-Direkt, 2005a; 2005b). Payment to the consortium was based on the realization of milestones, but given that there were no acceptance criteria defined for these milestones, the government was not able to take proper legal measures when the consortium did not meet their expectations. The contract did not take this aspect into account, and the signed contract was not reviewed by an independent third party law firm (P-Direkt, 2007). Some critical remarks by other third-party consultancy firms about the risks were ignored and in that regard the risk management and quality assurance processes were not properly part of a formal governance process.

The architectural design created by the consortium for the ICT infrastructure was not approved by the government on two consecutive occasions because it didn't meet their expectations, and the consortium decided to retract itself from this process as no agreement could be made about the next steps. The state was obliged to pay 20.8 million euro compensation, mainly for retaining the right to interim products, licenses, and documentation that could later still be used. At the end of 2005, the Minister responsible for this project confirmed that he still wanted to go forward with the SSC and demanded an investigation into why the project failed.

There were many lessons learned and a variety of shortcomings in the decision-making process. The strategy, the management and control on the part of the government were contributory factors in the failure of the tendering and implementation process. On a number of crucial occasions, decisions were taken under excessive time pressure, and as such the decision process did not meet the quality demands of the central government, also because insufficient account was taken of the criticism from different external experts about the management of the tendering process. Unsolved issues with the consortium were put off until a subsequent phase, including agreements about the expected performance and acceptance criteria by which this performance could be assessed (P-Direkt, 2007). Moreover, the information given about the progress of the SSC was often too optimistic. Working together with a private party consortium required a professional government commissioning practice, but this was not the case, and there was no adequate project management. There was insufficient quality assurance and risk management of the products or services and insufficient information provision to all the stakeholders involved. Moreover the expectations with respect to the timeline of the project and its milestones were not properly managed and not enough support was created among the most important internal and external stakeholders (P-Direkt, 2005b).

There were dependencies of P-Direkt with other HR projects that were managed outside the formal responsibility of P-Direkt, though they were important elements within the new HRM system. This implied that P-Direkt was not able to adjust certain aspects of their project but had to escalate this to the responsible people within the other projects. This layered project management approach was causing inefficiencies (P-Direkt, 2007). Moreover, because the dependencies with certain projects were critical and these projects were not able to meet their planning, the planning for P-Direkt regarding which services should be operational at a certain date also needed to be changed. Coordination requires good communication about the progress of each of the projects and the use of quality management tools, which was not the case. There was no unified overall vision of quality management, which therefore did not result in a consistent and coherent quality management process (P-Direkt, 2007). P-Direkt's cost savings were partially based on the assumption that the ministries did not have to have any HR activities anymore at all, but P-Direkt was not able to provide the ministries with the dates that they could discontinue their services and fully rely on the services provided by P-Direkt. The ministry of finance had already started their own HR project, and moreover, there was a far longer period where both P-Direkt as well as the individual ministries executed several complementary HR activities (Lievense, 2005). In Table 16.2, the lessons learned have been summarized using Baldwin et al.'s (2001) four dimensions.

Table 16.2   Lessons Learned from the P-Direkt Case Study

Dimension	*Lessons learned*
Strategic and organizational	• The (master) planning was too ambitious • Too many things were tried to be changed at the same time • Role of the project principal was too weak • Improve internal communication as the individual ministries were not able to keep up with the decision speed • Project management tools were either not available or still in development • Knowledge was too dependent on too many external people • Too many project leaders making it unclear who is responsible and accountable • The project management governance was not the same for the different individual sub-projects and for the different ministries • Either no clear responsibilities (and accountabilities) or the wrong responsibilities were assigned to different parties involved

(continued)

Table 16.2   (continued)

Dimension	Lessons learned
Strategic and organizational (continued)	• The HR department was not enough involved, and the project therefore lacked HR experts able to properly review the proposed ideas and solutions • Unclear governance model and no clear alignment between the strategic, tactical and operational levels across the different ministries • There was no experience with performance-based contracting • Division of responsibilities between the stakeholders involved was insufficiently defined • There was unclarity about the way the service delivery model and the way the services were going to be provided to the organization
Political	• Insufficient attention for the users and change management was given • No integral and consistent project management approach and methodology • Due to too much political pressure and ambition, reports were too optimistic and positive about the project benefits and the progress made during the project preparation phase • The third parties involved were not able to provide relevant input as the design choices were already made • Before any key project decision could be taken, a number of conditions had to be satisfied that the government had defined already in advance • Ensure an open relationship with the external service provider and enough countervailing power between all parties when using a performance-based contract. • More communicating about the relevance and necessity of the new project to the internal organization to get more understanding and support • Share relevant knowledge with third parties as these were not up to date about certain (legal) project requirements
Technical	• Overestimation of the possibilities of ICT • Consolidation and standardization efforts of the different ICT systems across the ministries had not taken place • Acceptance criteria, interfaces and technical standards were not clearly defined • Dogmatically trying to keep the scope the same as it was initially agreed on, resulting in less efficiently working processes when these are separated in an illogical and unnatural way
Economic	• The business case was ambiguous and not convincing • No regular check and update of the business case was performed • Unclarity about the funding model and the costs for the ministries • Bonus constructions need to part of a performance-based contract with a third party to ensure that the third party is incentivized to use innovative tools, methods and quality checks

5.2   Phase II: Redesign and Re-initiation of P-Direkt

Based on the lessons learned, a new project approach was defined (P-Direkt, 2008; 2011). An important change in the strategy was to have a more phased approach of the project using a growth model and a realistic planning. Three stages were defined, and in the first stage there was a focus on simplifying, digitalizing, and bundling the HRM activities within each of the individual ministries, with the main purpose to come to one ICT standard for the salary administration. Moreover, several ministries had to implement a self-service concept and helpdesks. The ministries themselves were responsible for the implementation and received support from P-Direkt. This first stage was planned to take 1 to 2 years, and this went according to plan. In 2008, twenty-six standard HRM-processes were defined for the central government, there was a self-service portal for the different ministries and a central digital personnel dossier service, and the civil servants of a number of ministries were getting paid via P-Direkt (Annual Report P-Direkt, 2007; 2008). At this stage the different ministries were able to choose out of different temporary scenarios to connect to P-Direkt, depending on how much progress they had made and what salary administration system they used.

The second stage started in 2009 and was to implement one HRM administration and contact center for all participating ministries. This included the physical migration of personnel to a limited number of SSC locations. The activities of P-Direkt were performed by four main departments, including a development department where services are developed and a services delivery systems department where the services are managed and maintained after development. Moreover there is a P-services department responsible

Table 16.3   Main Characteristics of the New Project Approach after the Re-initiation of P-Direkt

Dimension	Main characteristics of the new project plan and methodology
Strategic and organizational	• Using an incremental growth model and defining projects with few mutual dependencies • Realistic master planning • Better usage of existing HR knowledge, experience and people • Introducing uniform HR processes across all participating ministries • New governance model • Professional project and program management • Introducing an implementation of a support helpdesk
Political	• Attention for change management • Connecting to the demands of each of the different ministries
Technical	• Use of technical standards and interfaces, so that each ministry could connect to P-Direkt
Economic	• New funding model and clarity about who is paying what

for the non-automated services of P-Direkt that includes the helpdesk, and finally there is a department for simplifying and unifying processes, taking into account the legal and regulatory requirements (Annual Report P-Direkt, 2009; 2010). Table 16.3 provides the main characteristics of the new project plan and methodology (P-Direkt, 2008; 2011).

6 CONCLUSION

Shared service centers provide a solution for public sector organizations that lack resources and want to reduce costs and increase service levels at the same time. The implementation of a large-scale SSC with many different stakeholders is a complex transformation project. In this chapter we explored the largest Dutch governmental HR SSC addressing the whole government in the Netherlands that initially failed and only became successful after redefining the scope, governance, and implementation strategy. We identified the lessons learned from a organizational, strategic, political, economic, and technical perspective and also identified the main changes that have been made when the SSC was re-initiated.

Already before the decision was made to implement the SSC, a number of critical actions were not finalized. During the implementation phase itself, there were many lessons learned. These include a realistic master planning with few dependencies, strong change and project management with enough expert people and good communication toward all stakeholders, a governance structure with clear responsibilities for all parties and people involved, having a clearly defined services model and business case. When the shared service center P-Direkt was re-initiated in 2007, the new approach was characterized by significant strategic and organizational changes that include a more phased approach using an incremental growth model, fewer project dependencies, a realistic master planning, better use of existing HR knowledge, the introduction of uniform HR processes, professional project and program management, and a new governance model. Also, clarity about the funding model, attention for demand management, and the use of standards were important elements of this new approach. Even though big public sector IT projects can be done in different ways, certain basic project measures and mechanisms need to be put in place.

Because of the failure of P-Direkt, a lot of attention was given to avoid these failures in the future for such big IT projects. In the last years, most big ICT projects are regularly evaluated, and increasingly more standard project methods are used such as ITIL and PRINCE. Also, project leaders of big IT projects are sharing their experiences (P-Direkt, 2007). P-Direkt is the biggest SSC in the central government and is currently considered successful in terms of achieved cost savings and service quality. As such, it is a reference example for a public sector ICT project and increasingly more governmental SSCs are introduced. Given that P-Direkt required a lot of standardization, a lot of the ministries are currently using the same systems, and further IT integration can be expected beyond the HRM domain.

There has been scant attention given to the identification of failure factors for SSCs. This explorative research contributes to the limited body of research on large governmental HR SSCs available, and this analysis can be used by governments to support a decision-making and implementation process for such a large center. The factors can be extended in further research and can be used as a starting point for developing effective transformation strategies. Also comparisons with private sector projects and with case studies in other countries would be useful for generalization purposes.

REFERENCES

Annual Report P-Direkt (2007). Retrieved September 13, 2011, from http://www.p-direkt.nl/aspx/download.aspx?file=/contents/pages/99942/jaarver-slagp-direkt2007.pdf

Annual Report P-Direkt (2008). Retrieved September 13, 2011, from http://www.p-direkt.nl/aspx/download.aspx?file=/contents/pages/99940/p-direkt-jaarverslag2008.pdf

Annual Report P-Direkt (2009).Retrieved September 13, 2011, from http://www.p-direkt.nl/aspx/download.aspx?file=/contents/pages/105452/p-direktjaarver-slag2009_defvoorweb.pdf

Annual Report P-Direkt 2010 (2010). Retrieved September 13, 2011, from http://www.p-direkt.nl/aspx/download.aspx?file=/contents/pages/106126/jaarver-slagpdirektinteractief2010.pdf

Baldwin, L. P., Irani, Z., & Love, P. E. D. (2001). Outsourcing information systems: Drawing lessons from a banking case study. *European Journal of Information Systems, 10*(1), 15–24.

Baskerville, R. (1999). Investigating information systems with action research. *Communications of the AIS, 2*(19), 2–31.

Benbasat, I., Goldstein, D. K., & Mead, M. (1987). The case research strategy in studies of information systems. *MIS Quarterly, 11*(3), 369–386.

Bergeron, B. (2003). *Essentials of shared services.* John Wiley & Sons, Hoboken, New Jersey.

Christensen, T., & Lægreid, P. (2007). The whole-of-government approach to public sector reform. *Public Administration Review, 67*(6), 1059–1066.

Donner, J. P. H. (2011). *Uitvoeringsprogramma Compacte Rijksdienst: letter to the parliament.* Retrieved September 13, 2011, from http://www.rijksoverheid.nl/documenten-en-publicaties/jaarplannen/2011/02/14/uitvoeringsprogramma-compacte-rijksdienst.html

Fowler, A., & Jeffs, B. (1998). Examining information systems outsourcing: A case study from the United Kingdom. *Journal of Information Technology, 13*, 111–126.

Hirschheim, R., & Lacity, M. (2000). The myths and realities of information technology insourcing. *Communications of the ACM, 43*(2), 99–107.

Irani, Z., Love, P. E. D., & Jones, S. (2008). Learning lessons from evaluating eGovernment: Reflective case experiences that support transformational government. *The Journal of Strategic Information Systems, 17*(2), 155–164.

Janssen, M., & Joha, A. (2006). Motives for establishing shared service centers in public administrations. *International Journal of Information Management, 26*(2), 102–116.

Janssen, M., Joha A., & Weerakkody, V. (2007). Exploring relationships of shared service arrangements in local government. *Transforming Government: People, Process & Policy*, (TGPPP, ISSN 1750–6166), Vol.1, No. 3, pp. 271–284.

Lee, J. N., Huynh, M. Q., Kwok, R. C. W., & Pi, S. M. (2003). IT Outsourcing Evolution. Past, Present and Future. *Communications of the ACM, 46*(5), 84–89.

Lievense, P. (2005). P-Direkt: Wat er mis ging. *Digitaal Bestuur*, (2). Retrieved September 13, 2011, from http://peterlievense.nl/p-direkt-wat-er-mis-ging

Miles, M. B., & Huberman, A. M. (1994). *Qualitative Data Analysis*. Newbury Park, CA: Sage.

Orlikowski, W. J., & Baroudi, J. J. (1991). Studying information technology in organizations: Research approaches and assumptions. *Information Systems Research, 2*, 1–28.

P-Direkt (2002). Personeelsbrief 2003. Retrieved September 13, 2011, from https://zoek.officielebekendmakingen.nl/kst-28610–1.pdf.

P-Direkt (2003). Kabinetsbesluit tot oprichting van een Shared Service Center HRM voor Personeelsregistratie en Salarisadministratie (P&S). Retrieved September 13, 2011, from https://zoek.officielebekendmakingen.nl/kst-28610–2.pdf

P-Direkt. (2004a). Personeelsbrief 2003; Brief minister over shared service center (SSC) HRM. Retrieved September 13, 2011, from https://zoek.officielebekendmakingen.nl/kst-28610–5.pdf

P-Direkt. (2004b). Second opinion—Voortgangsrapportage SSC HRM. Retrieved September 13, 2011, from https://zoek.officielebekendmakingen.nl/kst-28610–5-b1.pdf

P-Direkt. (2005a). Brief minister met de tweede voortgangsrapportage over de oprichting van P-Direkt. Retrieved September 13, 2011, from https://zoek.officielebekendmakingen.nl/kst-28610–7.pdf

P-Direkt. (2005b). "Lessons Learned" P-Direkt: First opinion inzake verbeterpunten van 'de oprichting van P-Direkt'. Retrieved September 13, 2011, from www.sharedservicesbijdeoverheid.nl/resources/uploads/files/Lessons%2520Learned%2520P-Direkt.pdf.

P-Direkt. (2007). Aanbesteding ICT-component P-Direkt; Brief met rapport "Aanbesteding ICT-component P-Direkt." Retrieved September 13, 2011, from https://zoek.officielebekendmakingen.nl/kst-31027–1.pdf

P-Direkt. (2008). P-Direkt: nu en in de toekomst: Op weg naar een Shared Service Center HRM voor het Rijk. Retrieved September 13, 2011, from http://www.sharedservicesbijdeoverheid.nl/resources/uploads/files/toekomstvisiep-direkt.pdf

P-Direkt. (2011). Opbouw P-Direkt. Digitaal Bestuur Congres 2011. Retrieved September 13, 2011, from http://digitaalbestuurcongres.lynkx-01.nl/Uploads/Files/T04_20-_20Bronmans_26Boissevain_20-_20Les_201–10_20Opbouw_20P-Direkt.pdf

Weerakkody, V., & Dhillon, G. (2008). Moving from e-government to t-government: A study of process re-engineering challenges in a UK Local authority perspective. *International Journal of Electronic Government Research, 4*(4), 1–16.

Weerakkody, V., Janssen, M., & Dwivedi, Y. K. (2011). Transformational change and business process reengineering (BPR): Lessons from the British and Dutch public sector. *Government Information Quarterly, 28*(3), 320–328.

Yin, R. K. (2003). *Case study research: Design and methods* (3rd ed.). London: Sage Publications.

17 E-Strategic Management Lessons from Greece

Leonidas G. Anthopoulos, Dimitrios Triantafyllou, and Panos Fitsilis

CHAPTER OVERVIEW

E-government evolution follows strategic documents that define vision and mission statements for government transformation. These documents are generally called "e-strategies" and guide the investments on Information and Communications Technologies (ICT) at national and at supranational levels. Most e-strategies have closed their initial life-cycles, and they have been reengineered in order to achieve updated challenges such as improved and shared services, e-government adoption, and open and inclusive public administration. In Europe, the e-strategies have been defined centrally, trans-European projects have been launched, and Member States try to rearrange their national priorities in order to meet the European ones. Greek e-strategies concern an important European case that can show how e-strategic transformation is being evolved during the last decade. In this chapter the Greek e-strategies compared with means of effective strategic planning, and investigated in order for the reasons of the strategic updates to be recognized.

1 INTRODUCTION

Various e-strategies define the vision and the mission statements for e-government: U.S. "Expanding Government" (U.S. OMB, 2002) and "Open Government" (U.S. OMB, 2010; 2009); European "e-Europe" (Commission of the European Communities, 2000; 2001), "i2010" (Commission of the European Communities, 2005) and "Digital Agenda" (European Commission, 2010); British "Modernising Government" (U.K. Modernising Government Secretariat Cabinet Office, 1999) and "Transformational Government" (U.K. Cabinet Office, 2005); German "Bund Online" (German Federal Government, 2003) and "Deutschland Online" (ePractice, 2011); Australian "Government Online" (Australian Government, 2000); and Japanese "e-Japan" (Japanese Government, 2001) and "i-Japan 2015" (Japanese Government, 2009) are only some of the abovementioned strategic documents. These documents are called "e-strategies" and guide the investments on information and communications technologies (ICT) at national and at supranational levels. E-strategies have closed their initial life-cycles and have been reengineered in order to achieve updated challenges such as: improved and shared services, e-government adoption, open and inclusive public administration, etc.

In (Table 17.1) the vision and the mission statements of the above-mentioned e-strategies are summarized, and the Critical Success Factors (CSFs) that the political leaderships recognize are presented. Moreover, the updated strategic definition shows how governments realize and treat—with the ICT—challenges during the last decade.

Some important outcomes can be extracted from the above analysis (Anthopoulos, 2011): the priorities and the CSFs show that e-service delivery and infrastructure deployment were aimed during the first strategic versions. The updated e-strategies moved mainly to a service integration approach, while some adopted the "Open Government" principles.

Table 17.1 Analysis of Major E-Strategies

Strategy	Vision Statement	Mission Statement
USA—2002: Expanding Government	Citizen centered, results oriented and market based public administration	Supervisor: Office of Electronic Government CSFs: capital planning / investment control: Integrated Acquisition Environment (IAE), SmartBUY service integration: Federal Enterprise Architecture (FEA) information securityprivacy Accessibility: usa.gov
Update: 2009 Open Government Initiative	Update: transparency, participation, and collaborationCost: $71 billion/year	Update: best practices from the private sector; managerial methods: Open Government Directive, RIN public service transformation: Paper Reduction Act (PRA), customer satisfaction Government accountability: Federal IT Dashboard
UK—1999: Modernising Government	Improvement of citizens' and enterprises' everyday life via digital services, inclusive and integrated Government Cost: £1.7 billion	Supervisor: the Modernising Government Secretariat, Office of the e-Envoy, Cabinet Office CSFs: high quality and efficient public services: directgov.uk citizen-centered services Strategic policy making Joined up delivery of services: Government Secure Intranet (GSI) Interoperability: e-GIF Standardization: xGEA Enterprise Architecture

(continued)

Table 17.1   (continued)

Strategy	Vision Statement	Mission Statement
Update: 2007 Transformational Government Enabled by Technology	Update: accountability, economic productivity, social justice and public service reform, UK's leading role in Globalized Economy Updated Cost: £1.4 billion	Update: service design around citizens and businesses shared services managerial professionalism Public involvement Cost savings
2009: Digital Britain	Broadband universal access by 2012	Boost digital participation, Planning for investment to the next generation of broadband networks, direct access to public e-services.
Germany—2001: Bund Online 2005	Citizen-centered and open environment	Supervisor: Federal Ministry of Interior, IT Planning council (2010)
Update: 2006— Deutschland Online Update: 2007— Federal IT Strategy Update: 2009— Broadband Strategy of the Federal Government	Updated vision statement: inter-departmental service delivery and IT innovation's promotion	CSFs: Service digitization and availability Common components for payment transactions, data security, content and workflow management Central coordination for service transformation: SAGA Enterprise Architecture Fifteen (15) One For All (OFA) services Update: One-for-all (OFA) services Broadband diffusion Cross-agency service delivery
Europe—1998, 2003: e-Europe 2002, e-Europe+, e-Europe 2005	Knowledge based economy, capitalization of the ICT for better jobs and for quality public services	Supervisor: DG of the Information Society CSFs: Broadband diffusion, communication markets' deliberation ICT skills twenty (20) public services interoperable processes
Update: 2005 i2010 Update: 2010— Digital Agenda	Update: Common information space; Inclusive Information Society, ICT Innovation and Investment, effective, efficient, and transparent public administration, a flavor environment for communication between citizens and politicians, cross European services	Update: digital convergence, digital single market, interoperability and standardization, trust and security, ultra-fast networks, research and innovation digital literacy and social challenges, digital e-identity, e-authentication, rights management, open source software

(continued)

Table 17.1   (continued)

Strategy	Vision Statement	Mission Statement
Australia-2000: Government Online	Better services for citizens and enterprises	Supervisor: National Office for the Information Economy of the Australian Government (NOIE) CSFs: 400 digital services online Enterprise Architecture (AGA) Government-wide Intranet Electronic payments
Update: 2002: Better Services, Better Government	Update: e-Government for economic growth	Update: greater administrative efficiency, security and trust, responsive public services service integration participation
Japan-2001: e-Japan 2003: e-Japan II	"knowledge-emergent society" with ICT	Supervisor: Prime Minister Office, IT Strategy Headquarters CSFs: ultra-high-speed networks e-commerce service and information provision ICT literacy enterprise architecture program (2004)
Update: 2006— New IT Reform Strategy Update: 2009 i-Japan 2015	Update: Inclusive and Innovative Society	Update: citizen satisfaction e-local Government and standardization health and environmental challenges aging society 50 percent of form applications by 2010 Elimination of paper certificates by 2020 multi-channel and via three-"mouse clicks" services Government offices e-PO box Digital ID

However, although e-strategies seem to migrate from "service digitization" to "service transformation" and governments from "modern" to "accountable," there is no clear strategic management method that shows how this evolution is controlled. In this context, this chapter seeks for a strategic management model that can be applied on e-strategies either at an ex-post level, so that managers can determine the next steps for "e-evolution." In this context, an indicative strategic management method that is based on the strategic life-cycle is suggested, and it was applied on the Greek e-strategies in order for the reasons that lead to the selective updates to be recognized and to be evaluated. The Greek e-strategies can be considered representative European cases, where governments had to deal with both the national requirements and with the European goals such as the Lisbon's (European Council, 2000).

In the background section (Section 2) of this chapter, some useful strategic management methods and tools are presented, and a strategic management model is composed. In Section 3 this model is applied on the three Greek e-strategies in order for the updated versions to be compared and for the reasons that lie behind these updates to be realized.

2   BACKGROUND

Various strategic analysis methods such as the strategy map (Barrows & Frigo, 2008), the strategic life-cycle (Lysons & Farrington, 2006) and the balanced scorecard (Creamer & Freund, 2010; Huang, 2009; Kaplan & Norton, 1996) can be used for realizing, communicating, and visualizing a strategic plan and for strategic decision making. The strategic life cycle analyses a strategic implementation in the following phases (Figure 17.1): (a) analysis, (b) synthesis, (c) evaluation, (d) implementation, (e) control, and (f) review.

2.1   The Analysis Phase

This phase defines the CSFs according to both the external and the internal environments. Three alternative methods (David, 2011) can provide with data the strategic analysis: the External Factors Evaluation (EFE) Matrix, the Internal Factors Evaluation (IFE) Matrix and the Competitive Profile Matrix (CPM). These three tables contain internal and external CSFs that are obtained according to systematic investigation performed by the organization.

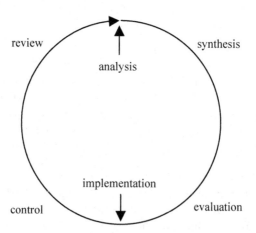

Figure 17.1   The strategic life-cycle.

The EFE matrix stores the external factors together with their significance. Demographic, environmental, financial, political, and legal could be some of these factors, whereas some concern chances and others threats. Initially, the identification and the classification of the factors to threats or chances are performed, and then weight values from 0 to 1 are assigned to them. The weight values reflect the significance of each factor, whereas the total sum of these values equals to 1. Later, each factor is characterized with an index value from 1 to 4. The weighted result for each value varies from 4 to 1, whereas the value of 2.5 is the baseline that reflects the organization's strength or weakness.

The selection of the appropriate strategy is usually based on intuition and/or on numerical analysis. The IFE matrix aims to close the gap between intuition and analysis (Mintzberg, 1994) with values subjectively defined by the strategic team. The IFE matrix follows the same implementation procedure with the EFE matrix.

The construction of the CPM finalizes the analysis phase. This matrix presents the strengths and weaknesses of an examined strategy compared to other strategies. The comparison is based on CSFs, which are evaluated with values from 1 to 4. The weighted results give the final ranking (David, 2011).

2.2 The Synthesis Phase

Under this phase both the vision and the mission statements are identified with the use of alternative methods such as (a) the Porter's Five Forces model (1996), (b) the Marketing Mix 7p's (Ivy, 2008; Rafiq & Ahmed, 1996), and (c) the strategy map (Kaplan& Norton, 1996).

In Porter's (1996) model, five forces define the organization's strategy together with its attractiveness and its profitability: (a) the threat of the entry of new competitors; (b) the threat of substitute products or services; (c) the bargaining power of customers (buyers); (d) the bargaining power of suppliers; and (e) the intensity of competitive rivalry. From these forces, only (b) and (c) comply with the e-strategic characteristics, since substitute products do not exist, while the supplier is the government that has no competitors.

The Marketing Mix 7p's (product, price, place, promotion, physical evidence, people-participants, process) is based on marketing theory and refers to the strategic, tactical and implementation's planning (Ivy, 2008; Rafiq & Ahmed, 1996). However, this method is difficult to comply with the e-strategic characteristics.

The strategy map (Kaplan & Norton, 1996) is a diagram—part of the Balanced Scorecard—that reflects the produced value process of an organization, and it is constructed with the assign of the strategic objectives to cause and effect. The strategy map can support the visualization and the communication of a strategic plan and consists of four pillars: (a) financial, (b) customer, (c) internal business process, and (d) learning and growth. This method was applied in the examined Greek case.

2.3   The Evaluation Phase

The evaluation process compares the strategic results to the strategic objectives (Nag, Hambrick, & Chen, 2007). The strategic evaluation consists of the ex-ante, the intermediate, the updated intermediate and the ex-post procedures. The ex-ante evaluation is based on estimates and on suggestions; it is performed on political and program planning, and it measures the applicability and effectiveness of the plan, the availability of resources, and the implementation's monitoring according to predefined directives. The intermediate evaluation analyses the ex-ante results and provides strategic updates, which compose the updated intermediate evaluation process. Finally, the ex-post evaluation measures the final results and the strategic impacts and has to be performed not later than 3 years from the strategic completion.

2.4   The Implementation Phase

The implementation phase concerns the set of actions that makes the strategic plan a reality (Nag et al., 2007). It can be considered a process that consists of the communication management between the stakeholders of the plan, the objectives' determination and review, the assignment of duties to the responsible parties, staff training, organizational transformations, and the continuous monitoring of the entire procedure (Lysons & Farrington, 2006).

3   A STRATEGIC ANALYSIS OF THE GREEK CASE

The Greek Government signed the eEurope strategy and developed its plan for the Information Society by 1998. The resulted e-strategy was called the "Information Society Framework Programme" (www.infosoc.gr), and it was supervised by the Special Secretariat for the Information Society located at the Ministry of Finance giving a clear directive that the national strategy had to align properly to the European obligations for funding. This initial e-strategy was funded with €1,150 million, and it mainly focused on infrastructure installation and to large-scale information systems. More than 4,000 projects were implemented under the first Greek e-strategy.

The second Greek e-strategy was initiated by 2005, it was called "Digital Convergence" and it was aligned to i2010 European strategy. This strategy, funded with €900 million about 2,000 projects, focused on social cohesion and on regional development and delivered significant outcomes such as the Greek e-Government portal (Ermis) and the Greek interoperability framework (e-GIF). This second e-strategy was updated by 2010 according to the Digital Agenda's and to U.S. Open Government's visions. This third Greek e-strategy (www.digitalplan.gov.gr) has not changed title from its predecessor; it has not started its implementation yet, for the purposes of this chapter it will be called "Digital Convergence II."

Each of the above strategic plans was analyzed in pillars, called "measures" in the Information Society, "fiber actions" in the Digital Convergence, and "horizontal interventions" in Digital Convergence II. Each pillar focuses on specific European challenges and objectives.

In this chapter a strategic review of the three Greek e-Strategies is being performed in order to document a suitable strategic management model, and to visualize Greek strategic development. In this context, official data from the Greek Special Secretariat for the Information Society websites has been used (http://www.infosoc.gr and http://www.digitalplan.gov.gr), which provided with strategic vision, with objectives, with budget allocation on pillars and projects, with projects' definition and with implementation timeframes. Published data concern e-strategic progress monitoring since 1999 and was collected on summer 2011. The introduced strategic management model consists of the tools and methods from the strategic life cycle, which were presented in the previous section.

3.1   The Analysis Phase

The performed analysis of the external environment in Greece supported the realization of the trends that affect the e-strategic planning and of the CSFs, whereas the investigation of the internal environment lead to the recognition of the untapped opportunities and of the hidden threats. Additionally, a comparison between the three Greek e-strategies was established, in terms of better recognition of the internal and external factors, as well as of efficiency in serving national vision. Besides, the primary objectives of strategic management concern (a) the capitalization of external and internal opportunities and (b) the avoidance or the minimization of weaknesses.

The external and the internal factors that influence the Greek e-Strategies were initially defined in order to structure and calculate the EFE (Table 17.2), the IFE (Table 17.3), and the CPM (Table 17.4) matrixes for the three e-strategies. Greek strategies recognize the European threats and opportunities and combine them with the national environment in order to define their visions and missions: For instance, the aging challenge (European Commission, 2009) concerns a threat, whereas globalization (Laudon & Laudon, 2002) and economic growth (Drucker, 1985; Porter, 2002) concern opportunities. The calculation of the weights that were assigned to each factor was based on the following simple formula:

$$W = \frac{x}{p} + \frac{Tx}{T}$$

where

> W represents the resulted weight;
> x, the number of projects that concern this factor;
> p, the total number of projects that ran under the strategy;
> T_x, the budget of the x projects;
> T, the total budget of the p projects.

The calculation of the factors of the Tables 17.2, 17.3, and 17.4 was based on the allocated funding to the corresponding strategic pillars. Data for the calculations was collected from the strategic annual reports (http://www.infosoc.gr/infosoc/el-GR/epktp/proodos_ylopoiisis).

Table 17.2　The EFE Matrix for the Greek Strategies

External Factors	Information Society			Digital Convergence			Digital Convergence II		
Opportunities	Weight	Rating	Results	Weight	Rating	Results	Weight	Rating	Results
Globalization	0,23	4	0,92	0,22	4	0,88	0,022	4	0,088
National Economic Growth	0,22	4	0,88	0,033	3	0,099	0	3	0
Supranational Economic Growth	0,018	3	0,054	0,04	3	0,12	0	4	0
European transactions	0,043	1	0,043	0,38	2	0,76	0,16	3	0,48
Schengen's membership	0,15	2	0,3	0,02	4	0,08	0,4	4	1,6
Participation in Internet Governance	0,018	3	0,054	0,041	4	0,164	0	4	0
Threats									
Aging	0,003	2	0,006	0,003	3	0,009	0	2	0
Rising Asia	0	4	0	0,022	4	0,088	0	4	0
High levels of poverty	0	4	0	0	3	0	0	3	0
Lack in natural resources	0,02	1	0,02	0,036	2	0,072	0	1	0
Economic and political stability	0,018	4	0,072	0,022	3	0,066	0	2	0
Currency outflow due to e-Commerce	0,19	1	0,19	0,033	1	0,033	0,4	1	0,4
Technological inflow	0,09	1	0,09	0,15	1	0,15	0,018	1	0,018
Scores: Lower=1, Below Average=2, Over Average=3, Highest=4									
Total	1		2,629	1		2,521	1		2,586

Table 17.3 The IFE Matrix for the Greek Strategies

Internal Factors	Information Society			Digital Convergence			Digital Convergence II		
Opportunities	Weight	Rating	Results	Weight	Rating	Results	Weight	Rating	Results
Training activities	0,11	4	0,44	0,068	3	0,204	0,016	3	0,048
Popularity	0,009	1	0,009	0,017	1	0,017	0	2	0
ICT contribution to national growth	0,068	3	0,204	0,02	3	0,06	0,028	3	0,084
Telecommunications' costs reduction	0,06	3	0,18	0,067	3	0,201	0	4	0
Market liberation	0,2	3	0,6	0,118	3	0,354	0,46	3	1,38
ICT industry's growth	0,1	1	0,1	0,041	2	0,082	0	3	0
Income from e-Commerce sales	0,24	3	0,72	0,48	3	1,44	0,41	3	1,23
Weaknesses									
Weberian administration structure	0,041	1	0,041	0,023	1	0,023	0,02	1	0,02
Organizational change	0,1	1	0,1	0,06	1	0,06	0,02	1	0,02
Digital skills held by the civil servants	0,044	2	0,088	0,034	2	0,068	0,016	2	0,032
national contribution (25 percent of strategic funding)	0,004	4	0,016	0	4	0	0	4	0
Legal framework adjustment	0,008	3	0,024	0,01	2	0,02	0,006	1	0,006
Complex public procurement system	0,008	1	0,008	0,032	1	0,032	0	1	0
Public Corruption	0,008	1	0,008	0,03	1	0,03	0,024	1	0,024

Scores: Lower=1, Below Average=2, Over Average=3, Highest=4

Total	1		2,538	1		2,591	1		2,844

Table 17.4   The CPM for the Greek Cases

Critical Success Factors	Information Society			Digital Convergence			Digital Convergence II		
	Weight	*Rating*	*Results*	*Weight*	*Rating*	*Results*	*Weight*	*Rating*	*Results*
Citizen and supplier demand	0,24	1	0,24	0,48	2	0,96	0,22	2	0,44
National political willing	0,125	4	0,5	0,14	4	0,56	0,24	4	0,96
Objectives' determination	0,125	4	0,5	0,14	3	0,42	0,24	4	0,96
Managerial efficiency	0,041	3	0,123	0,023	4	0,092	0,0137	4	0,0548
Organizational change	0,11	1	0,11	0,0684	2	0,1368	0,01	4	0,04
Effective planning	0,041	3	0,123	0,0232	3	0,0696	0,0147	4	0,0588
Skills and knowledge	0,114	3	0,345	0,0559	4	0,2236	0,0226	4	0,0904
ICT infrastructure	0,204	4	0,816	0,0695	2	0,139	0,239	1	0,239
Scores: Lower=1, Below Average=2, Over Average=3, Highest=4									
Total	1		2,754	1		2,601	1		2,843

The above results confirm the strong alignment of the Greek e-strategies to the European ones. The first e-strategy scores highest on the EFE matrix since it aligned fully to the European directives. On the other hand, the Information Society's low performance on the IFE and the CPM matrixes could be interpreted as low penetration and adoption of the strategic outcomes. The IFE and the CPM matrixes rank best for the Digital Convergence II; these calculations were based on hypothetical values, since strategic objectives and budget assignments have not yet been determined. Furthermore, the Information Society performs worse at both the IFE matrix and the CPM since it did not succeed in its targets, while many of its projects shifted to the Digital Convergence strategy.

3.2   The Synthesis Phase

The strategy map visualizes the synthesis of the Greek strategies. Authors studied the strategic documents and extracted the vision and the objectives, and assigned priorities and actions to the respective pillars (Figures 17.2, 17.3, and 17.4).

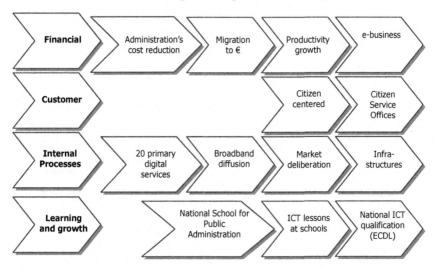

Figure 17.2 The strategy map of the Greek Information Society.

Information Society's strategic priorities were mostly financial due to the national priority of joining the Euro Group, while its internal processes concerned mostly the ICT market deliberation. The Information Society paid significant attention on training activities and on ICT skills' profiling, but t did not support customer-oriented objectives.

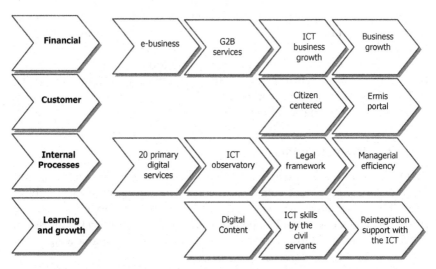

Figure 17.3 The strategy map of the Digital Convergence.

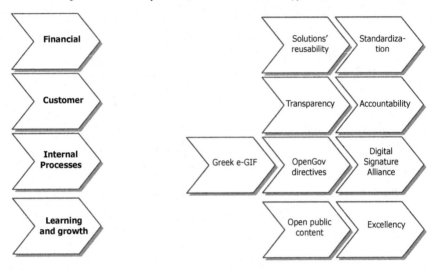

Figure 17.4   The strategy map of the Digital Convergence II.

The Digital Convergence supported strongly the development of the national ICT industry and delivered customer-oriented outcomes such as the Greek one-stop government portal (Ermis). Moreover, iznternal re-organization was supported with legal framework's adjustment and with managerial efficiency by the project organizations. Learning activities were weakened and mostly concerned digital content production.

Finally, the Digital Convergence II makes a strong transition to the open government directives. Accountability has been obtained with the publication of public spending (www.diavgeia.gov.gr), whereas transparency is supported with projects such as the Urban Planning e-Service and with public consultation of all political and administrative decisions (www.opengov.gr). Moreover, this recent e-strategy pays attention to standardization via the Greek e-GIF and with the determination of minimum standards for the ICT systems and e-services. Internal processes' transformation and integration are still bellow national expectations.

3.3   The Evaluation Phase

The Greek Information Society Observatory (www.observatory.gr) measures projects' deliverables and compares them to the European strategic objectives. The Observatory follows multi-criteria evaluation models defined by the European Development Cooperation Directorate (European Commission, 2005). Authors used Observatory's reports and delivered the following:

- Ex-post evaluation of the Information Society shows a prioritization on education, training, and employment, and 37 percent success to e-Government objectives.

- Intermediate evaluation of the Digital Convergence (Information Society Special Secretariat, 2010) returns difficulties in e-service deployment and high operational costs, due to ICT national market's inefficiencies. Strategic spending is poor after a 3-year period due to insufficient project planning and to complexities of the national procurement system. Ex-post analysis is not available since it requires a 3-year period after completion.

Authors also performed ex-ante evaluations according to the European Quality Grid (European Commission, 2006), which show that the Information Society performed satisfactorily, whereas political and managerial inefficiencies caused projects' progress to be and a shift to the Digital Convergence. The Digital Convergence had quite a clear strategic vision, and its integrity was inelastic against external threats due to accurate strategic objectives and to the inherited experience from the previous strategy.

Finally, the Digital Convergence II does not recognize the financial crisis although the European Digital Agenda—to which it aligns—does. Since 2009, the international fiscal crisis has revealed chronic problems of the Greek economy and of the public sector; however, a number of initiatives that aim to transform public Administration have been undertaken, such as (a) accountability (diavgeia.gr), (b) electronic prescriptions, (c) new tax processing system (TAXIS), (d) use of the European Public Procurement System (PEPPOL), and (d) the adoption of receipt citizen smart card for purchases. Despite measures and initiatives the national debt rose further.

3.4 The Implementation Phase

The implementation of the Greek e-strategies (Anthopoulos, Gerogiannis, & Fitsilis, 2010) and the major strategic deliverables were presented in Section 2.2. The strategic organization was complex and consisted of various stakeholders whose duties were overlapped: (a) the Special Secretariat for the Information Society had to provide with directives and obligations the Ministers; (b) the General Secretariat for Information Systems of the Ministry of Finance was responsible for tax based services; (c) the General Secretariat for e-Government of the Ministry of Interior was responsible for administrative services; and (d) the General Secretary for Telecommunications was responsible for ICT market deliberation. This authorization's overlap was accompanied by a complex procurement system and with difficulties in contributing 25 percent to national funding and lead to significant implementation delays. In order to visualize projects and budget distribution during strategic implementation, fifteen major ICT projects (Table 17.5) of a total funding of €658 million were investigated and presented on (Figure 17.5), showing huge differentiation in e-strategic performance, with best ranking by the years of 1999, 2006 and 2010.

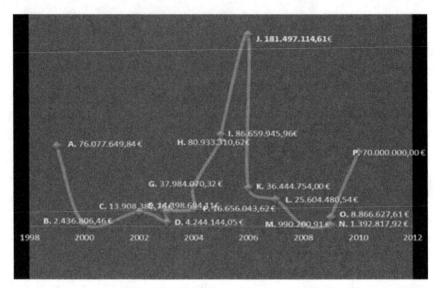

Figure 17.5   Spending distribution during e-strategic implementation.

Table 17.5   Major Large-Scale Projects Funded by the Greek E-Strategies

	Completion	Title	Client	Budget (€)
A	1999	ARIADNE	Ministry of Interior	76.077.649,84
B	2000	ULESSE (ODYSSEAS)	Ministry of Education	2.436.806,46
C	2002	«TAXIS-NET»	Ministry of Finance	13.908.382,76
D	2003	DIGITAL URBAN PLANNING	Ministry for Urban Planning	4.244.144,05
E	2003	e-Meteo	Ministry of Transportation	14.398.694,11
f	2004	e-BUSINESS	Ministry of Education	16.656.043,62
G	2004	ICT FOR BUSINESSES (A)	Ministry of Commerce	37.984.070,32
H	2005	ICT FOR BUSINESSES (B)	Ministry of Commerce	80.933.310,62
I	2005	SYZEFXIS	Ministry of Interior	86.659.945,96
J	2006	e-BUSINESS	Ministry of Commerce	181.497.114,61
K	2006	«BROADBAND SERVICES»	Ministry of Transportation	36.444.754,00
L	2007	«POLICE ONLINE»	Ministry of Social Security	25.604.480,54
M	2008	«e-GIF»	Ministry of Interior	990.200,91
N	2009	«e-SCHOOL»	Ministry of Education	1.392.817,92
O	2009	ERMIS	Ministry of Interior	8.866.627,61
P	2010	«JEREMIE»	Ministry of Finance	70.000.000,00

4 CONCLUSION

E-strategic transformation is being observed during the last decade in all major cases around the world. E-strategies declare vision and mission statements, together with priorities and objectives. In this chapter the Greek e-strategies were approached with a strategic management model in order to recognize the strategic change. The applied model uses known methods and can extract useful outcomes for the strategic transformation. The application of the presented model discovered the strengths and weaknesses for the examined Greek strategies and showed both reasonable and mistaken strategic updates. These findings can be used in future e-strategic updates in order to create a smooth transition path between previous and future objectives.

REFERENCES

Anthopoulos, L. (2011). An investigative assessment of the role of enterprise architecture in realizing e-government transformation. In P. Saha (Ed.), *enterprise architecture and connected e-government: practices and innovations.* IGI Global.

Anthopoulos, L. G., Gerogiannis, V. C., & Fitsilis, P. (2010). Measuring e-government adoption by governments: the Greek case. In *Comparative e-government, integrated series in information systems* (vol. 25, pt. 2, pp. 353–370). Springer Science & Business Media.

Australian Government. (2000). *Government Online.* Retrieved January 2011 from http://www.agimo.gov.au/archive/publications_noie/2000/04/govonline.html

Barrows, E. A., & Frigo, M. L. (2008). Using the strategy map for competitor analysis. *Harvard Business Review,* July 15, 2008. Retrieved August 2011 from http://hbr.org/product/using-the-strategy-map-for-competitor-analysis/an/B0807E-PDF-ENG

Commission of the European Communities. (2000). *eEurope 2002 Update.* Retrieved December 2010 from http://eur-lex.europa.eu/LexUriServ/LexUriServ.do?uri=COM:2000:0783:FIN:EN:PDF

Commission of the European Communities (2001). *eEurope+ 2003: A co-operative effort to implement the Information Society in Europe.* Retrieved, December 2010, from http://ec.europa.eu/information_society/eeurope/i2010/docs/2002/action_plan/eeurope_2003.pdf

Commission of the European Communities. (2002). *eEurope 2005: An information society for all.* European Commission—COM 263, 2002. Retrieved December 2010 from http://eur-lex.europa.eu/LexUriServ/LexUriServ.do?uri=COM:2002:0263:FIN:EN:PDF

Commission of the European Communities. (2005). *i2010—A European Information Society for growth and employment.* Retrieved December 2010 from http://ec.europa.eu/information_society/eeurope/i2010/key_documents/index_en.htm

Creamer, G., & Freund, Y. (2010). Learning a board balanced scorecard to improve corporate performance. *Decision Support Systems, 49,* 365–385.

David, R. F. (2011). *Strategic management (concepts and cases),* Global Edition (13th ed.). Pearson Higher Education.

Drucker, F. P. (1985). *Innovation and entrepreneurship: Practice and principles.* New York: Harper & Row.

ePractice.eu (2011). *eGovernment Factsheet—Germany—Strategy.* Retrieved, May 2011 from http://www.epractice.eu/en/document/288242

European Commission. (2005). *Guidelines of project/programme evaluations.* Retrieved September 2011 from http://ec.europa.eu/europeaid/evaluation/methodology/egeval/guidelines/gba_en.htm

European Commission. (2006). *Indicative guidelines on evaluation methods: ex ante evaluation.* Retrieved September 2011 from: http://ec.europa.eu/regional_policy/sources/docoffic/2007/working/wd1_exante_en.pdf

European Commission. (2009). *2009 ageing report: Economic and budgetary projections for the EU-27 member states (2008–2060).* Retrieved September 2009 from http://ec.europa.eu/economy_finance/publications/publication14992_en.pdf

European Commission. (2010). *A digital agenda for Europe.* Retrieved January 2011 from http://eur-lex.europa.eu/LexUriServ/LexUriServ.do?uri=COM:2010:0245:FIN:EN:PDF

European Council (2000). *Lisbon European Council 23 and 24 March 2000: Presidency conclusions.* Retrieved September 2011 from http://www.europarl.europa.eu/summits/lis1_en.htm

German Federal Government. (2003). *BundOnline 2005. 2003 implementation plan.* Retrieved September 2011 from http://www.bunde.de

Huang H. C. (2009). Designing a knowledge-based system for strategic planning: A balanced scorecard perspective. *Expert Systems with Applications, 36*, 209–218.

Information Society Special Secretariat. (2010). *Intermediate evaluation report of the digital convergence* [in Greek]. Retrieved September 2011 from http://www.opengov.gr/ypoian/?p=429

Ivy, J. (2008). A new higher education marketing mix: The 7Ps for MBA marketing. *International Journal of Educational Management, 22*(4), 288–299.

Japanese Government. (2001). *e-Japan Strategy.* Retrieved January 2011 from http://www.kantei.go.jp/foreign/it/network/0122full_e.html

Japanese Government. (2009). *i-Japan Strategy 2015.* Retrieved January 2011 from http://www.kantei.go.jp/foreign/policy/it/i-JapanStrategy2015_full.pdf

Kaplan, S. R., & Norton, P. D. (1996). Translating strategy into action. The balanced scorecard. *Library of Congress Cataloging-in-Publication Data,* pp. 8–12, 30–32.

Laudon, K., & Laudon, J. (2002). management information systems: Managing the digital firm (7th ed.). Prentice Hall, New Jersey, USA.

Lysons, K., & Farrington, B. (2006). *Purchasing and supply chain management,* Chapter 2. Prentice Hall, Harlow, England.

Mintzberg, H. (1994). *The rise and fall of strategic planning.* Prentice Hall.

Nag, R., Hambrick, D. C., & Chen, M.-J. (2007). What is strategic management, really? Inductive derivation of a consensus definition of the field. *Strategic Management Journal, 28*(9), 935–955.

Porter, M. (2002). *Building the microeconomic foundations of prosperity: Findings from the business competitiveness index from the global competitiveness report 2002–2003.* Retrieved September 2011 from http://courses.wcupa.edu/rbove/eco343/030compecon/gen-eral%20compar/030900compet3.pdf

Porter, M. (1996). What is strategy?. *Harvard Business Review* [online]. Retrieved September 2011 from http://www.ipocongress.ru/download/guide/article/what_is_strategy.pdf

Rafiq, M., & Ahmed, K. P. (1995). Using the 7Ps as a generic marketing mix: An exploratory survey of UK and European marketing academics. *Marketing Intelligence & Planning, 13*(9), 4–15.

U.K. Cabinet Office. (2005). *Transformational government enabled by technology.* Retrieved September 2010 from http://archive.cabinetoffice.gov.uk/e-government/strategy/

U.K. Digital Britain Final Report. (2009). Building Britain's future. Retrieved January 2012 from http://www.official-documents.gov.uk/document/cm76/7650/7650.pdf

U.K. Modernising Government Secretariat Cabinet Office. (1999). *Modernising government.* Retrieved August 2010 from www.nationalschool.gov.uk/policy-hub/docs/modgov.pdf

U.S. Office of Management and Budget (OMB) (2002). e-Government Strategy: Simplified Delivery of Services to Citizens. Retrieved, August 2010 from http://www.usa.gov/Topics/Includes/Reference/egov_strategy.pdf

U.S. Office of Management and Budget (OMB). (2009). *Open Government Directive. Memorandum for the Heads of Executive Departments and Agencies.* Retrieved December 2010 from http://www.whitehouse.gov/omb/assets/memoranda_2010/m10–06.pdf

U.S. Office of Management and Budget (OMB). (2010). *Memorandum for Chief Acquisition Officers and Chief Information Officers: Improving the Accessibility of Government Information.* Retrieved August 2010 from http://www.cio.gov/documents_details.cfm/uid/EC4F5AF8–5056–8F64–36567BC324976D2A/structure/Laws,%20Regulations,%20and%20Guidance/category/Accessibility

18 State Response to Obama's Broadband Access Policy
A Study in Policy Implementation

Ramona McNeal

CHAPTER OVERVIEW

The focus of the Obama administration's policy for addressing Internet inequalities within the United States places an emphasis on addressing infrastructure barriers to residential areas. Under the American Recovery and Reinvestment Act of 2009, grants and loans have been provided to states and local governments to extend high-speed broadband access to rural areas that have not been served by existing broadband providers. The response by the states to these programs has varied significantly. Some states have not followed up on these monies while others have used these programs as an opportunity to encourage local communities to pursue government ownership of broadband facilities or to finance the construction of infrastructure necessary for broadband services. This chapter explores factors that influence state-level response. Implementation theory suggests many factors may influence the extent that the policy is carried out including attitudes of the implementers towards the law, public opinion and state resources. Multivariate logistic regression analysis of fifty state data is used to test rival explanations for state response as of December 2010. Goggin et al.'s (1990) Communications Model is utilized in order to control for the influence of the federal government in this policy area.

1 INTRODUCTION

Electronic government or e-government, which refers "to the delivery of information and services via the Internet or other digital means" (West, 2004, p. 2), has been a force in public administration for roughly 20 years. The public sector has increasingly gone online to provide information, deliver services, and interact with citizens, businesses, and other government agencies (McNeal, Hale & Dotterweich, 2008). In the United States the move to adopt e-government practices at all levels of government began at the urging of the Clinton administration. At the time, numerous benefits were predicted including the reduction of government costs and increased efficiency (Pardo, 2000; Norris, 2001).

Although e-government came with many promises, implementation of these practices faced numerous barriers. One crucial hurdle was that it necessitated that citizens have Internet access. Bringing everyone online would not be an easy task. Even though Americans have been increasingly going online, inequalities in usage still persist. The latest National Tele-communication and Information Administration (NTIA) study (2010, pp. 3) finds that 30 percent of all U.S. citizens still do not have access to the Internet, whereas 40 percent do not have broadband access at home. Those individuals without Internet access are primarily elderly, less-affluent, less-educated, minorities and those who live in rural areas.

One barrier to Internet access that has proven particularly difficult to conquer is geography. Individuals who live in rural areas face unique chal-lenges to gaining online access. Early research (Stover, 1999) found that Internet access in rural areas was hampered by limited choices of service providers and connection fees that are considerably higher than in urban/suburban areas. The underlying cause is low levels of commercial invest-ment for basic telecommunication infrastructure. Telephone and other tele-communication service providers have little incentive to invest in sparsely populated rural areas. Additionally, Nicholas (2003) found that government policy aggravated the rural/urban divide. State government officials often ignored federal policy encouraging competition among telecommunication service providers. Instead, some state policies protected the monopolies of rural telephone companies and discouraged competition.

Among the competition discouraged by state laws has been municipal owned broadband service. Some local and regional governments have tried to expand Internet access through providing communication services them-selves. As of 2009, there were 85 local and regional governments providing broadband service (Fiber-to-the-Home Council, 2009). Incumbent tele-communication service providers have lobbied state legislatures to outlaw this practice with some success. By January 2011, 18 states have passed laws that either restrict or prohibit municipal owned broadband service (Baller Herbst Law Group, 2011).

Although some state policies have increased the access divide between rural and suburban/urban areas, others are lessening disparities. Exam-ples include the NOANet in the Pacific Northwest and One Community in Ohio which are state-sponsored programs that help reduce the cost of providing Internet service by allowing providers to patch into exist-ing infrastructure that was created for government needs "backhaul capacity" (Federal Communication Commission, 2010). Recently, the Obama administration has attempted to encourage actions to increase Internet access in rural areas through the American Recovery and Rein-vestment Act. Under this act, grants and loans have been provided to states and local governments to extend high-speed broadband access to underserved rural areas (Recovery Accountability and Transparency Board, 2010).

The implementation of this policy depends on the cooperation of state and local governments. The response of the states has varied from creating administrative boards necessary to receive federal monies to building state-owned utilities that will provide broadband Internet service. One factor that might be influencing state response is the action of interest groups within the state. Historical patterns show that telecommunication service providers have been successful in limiting both the expansion of municipal own broadband service and promotion of competition among service providers in rural areas. The goal of this research is to determine whether states (perhaps under pressure from interest within the state) will continue on their current policy paths with regard to this policy area or are they altering their strategies following the passage of the American Recovery and Reinvestment Act? This chapter explores this topic starting with a general discussion of federal policies within the United States aimed at increasing Internet usage.

2   FEDERAL INTERNET ACCESS POLICY

Federal Internet policy began under the Clinton administration which adopted policies expressly designed to increase Internet access by providing public access through schools, libraries and community technical centers (CTCs). Programs put into place to increase access to disadvantaged groups included the Technology Opportunities Program (TOP), the Community Technology Center (CTC) initiative and the E-rate. The CTC and TOP programs made available matching grants for the creation and maintenance of community centers where the public can go for computer access and training. In addition, the TOP program offered grants for projects that use technology to solve social problems and improve communities (Dickard, 2003). The largest federal program created to address the digital divide is the Schools and Libraries Universal Fund or the "E-rate." It was created under the Telecommunications Act of 1996 and was set up as a $2.25 billion annual fund to provide discounts (between 20 percent and 90 percent) to schools and libraries for connectivity costs for the Internet (Carvin, Conte, & Gilbert, 2001).

Programs meant to expand Internet access were downsized or eliminated under the George W. Bush administration. During his tenure, the problem of disparities in Internet usage was recast in terms of technological literacy. His administration worked to reduce inequalities in usage by improving computer skills through the No Child Left Behind Act (NCLB). This act expanded the definition of literacy to include technical competence and information literacy and provided money to schools for a broader variety of Internet resources such as teacher training, support staff, and software (Dickard, 2003).

The Obama administration has redirected the federal government response to Internet inequalities to a strategy more closely resembling Bill Clinton's by focusing on increasing Internet access but with an emphasis of addressing infrastructure barriers to residential areas. Under the American Recovery and Reinvestment Act of 2009, $7.2 billion was provided to states and local governments to extend high-speed broadband access to rural areas that have not been served by existing broadband providers. The money was distributed through the Broadband Technology Opportunities Program (BTOP) and the Broadband Initiatives Program (BIP). The two programs provide grants and loans to state and local communities to either update existing telecommunication infrastructure or to put into place necessary infrastructure to provide broadband service to areas that do not currently have broadband access or are underserved. The Obama administration has also enlisted the aid of the private sector through awarding $100 million dollars under the Recovery Act to four satellite companies to help broadening access to broadband in rural area (Recovery Accountability and Transparency Board, 2010). Additionally, these programs are complemented by the State Broadband Initiative. This program was created in 2009 as a joint venture between the Recovery Act and the Broadband Data Improvement Act. Currently, it has awarded $293 million in grants to support the use of broadband for projects that help the states compete in the digital economy, including expansion of Internet access (NTIA, 2011a).

3 COMMUNICATIONS MODEL

While each of the three administrations took a different approach to addressing the issue of inequality in Internet usage, the success of each of the policies relied heavily on the cooperation from state and local governments. In exploring variation to state compliance with the current administration's policy, this study turns to Goggin et al.'s (1990) Communications Model designed to frame intergovernmental policy. The goal of this model is to depict implementation over time and determine why there is variation in how states implement federal laws. The dependent variable under this framework is state implementation. Specifically, the dependent variables include outputs and outcomes. Outputs can be characterized as agency efforts. Outcomes involve the impact that the law had on society (1990).

The intervening variables are state organizational and ecological capacities or resources that allow the state to ignore messages from other political actors. State organizational capacity refers to items such as a state's administrative efficiency and competency. State ecological capacity refers to factors such as the partisan make-up of the governor's office and the state legislature (1990). The independent variables are federal-level and state-level inducements and constraints. An example of a federal level inducement is the allocation of resources to implement a law. Conversely, a restraint would include sanctions against states that fail to implement a law as directed (Goggin et al., 1990).

Goggin et al. (1990) argue that communications takes center stage in implementation. The message and content of the policy, in addition to the level of communication federal agencies have with state and local implementation agencies, is also likely to affect the success or failure of the implementation of a law. If state and local implementers regard the message and content as credible, their execution of the law is more likely to mirror its original intent. Typically, higher levels of communication facilitate better implementation. Also, the less communication there is, the more likely that competing messages from other political actors will result in the implementation of policy that deviates from its original design (Goggin et al., 1990).

A review of the Communication Models suggests a number of factors that can influence state compliance with federal policy. In the next section, their influence—including that of state organizational and ecological capacity on the state-level response to one such U.S. telecommunication policy, the Obama administration's programs to extend Internet access—will be examined. Multivariate logistic regression analysis of fifty state data will be used to test rival factors for state response as of December 2010.

4   DATA AND MEASUREMENT

The dependent variable is constructed to measure the extent of broadband/high-speed Internet access policy in a state. It measures whether the state has taken action that is in compliance with the Obama's administration policy to expand broadband access either through authorizing financial support to provide infrastructure to facilitate broadband access or working with local government to provide municipal owned broadband service. It is coded 1 if such actions were taken and 0 otherwise. The dependent variable was created from a summary of current state broadband laws available through the National Council of State Legislatures (2010a). Because of problems related to multicollinearity, two models will be presented. The dependent variable remains the same but several independent and control variables change between models.

The main independent variables under the Communication Model are federal-level and state-level inducements and constraints. The federal government can compel the states to act through inducements such as grants, constraints such as sanctions, or a combination of both. The Obama administration is relying entirely on inducements in the form or grants and loans to encourage state compliance. In Model 1, two variables are included to measures these inducements. The first measure is the amount of grants in 100's of millions of dollars awarded to each state under the State Broadband Initiative program (NTIA, 2011a). The second is the amount of grants rewarded to the states for infrastructure under the BTOP program in millions of dollars (NTIA, 2011b). This second measure is not included in Model 2.

Actors at the state and local level (interest groups, local officials and agencies) can shape the implementation of legislation. Depending on how legislation impacts local groups, they may act either to boost or to hinder implementation. Because e-government may have the ability to increase political engagement and facilitate a more participatory democracy (Pardo, 2000), it is expected that good government groups would play an important role in supporting the extension of broadband. The number of good government groups in a state was included as a control for interest group strength (Project Vote Smart, 2009). One group proven to influence state Internet access policy is the telecommunication service providers. Acting as a proxy for the strength of telecommunication service providers is whether or not a state has passed laws that either restrict or prohibit municipal owned broadband service (a policy that was hard fought for by service providers). The measure is coded 1 if the state has such a law and 0 otherwise (Baller Herbst Law Group, 2011).

Although actors at the federal, state, and local levels may attempt to influence state policy, states may still disregard these players and enact its own preferences. This can occur if the "messages" sent by these actors are not considered credible. Credibility is based on a number of factors including clarity of message, accompanying resources to implement a policy and whether the "message" came from an actor who is perceived to be credible and legitimate. How much leeway a state has in disregarding such messages is based on state resources. The ability of states to discount outside messages is defined by Goggin et al. (1990, p. 119) as state capacity. This capacity falls into two categories: ecological capacity and organizational capacity. Ecological capacity concerns the "contextual environment in which state government operates" (Goggin et al. 1990, p. 911). The state operates within three environments: economical, situational and political. Economical capacity concerns the availability of monetary resources. The ability of a state to decline federal grants and loans for Internet access depends on state wealth. Following Walker (1969) in Model 2, educational attainment measured as the percent of the state population over the age of 25 with a bachelor's degree or higher (U.S. Census Bureau, 2012) is included as a measure of societal resources.

The political environment includes both the attitudes of the citizens as well as public officials. A number of factors can influence the opinion of policymakers. The first is partisanship. A measure of party control of the government is included, coded 1 if the Republican Party controls both houses of the legislature and the governorship, 0 if control is divided between the two parties, and–1 if the Democratic Party controls both houses of the state legislature and the governorship (National Council of State Legislatures, 2010b). Research on partisanship and e-government (McNeal et al., 2003; Tolbert, Mossberger, & McNeal, 2008) found a positive relationship between Republican controlled legislatures and implementation of e-government policies. Both studies concluded that states with Republican controlled legislatures were more likely to be innovators in e-government because of the belief that e-government would increase both efficiency and cost savings. To control for the possible response to citizen concerns, included in the models is the voting age turnout in the state for the 2010 midterm election (United States Election Project, 2011).

The final area of ecological capacity is state situational capacity. Goggin et al. (1990, pp. 145–6) include in this category such factors as public awareness. States are more likely to respond to an issue if the public believes that a problem exists. Measures of demand, such as the number of Internet users in a state or problem severity, may also affect policy adoption and the scope of implementation (Goggin et al., 1990). Several measures were included for barriers to Internet access. The first is the average number of computers available for public use per public library in 2009 (U.S. Census Bureau, 2012). The greater the access to the Internet in public places such as the library, the severity of the problem may not seem as acute. The second measure is the percentage of rural areas in a state with three or fewer wireless providers (NTIA, 2011c). Citizens living in rural areas often have limited choices for service providers and therefore connection fees that are considerably higher than in urban/suburban areas (Stover, 1999). Because the cost of Internet service tends to be lower in more densely populated areas, a measure of state population density calculated by the population per square mile was included (U.S. Census Bureau, 2011). In states with greater population density, there may be less of a pressing need to implement these policies. In Model 2, a fourth variable measuring the percentage of households with Internet access within the state in 2009 was included (U.S. Census Bureau, 2012). The greater the percentage of households with Internet access, the less likely the state will feel that it needs to implement additional policies to further extend broadband access.

While ecological capacity focuses on the environment in which policy implementation takes place, organizational capacity concerns the resources available to the state agencies that oversee policy implementation. Institutional capacity includes items such as a state's administrative efficiency and competency (Goggin et al., 1990). As a measure of ecological capacity, included is an indicator of whether the state has an existing broadband task force, commission, or authority to oversee state-level broadband initiatives (National Council of State Legislatures 2010c). It is coded 1 if such an agency exists and 0 otherwise.

Markell (1993) suggests that measures of resources include a strong record of policy implementation. States that have a history of innovation in an issue area may be more likely to continue placing new ideas on the table and implement additional programs. Several measures of innovation in e-government are included. In Model 2 is included an index that measure state innovation in electronic commerce (Atkinson & Wilhelm, 2002). The second measure is West's (2007) innovation index—a measure of the overall state ranking of government websites. The final measure is a count of social network sites such as Facebook and Twitter being utilized by legislative agencies and caucuses in a state (National Council of State Legislatures, 2011).

5 FINDINGS AND DISCUSSION

In Table 18.1, the dependent variable is coded so that higher scores are associated with increased likelihood of adopting state policies that are in compliance with the Obama administration's policy goals of extending Internet access to underserved areas. Because the dependent variable is binary, logistic regression models are used. Although two models were explored because of muticollinearity concerns, the findings were the same. The same subset of variables was found to be significant in both models. The findings suggest that a limited number of variables including State Broadband Initiative grants, good government interest groups, Republican control of state government, number of computers per library, West's

Table 18.1 State-Level Broadband Access Policy Implementation

Variables	Gov't Ownership or Financing (Model 1)		Gov't Ownership or Financing (Model 2)	
	b (se)	p>|z|	b (se)	p>|z|
Federal-Level Inducements and Constraints				
State Broadband Initiative Grants	.22(0.09)	.019	.27(0.13)	.042
BTOP Infrastructure Monies	.02(0.14)	.225	—	—
State-Level Inducements and Constraints				
Barrier Laws	4.12(2.76)	.132	2.87(2.02)	.156
Good Government Interest Group Strength	-1.46(0.68)	.033	-1.28(0.60)	.034
Ecological Capacity				
Republican Government Control	3.97(2.41)	.098	3.03(1.69)	.073
Voter Age Population Turnout	-.45(0.31)	.140	-.35(0.24)	.145
Percent With Bachelor's Degree	—	—	-.34(0.46)	.457
Rural Broadband Availablity	.06(0.05)	.250	.06(0.05)	.166
Population Density	3.4E-3(3.7E-3)	.342	4.5E-3(5.2E-3)	.391
Percent of Households With Internet Access	—	—	.13(0.17)	.449
Average Number of Computers Per Library	-1.27(0.73)	.083	-.91(.52)	.073
Organizational Capacity				
Task Force	-3.20(2.74)	.242	-1.91(2.19)	.381
Electronic Commerce Score	—	—	-.14(0.37)	.709
West E-government Score	.29(0.15)	.060	.22(0.12)	.048
Legislative Social Media Use	2.35(1.22)	.055	2.07(0.98)	.035
Constant	-2.89(8.57)	.736	-7.21(10.50)	.492
Pseudo R^2	.6589		.6356	
LR Chi^2	35.94	.0003	34.67	.0016
N	49		49	

measure of e-government and the extend of legislative social media use influence state compliance with this federal policy.

Logistic regression estimates with standard errors in parentheses. Reported probabilities are based on two-tailed tests. Statistically significant coefficients at .10 or less in bold.

Some of the findings were expected. Measures of demand or need were not found to be related to adoption in this policy area which is consistent with the e-government literature (McNeal et al., 2003; Tolbert et al., 2008). The only exception was the measure for average number of computers per library and it was negatively related to policy adoption. The findings suggest that the greater availability of computers at public libraries, the less likely that the state will take policy action to extend broadband access. Need or citizen demand has not typically been found to bring about adoption of e-government initiatives. Although this finding is consistent with the e-government literature, it contradicts Goggin et al. (1990) who argue that public awareness of a problem is a significant predictor of political activities. It is likely that because both e-government and telecommunication policy are technical, they are unlikely to be salient with the general public. Like the general public, interest groups were not found to play an important role in the implementation of this policy. Surprisingly, the measure of telecommunication service providers was not found to be significant and the measure for good government interest groups was found to be significant but not in the direction predicted.

Goggin et al. (1990) argue that even though actors at the federal, state, and local levels may attempt to influence state policy, the state may ignore these messages and enact its own preferences. The findings are in fact suggesting this is happening for actors within the state for this issue area. There is evidence however that federal-level inducement has had some influence on state behavior. In both models, states who had accepted larger grants from the State Broadband Initiative program where more likely to implement policy that was consistent with the goals of the federal government. On the other hand, monies collected for infrastructure from BTOP were not related to state policy actions. The main difference between these two programs is flexibility. Monies from BTOP is for extending or updating telecommunication infrastructure, whereas grants from the State Broadband Initiative is for a variety of projects that help the states compete in the digital economy, which may include expansion of Internet access.

Whereas Goggin et al. (1990) argue that states may choice to ignore messages from other political actors, how much freedom they have to do so is based on state resources (state capacity). Nevertheless, the findings point to only a few examples of state capacity which are related to the level of state compliance. The first is Republican-controlled state governments. This finding, although not intuitive, is consistent with the e-government literature that finds that states with greater proportions of Republicans in the state legislature are more likely to innovate in the area of e-government (McNeal et al., 2003; Tolbert et al., 2008; Hale & McNeal, 2011). This result has been attributed to the cost-cutting capacity and efficiency associated with e-government. The final two examples of state capacity found to influence implementation of these programs are West's (2007) innovation index—a measure of the overall state ranking of government websites and the extent to which legislative agencies and caucuses rely on social media. Both are indicators of the extent to which e-government has been adopted in the state.

6 CONCLUSION

Because the United States has a federalist system, implementation of national policies often requires the cooperation of other levels of government. Whether they chose to cooperate depends on how credible they believe the federal government's request for assistance is and if they have sufficient resources that permit them the freedom to ignore these messages. The results from this study find that the policies under the Obama administration have not altered the path that the states have chosen in the adoption of e-government strategies. Those states that have already taken greater steps toward adopting e-government approaches for delivering informational services are the ones most likely to adopt policies that are consistent with the current administration's goals of extending broadband service. Two factors may be resulting in states staying on their current policy paths. The first is that this is a highly technical area and less likely to be salient among the general public. There may be little demand for change coming from within the state. The second is that whereas e-government strategies can result in cost-cutting and efficiency, it requires significant initial investments. During these difficult economic times, states may be unwilling to undertake new projects that are expensive even with the promise of future savings.

These findings must, however, be considered with the understanding that this study is preliminary. The goal of the Goggin et al. (1990) Communication Model is to depict implementation over time and determine why there is variation in how states implement federal laws. This study relies on a cross-sectional study that depicts state action at one point in time. In addition, the dependent variables under this framework include both outputs and outcomes. This study has only examined outputs by the state government or policy adoption. Outcomes include the impact a law has on society. These limitation results from this policy area being relatively new; the Recovery Act was only enacted in 2009. Future research can improve upon this initial study through utilizing a time-series approach and including measures of outcomes such as percentage of households with Internet access, and availability of service providers in rural areas as dependent variables.

REFERENCES

Atkinson, R. D., & Wilhelm, T. (2002). *The best states for e-commerce*. Washington, DC: Progressive Policy Institute.

Baller Herbst Law Group. (2011). State restrictions on community broadband services or other public communications initiatives. Retrieved March 23, 2011, from http://www.baller.com/pdfs/BallerStateBarriers(1-1-11).pdf

Carvin, A., Conte, C., & Gilbert, A. (2001). The E-rate in America: A tale of four cities. In B. M. Campaign (Ed.). *The digital divide: Facing a crisis or creating a myth?* (pp. 223–242). Cambridge, MA: MIT Press.

Dickard, N. (2003). Edtech 2002: Budget challenges, policy shifts and digital opportunity. In N. Dickard (Ed.), *The Sustainability challenge: Taking ddtech to the next level*. Benton Foundation and the Education Development Centers for Children and Technology. Retrieved May 7, 2004, from http://www.benton.org/publibrary/sustainability/sus_challenge.html

Federal Communication Commission. (2010). National broadband plan: Connecting America. Retrieved March 25, 2011, from http://www.broadband.gov/

Fiber-to-the-Home Council, (2009). Municipal fiber to the home deployments. Retrieved August 20, 2010, from http://www.ftthcouncil.org/sites

Goggin, M., Bowman, A .O., Lester, J. P., & O'Toole, L. J., Jr. (1990). *Implementation theory and practice: Toward a third generation*. New York: HarperCollins Publishers.

Hale, K., & McNeal, R. (2011). Technology, politics, and e-commerce: Internet sales tax and interstate cooperation. *Government Information Quarterly*, 28(2), 262–270.

Markell, D. (1993). The federal superfund program: Proposals for strengthening the federal/state relationship. *William and Mary Journal of Environmental Law*. 18, 1–82.

McNeal, R., Tolbert, C., Mossberger, K., & Dotterweich, L. (2003). Innovating in digital government in the American states. *Social Science Quarterly*. 84(1), 52–70.

McNeal, R., Hale, K., & Dotterweich, L. (2008). Citizen-government interaction and the Internet: Expectations and accomplishments in contact, quality and trust. *Journal of Information Technology & Politics*. 5(2): 213–229.

National Council of State Legislatures. (2010a). Broadband statutes. Retrieve April 19, 2010, from http://www.ncls.org/dafault.aspx?tabid=13455

National Council of State Legislatures. (2010b). Partisan composition of state legislatures. Retrieved April 19, 2010, from http://www.ncls.org

National Council of State Legislatures. (2010c). State broadband task forces, commissions or authorities and other broadband resources. Retrieved April 19, 2010, from http://www.ncsl.org/issues-research/telecommunications-information-technology/state-broadband-task-forces-commissions-or-autho.aspx

National Council of State Legislatures. (2011). Legislative social media sites. Retrieved July 20, 2011, from http://www.ncls.org/default.aspx?tabid=13409

National Telecommunications and Information Administration (NTIA). (2010). *Digital nation: 21st Century America's progress toward universal broadband Internet access*. Retrieved January 20, 2011, from http://www.ntia.doc.gov

National Telecommunications and Information Administration (NTIA). (2011a). State broadband initiative. Retrieved March 5, 2011, from http://www2.ntia.doc.gov/SBDD

National Telecommunications and Information Administration (NTIA). (2011b). Grants awarded: broadband infrastructure projects. Retrieved April 18, 2011, from http://www2.ntia.doc.gov/awards

National Telecommunications and Information Administration (NTIA). (2011c). National broadband map. Retrieved April 9, 2011, from http://www.broadbandmap.gov

Nicholas, K. (2003). Geo-political barriers and rural Internet access: The regulatory role in constructing the digital divide. *The Information Society.* 19, 287–295.

Norris, P. (2001). *Digital divide: Civic engagement, information poverty, and the Internet worldwide.* New York: Cambridge University Press.

Pardo, T. (2000). Realizing the promise of digital government: It's more than building a website. *Information Impacts Magazine.* Retrieved March 12, 2004, from http://www.cisp.org/imp/october_2000

Project Vote Smart. (2010). Issue organizations. Retrieved February 17, 2010, from http://www.votesmart.org/issue_group.php

Recovery Accountability and Transparency Board. (2010). Recovery funds satellite broadband to rural America. Retrieved February 12, 2011, from http://www.recovery.gov

Stover, S. (1999). *Rural Internet connectivity.* Rural Policy Research Institute. Retrieved April 10, 2001, from http://www.rupi.org/

Tolbert, C. J., Mossberger, K., & McNeal, R. (2008). Innovation and learning: Measuring e-government performance in the American states 2000–2004. *Public Administration Review.* 68(3): 549–563.

U.S. Census Bureau. (2011). Population density. Retrieved December 18, 2011, from http://2010.census.gov/2010census/data

U.S. Census Bureau. (2012). *Statistical Abstracts in the United States 2012.* Washington, DC: U.S. Government Printing Office.

U.S. Election Project. (2011). Voter-age turnout in the states. Retrieved May 15, 2011, from http://www.elections.gmu.edu/voter-turnout.htm

Walker, J. (1969). The Diffusion of innovation among the American states. *American Political Science Review.* 63(3): 880–899.

West, D. (2004). E-government and the transformation of service delivery and citizen attitudes. *Public Administration Review.* 64(1): 15–27.

West, D. (2007). State and federal e-government in the United States, 2007. Center for Public Policy, Brown University. Retrieved February 19, 2008, from http://www.brown.edu/Departments/Taubman_Center/minisite/policyreports/index.html

Contributors

EDITORS

Christopher G. Reddick is an Associate Professor and Chair of the Department of Public Administration at the University of Texas at San Antonio. Dr. Reddick's research and teaching interests are in information technology and public sector organizations. Dr. Reddick recently edited the two volume book entitled *Handbook of Research on Strategies for Local E-Government Adoption and Implementation: Comparative Studies*. He is also author of the book *Homeland Security Preparedness and Information Systems*, which deals with the impact of information technology on homeland security preparedness.

Vishanth Weerakkody is a Senior Lecturer and Director of Undergraduate Studies at the Business School at Brunel University, UK. His current research interests include electronic government, process transformation and change, and technology adoption and diffusion in the public sector. As well as being Editor-in-Chief of the International Journal of Electronic Government Research, he is Associate Editor for a number of leading journals. He has edited several books and published over 100 articles in peer reviewed journals and conferences on the themes of public sector transformation and e-government. At present, he serves as Track Co-Chair for e-government at a number of International Conferences including the Americas Conference on Information Systems and the European Conference on Information Systems. Prior to his career in academia, Dr Weerakkody spent several years working in the IT industry as a systems and process analyst.

CONTRIBUTORS

Laura Alcaide Muñoz is Lecturer in Financial Economic and Accounting Department of the University of Granada. She is interested in how e-government has favored the process of reform and modernization of public administrations, giving rise to greater accessibility to public information and services, and information transparency, this latter aspect being a key factor in the accountability of public administration. She has been author of articles published in *International Journal of Digital Accounting Research* and *Administration & Society* and a chapter in a book published by IGI Global.

Leonidas G. Anthopoulos is an Assistant Professor at the Project Management Department of the TEI of Larissa (Greece). At his previous job positions at the Hellenic Ministry of Foreign Affairs, the Information Society S.A. (Greece) etc. he was responsible for planning and managing multiple IT and e-government projects, and complex computer systems for Greek government and for various public organizations. He is the author of several articles published in prestigious scientific journals, books, and international conferences. His research interests concern, among others, e-government and e-Strategic management, enterprise architecture, social networks and engineering project management.

Ari-Veikko Anttiroiko is an Adjunct Professor and a Senior Lecturer at the School of Management, University of Tampere, Finland. Anttiroiko's research areas include local governance, globalization, e-government, public sector innovations, and high-tech center studies. He is a Co-editor of *e-Transformation in Governance* (2004), *e-City* (2005), the *Encyclopedia of Digital Government* (2007), *Innovations in Public Governance* (2011), and *Innovative Trends in Public Governance in Asia* (2011). He is the editor of the comprehensive reference book *Electronic Government: Concepts, Methodologies, Tools, and Applications* published in six volumes (IGP 2008). He has memberships in several editorial boards of international journals.

James Backhouse holds degrees from the Universities of Exeter, London and Southampton. He was awarded a PhD (Semantic Analysis in Information Systems Development) from the London School of Economics, where he is Emeritus Reader in the Department of Management. The author of many publications in the field of information and security, his research currently examines information security from a social sciences perspective and centers on power, responsibility and trust and identity. His work has been published in *MISQ, EJIS, ISJ, CACM*, and *JAIS*, among others. He is currently Senior Associate Editor of the *European Journal of Information Systems* and was until 2010 an Editor-in-Chief of the online Springer journal *Identity in the Information Society.*

Frank Bannister is an Associate Professor of Information Systems and Head of the Information Systems Department in Trinity College. Dublin. Prior to becoming an academic he worked in the Irish civil service and as a management consultant. His research interests include e-government, e-democracy, IT value and evaluation, and online privacy and trust. He is Editor of the *Electronic Journal of e-Government* and Co-director of the permanent study group on e-government in the European Group for Public Administration. Frank is a fellow of Trinity College, a fellow of the Institute of Management Consultants in Ireland, a fellow of the Irish Computer Society, and a Chartered Engineer.

John Carlo Bertot is Professor and Co-director of the Information Policy and Access Center in the College of Information Studies at the University of Maryland. He is President of the Digital Government Society of North America and serves as chair of the International Standards Organization's Library Performance Indicator (ISO 11620) working group. He is Editor of *Government Information Quarterly* and Co-editor of *The Library Quarterly*. Over the years, He has received funding for his research from the National Science Foundation, the Bill & Melinda Gates Foundation, the Government Accountability Office, the American Library Association, and the Institute of Museum and Library Services.

Lemuria Carter is an Associate Professor at North Carolina Agricultural and Technical State University. Her research interests include technology adoption, e-government, and online trust. She has published in several top-tier information journals, including the *Journal of Strategic Information Systems, Information Systems Journal, Communications of the ACM,* and *Information Systems Frontiers.* She has served as track and mini-track chair for the Americas Conference on Information Systems and the Hawaii International Conference on System Sciences.

Yu-Che Chen is an Associate Professor in the Division of Public Administration at Northern Illinois University. Dr. Chen received his Master of Public Affairs and PhD in Public Policy from Indiana University. His research and teaching interests are in electronic government and collaborative public management. His most recent co-edited book is entitled *Electronic Governance and Cross-boundary Collaboration.* His e-government research can be found in scholarly journals such as *Public Administration Review* and *American Review of Public Administration.* He is the Chair of the Technology Advisory Committee for the American Society for Public Administration (ASPA).

Regina Connolly is a Senior Lecturer in Information Systems at Dublin City University Business School and Program Director of the MSc in Electronic Commerce. In her undergraduate degree she received the Kellogg Award for outstanding dissertation and her MSc degree was awarded with distinction. She earned her PhD in Information Systems from Trinity College

Dublin. Her research interests include e-government, IT value and evaluation in the public sector, online trust and privacy issues, website service quality, and strategic information systems. She is Editor-in-Chief of the *Journal of Internet Commerce*. She has served on the expert eCommerce advisory group for Dublin Chamber of Commerce, which has advised national government on eCommerce strategic planning.

Carlotta del Sordo, BA Business Economics, University of Bologna, Italy, Ph.D. Management of the Public Sector, University of Salerno, Italy, visiting scholar at Boston University, US, Accounting Department. Lecturer in Business Economics, Department of Management, University of Bologna, Italy; current research interests are Management accounting theory and Management control in public sector.

Andres Dijkshoorn is trainee Research Assistant and PhD candidate in the Faculty of Social Sciences (Comparative Public Service Innovation research group) at Erasmus University Rotterdam. His research focuses on the diffusion of personalization in Dutch municipal e-government initiatives. Dijkshoorn has contributed to various books and research reports and has published various papers in national and international conference proceedings.

Panos Fitsilis, Professor at TEI Larissa, Greece, and Director of School of Business and Economics, has extensive project management experience with the development and deployment of large IT systems. He worked, as business unit manager at large software development companies and was responsible for the development, deployment, and operation of a number of prestigious IT systems for European Commission. He is the author of three books and author of many articles published on scientific journals and international conferences. His research interests include project management, software engineering, e-government systems, and business process reengineering.

Enrico Deidda Gagliardo is Associate Professor of Programming and Control in the Public Sector at the University of Ferrara, Italy, and Director of the postgraduate course entitled "Public Admnistration's Performance Improvement." His research field and publications focus on multidimensional programming and control in the public domain and public value creation and measurement. He has also conceived a software solution for local government's performance programming, management, and control, focusing both on financial and non-financial performance.

J. Ramon Gil-Garcia is an Associate Professor in the Department of Public Administration and the Director of the Data Center for Applied Research in Social Sciences at Centro de Investigación y Docencia Económicas (CIDE) in Mexico City. He is also a Research Fellow at the Center for Technology in Government, University at Albany, State University of New York (SUNY) and a Faculty Affiliate at the National Center for Digital Government, University of Massachusetts, Amherst. His research interests include collaborative electronic government, inter-organizational information integration, adoption and implementation of emergent technologies, digital divide policies, new public management, and multi-method research approaches.

Natalie N. Greene is a doctoral student at the University of Maryland's College of Information Studies. She is a Graduate Research Associate at the Information Policy & Access Center in Maryland's iSchool, where she is working on a project studying the potential partnerships between public libraries and government agencies funded by the Institute of Museum and Library Services. She received her Masters of Library Science at the University of Maryland–College Park, specializing in e-government and school library media, for which she is certified in the state of Maryland.

Ruth Halperin is currently a lecturer at Haifa University, Israel. She holds a PhD in Information Systems from the London School of Economics and Political Science, where she had been employed as a Research Fellow in the Information Systems and Innovation Group of the Department of Management. Her current research interests are in information risk; security and privacy; digital identity and systems design and implementation. She has published in the areas of risk perceptions, interoperable identity management systems, and profiling. Prior to joining academia, she was a Project Manager of a leading software development company specializing in e-learning and KM technologies.

Vincent Homburg is Associate Professor in the Faculty of Social Sciences (Comparative Public Service Innovation research group) at Erasmus University Rotterdam, the Netherlands. Homburg edited *The Information Ecology of E-Government* (IOS Press, 2005, together with Victor Bekkers) and *The New Public Management in Europe* (Palgrave MacMillan, 2007, together with Christopher Pollitt and Sandra van Thiel) and published *Understanding E-Government* (Routledge, 2008). He has furthermore published over forty book chapters and articles in national and international journals (among others *The Information Society*, *International Journal of Public Administration*, *Information Polity*) focusing on electronic government and public management.

Tommi Inkinen is Professor of Economic Geography at the department of Geosciences and Geography, University of Helsinki, Finland. His research interests focus on human and economic geography, including the regional structuring of innovation systems, technology implementation and information networks as well as electronic government and governance. He has also worked with the questions of logistics and transport. He has published extensively on these topics in national and international journals and books. He is a steering group member of the International Geographical Union's (IGU) Global Information Society Commission and the Editor-in-Chief of peer reviewed quarterly journal *Terra: A Geographical Journal.*

Paul T. Jaeger, PhD, JD, is Assistant Professor and Co-director of the Information Policy and Access Center and in the College of Information Studies at the University of Maryland. His research focuses on the ways in which law and public policy shape information behavior. He is the author of more than 120 journal articles and book chapters, along with seven books. His most recent book is *Disability and the Internet: Confronting a Digital Divide* (Lynne Reiner, 2011). Dr. Jaeger is Co-editor of *Library Quarterly* and Co-editor of the Information Policy Book Series from MIT Press.

Marijn Janssen is Director of the interdisciplinary Systems Engineering, Policy Analyses and Management (SEPAM) Master program and is an Associate Professor within the Information and Communication Technology section of the Technology, Policy and Management Faculty of Delft University of Technology. His research interests are in the field of ICT and governance in particular orchestration, (shared) services, intermediaries, open data and infrastructures for coordinating public-private service networks. He serves on several editorial boards and is involved in the organization of a number of conferences. He published more than 200 refereed publications. For more information, see: www.tbm.tudelft.nl/marijnj.

Anton Joha is a senior researcher and consultant at consultancy firm EquaTerra in London. His projects are mainly in the field of outsourcing, shared services, IT governance, and cloud computing. He holds an MSc in Management Information Systems from Delft University of Technology, The Netherlands.

Dennis Linders is a PhD candidate at the University of Maryland, iSchool and a Junior Professional Associate in Urban Development at The World Bank. His research focuses on e-government, open government, smart cities, ICT for development, and ICT-facilitated strategic planning.

Antonio M. López-Hernández is Professor of Accounting at the University of Granada. He is a foundational member of the Spanish Association of Accounting University Teachers and a member of European Accounting Association. He teaches public sector management and control. He research interests are focused on e-government, performance management systems, and financial information in federal and local government.

He has published in journals such as *The International Journal of Public Sector Management, Government Information Quarterly, International Review of Administrative Science, American Review of Public Administration, International Public Management Journal, Online Information Review, Public Administration and Development, Public Money & Management,* and *Public Management Review.* He is also the author of several chapters for books published by publishers such as Kluwer Academic Publishers, Springer, and IGI Global.

Luis Felipe Luna-Reyes is a Professor of Business at the Universidad de las Américas Puebla in Mexico. He holds a PhD in Information Science from the University at Albany. Luna-Reyes is also a member of the Mexican National Research System. His research focuses on electronic government and modeling collaboration processes in the development of information technologies across functional and organizational boundaries.

Ramona McNeal is an assistant professor in the Department of Political Science at the University of Northern Iowa. Her chief research interest is the impact of technology on participation, including its relationship to voting, elections, and public opinion. She also studies e-government, campaign finance reform and telecommunications policy. She has published work in a number of journals including *Journal of Information Technology & Politics, Social Science Quarterly, Political Research Quarterly, State Politics & Policy Quarterly,* and *Public Administration Review.* She is a co-author of *Digital Citizenship: The Internet, Society and Participation* (MIT Press, 2007) with Karen Mossberger and Caroline Tolbert.

Jeremy Millard is Chief Policy Analyst at the Danish Technological Institute, and Associate Research Fellow with Brunel University. Jeremy has forty years of experience working with new technology and society in Europe and globally. During the last few years, he has undertaken an e-government 2020 Vision Study on Future Directions of Public Service Delivery for the European Commission, worked as an expert on inclusive e-government and for the Ambient Assisted Living evaluation, and is currently directing a study on new business and financing models related to ICT for ageing well.

Porche Millington is a Senior Economics major at North Carolina Agricultural and Technical State University. Her current research interests include Information Technology (IT) in improving healthcare and government services. She is a novice to research but looks forward to her continuing growth and future research.

Rania Mousa, PhD, is an Assistant Professor of Accounting at Schroeder Family School of Business Administration at University of Evansville,

Indiana. Dr. Mousa received her Master of Business Administration from Illinois Institute of Technology, and PhD in Accounting Information Systems from University of Birmingham, United Kingdom. Her research and teaching interests are in electronic business reporting, e-government and adoption of Extensible Business Reporting Language (XBRL). Rania has been awarded 2011's Vangermeersch Manuscript Award by the Academy of Accounting Historians for her paper titled, "The Development of Electronic Filing Process: HM Revenue & Customs, 1960s–2010."

Philip O'Reilly is a former Assistant Secretary General responsible for Information Systems (equivalent to Chief Information Officer) of the Irish Department of Agriculture, Food and the Marine—a post which he held from 2000 to 2010 and during which he was responsible for leading a strategic review and complete redesign of the Department's systems and for the restructuring of its ICT organization. Before joining Agriculture, he served for a number of years as Head of Logistics for the Irish Revenue Commissioners (tax authorities). Prior to that he was responsible for a number of ICT projects for the Department of Social Welfare. Philip holds a Master of Business Administration and a master's degree in Public Sector Strategic Management.

Rebecca Levy Orelli, BA Business Economics, University of Bologna, Italy, PhD Management of the Public Sector, University of Salerno, Italy, visiting scholar at London School of Economics, Accounting Department. She is Lecturer in Business Economics, Department of Management, University of Bologna, Italy, and is affiliated with EBEN. Her current research interests are new public management and public services changes in local governments, management accounting, and management control in public sector.

Emanuele Padovani is Associate Professor of Accounting and Control in the Public Sector at the University of Bologna, Italy. He has done extensive research and consultancy activities on public management with specific reference to management control, outsourcing, and financial and non-financial performance measurement and management. He is now working on the development of management control systems based on e-government in healthcare. For more information, see: www.unibo.it/docenti/emanuele.padovani > curriculum

Manuel Pedro Rodríguez Bolívar is Associate Professor at the University of Granada. His main research interests are focused on e-government, public sector management, and international public sector accounting. He is author of numerous articles in leading international journals, including *Business & Society*, *Public Money & Management*, *Government Information Quarterly*, *Public Administration and Development*, *Online*

Information Review, International Review of Administrative Sciences, American Review of Public Administration, Academia Revista Latinoamericana de administración, Administration and Society or *ABACUS*. He has also written several book chapters for books published by international publishers such as Kluwer Academic Publishers, Routledge, Springer, and IGI Global and has written books published by the Ministry of Economy and Finance of Spain.

Jeffrey Roy is Professor in the School of Public Administration, Faculty of Management at Dalhousie University where he specializes in models of corporate and collaborative governance and digital government reforms. In addition to teaching and research, he has consulted to governments at all levels, the private sector, as well as the United Nations and the OECD. He is also an Associate Editor of the *International Journal of E-Government Research*, a featured columnist in Canadian Government Executive, and author of three recent books examining digital government. His research work has been funded by several funding bodies including the Social Sciences and Humanities Research Council of Canada and the IBM Center for the Business of Government.

Dimitrios Triantafyllou is a postgraduate student at the MSc in Project and Program Management of the Project Management Department of the TEI of Larissa. He holds a bachelor's degree in economics and has worked for various financial organizations including the Bank of Cyprus in Greece.

Susan Copeland Wilson is a Senior Legislative Affairs Analyst and Emergency and Continuity Planner for the Federal Aviation Administration. As a doctoral candidate at the University of Maryland's College of Information Studies, her research areas include the role of trust and accountability in government information, e-government, and the intersection of e-government and poverty.

Index

Printed in the United States
by Baker & Taylor Publisher Services